READING

PERFORMANCE

AND

HOW

TO

ACHIEVE

IT

Barbara D. Bateman, Editor

BERNIE STRAUB PUBLISHING CO., INC. & SPECIAL CHILD PUBLICATIONS

© 1973

BERNIE STRAUB PUBLISHING CO., INC. &
SPECIAL CHILD PUBLICATIONS
4535 Union Bay Place N.E.
Seattle, Washington 98105

Standard Book Number: 0-87562-039-6
Library of Congress Catalog Card Number: 72-79162

Printed in the United States of America

CONTENTS

SECTION 3
TOWARD TEACHING

SECTION 4
TEACHING

INTRODUCTION

This book of readings was compiled because of the editor's conviction that educators can and should reduce the frequency of reading failures in our public schools. The purpose of these selections is to demonstrate and highlight needed changes in philosophy and procedures of reading instruction. To read these articles with maximum comprehension and appreciation one should be somewhat familiar with current philosophies and methods of teaching reading. However, the editor recognizes that many who are interested in this area are not necessarily well acquainted with the many and various reading programs in use today. It is also reluctantly acknowledged that exposure to college courses in "reading methods" does not insure competency in teaching reading by even one method, let alone several. If the reader lacks familiarity with reading programs or research in reading, he is urged to examine Jeanne Chall's LEARNING TO READ: THE GREAT DEBATE (McGraw-Hill, 1968) before, during, and after studying the articles in this volume.

Readers who are primarily concerned with the problems of teaching developmental reading to all children, and secondarily concerned with the disabled reader, may wish to begin this volume with the final section of papers. The thrust of the entire volume is that we must begin to teach as suggested in the last section so that we will no longer face many of the problems described in the first selections.

Some readers will use this book primarily for reference to already familiar papers and bibliographies. But others will be studying the articles in a "new-learning context." The study questions at the end of each article have been prepared to assist the reader who is in the process of learning about the large and confusing field of reading and its disorders. It is easy to ignore such study questions; it is also easy, unfortunately, to miss crucial concepts and issues imbedded in a complicated article full of new terminology. The study questions are intended to emphasize and clarify points in each article. However, even more importantly, they highlight the cumulative evidence in the articles which culminates in the position of the papers in the final section.

If the reader accurately decodes and astutely comprehends the divergent messages in these selections, he should be better able to answer the question: "What can educators do to improve the teaching of reading and thereby reduce the number and severity of reading problems?"

The first section of papers presents three overviews dealing with the etiology (causes) of reading problems. The second section treats characteristics and implied diagnosis of children with reading difficulties. The third section presents efforts to move from etiology and diagnosis of reading disorders toward remediation. The final section deals with the nature of the reading process and implications for adequate teaching of reading and prevention of reading failure.

The volume begins and ends with the thesis that some portion of reading failure is due to inadequate instruction and that top priority in the field should be given to decreasing reading failure resulting from faulty teaching. The articles in the final two sections of the volume—"Toward Teaching" and "Teaching"—clearly indicate some of the steps required to prevent reading failure. Some of our current practices must be changed if we are to decrease our present failure rate. This conclusion is logically inescapable.

Many reviews of reading disorders are gallant efforts to sort confusion into orderly paragraphs and subheadings. This is necessarily the case because the field of reading problems *is* confused, even its boundaries. Reading disorders are ill defined. Diagnostic perplexities include all the major question words: Who should diagnose whom? When? Where? How?—and above all, Why? Statistics on the frequency of reading failure suggest that prevention and treatment procedures share the difficulties found in definition and diagnosis.

Causes, Severity and Classification of Specific Reading Disorders

The opening section presents three reviews: Westman on physical, emotional, family, and school factors in the etiology of reading retardation; Hill on a continuum of severity of reading disability and administrative provisions; and Bannatyne on a four-fold classification of the species of dyslexia.

10

A major emphasis throughout this volume is the role of auditory skills in learning to read and the importance it should be given in the teaching of reading. In the first article, Westman cites the important role of audition in the development of concept formation and in the ability to manipulate symbols. Bannatyne is explicit: ". . . learning to read and spell are nothing more than arbitrary, irregular, sequencing processes *mostly auditory* in nature." This describes precisely the view of reading which guided the selection of the articles in this volume and it is the view the editor believes should guide initial instruction in reading. Surely all educators know that it is much easier to teach correctly the first time than it is to undertake remediation with a young-ster who has already met failure.

Hill deals with reading disorders on a continuum of severity, rather than their etiology, and evolves a school framework for treating reading problems of varying degrees of severity. Bannatyne's position is that different etiological types of dyslexics require different remedial techniques.

After completing these three papers the reader will realize that 1) the termin-ology used to describe children who are not reading as well as possible is con-fused and confusing; 2) many factors and combinations of factors have been attributed to the cause of poor reading; 3) some hold that the cause of a reading disability must be taken into account in planning remedial education strategies. This last premise will be examined and questioned in later sections.

Some Characteristics of Poor Readers

In the first group of papers Hill concludes with a plea for more sophisticated research in our studies of the characteristics of children with reading difficulties. In the second section Shimota has employed just such a sophisticated design in which emotional factors were controlled by using a sample group of institution-alized, emotionally disturbed subjects. Within that sample, adequate and dis-abled readers were compared. Almost every factor studied occurred as fre-quently in the able as in the disabled readers. Shimota suggests that perhaps reading disabilities arise as a result of the teaching methods used. This study poses the important question of which characteristics, if any, are peculiar to poor readers and of focusing attention on the main issue—what to do about poor reading.

Kass' study represents an extremely important group of investigations leading to a data-based formulation of reading as a code-breaking process, signaling the difficulties presented when teachers or programs fail to recognize the fundamental nature of the reading task. Kass found that disabled readers had difficulty in rote, automatic, and sequential tasks; but perhaps more surprising was the fact that they performed well on decoding meaningful visual stimuli. Kass gives an outstanding description of the Illinois Test of Psycholinguistic Abilities and its use in reading diagnosis.

Bryant describes dyslexia as relating only to code-breaking disabilities and differentiates it from reading problems which are related to inadequate instruction. Others argue, however, that if a task is teachable and if an individual has not learned it, then that individual obviously has not had adequate instruction. In that view, all reading problems are—by definition—a matter of inadequate teaching. (In the last section of this volume, Engelmann takes just this position.) Bryant's paper is one of those most frequently cited by clinicians and teachers since he gives specific and useful teaching suggestions. He describes the difficulties dyslexic children encounter with sound-symbol associations, details within a word, and directionality in letters of similar shape. His descriptions are all behavioral and specific enough so that teaching strategies can be readily generated. The question left unasked and unanswered, however, is whether the teaching strategies for these difficulties would be any different if the child had these behavioral deficits as a result of dyslexia, or brain damage, or poor motivation, or absenteeism, or any other factor or set of factors.

McLeod's study on reading problems in young children contributes further data, similar to Kass', that reading is related to automatic and sequential skills rather than just to measures of general mental development and visual perception. He also presents a predictive Dyslexia Schedule which can be used with preschoolers to detect "dyslexia-proneness." McLeod argues persuasively that predicting and treating reading disorders is more important than itemizing characteristics of those said to be dyslexic. At the same time it is true that knowledge of the characteristics of dyslexics is one approach to predicting which children will have difficulty and to establishing early intervention programs.

In the next paper, de Hirsch also discusses the early prediction of reading failure. Whereas McLeod used questions asked of the parents, de Hirsch uses a test battery called the Predictive Index which is administered directly to 5-year-olds. The position taken by de Hirsch is that teaching methods must be determined by the child's strengths and weaknesses as shown by educational diagnosis. She recommends a transition class in which instruction would be differentially geared to those children with deficiencies in auditory perception, visual perception problems, expressive language, and so on.

Krippner presents a frank and thorough airing of some of the issues surrounding vision and vision training. His conclusion is that the cold war between the supporters and the detractors of visual training will continue. This paper is included in the section on characteristics of poor readers because the controversy surrounding the role and efficacy of visual training stems in part from conflicting views about the vision status of poor readers.

The papers in these first two sections agree that a thorough study of the child does help in selecting teaching methodology. Lest this premise be uncritically accepted because it has been heard so often, the reader is alerted that some of the remaining papers will soundly challenge matching child and technique. The question is far from resolved.

The papers also reveal that: 1) children with reading disorders or potential reading disorders are said to have certain characteristics which differentiate them from adequate achievers in reading and 2) some hold that the teaching method used should be derived from a knowledge of the child's patterns of strengths or weaknesses or from a knowledge of groups of children with reading problems. Hill and Shimota have shown that the first point is not quite universally certain or accepted. As we move into the next section of papers, doubt emerges regarding the second point, too—the efficacy of deriving teaching procedures from diagnosis of the child. Here, too, opinions differ.

Toward Teaching

When diagnosis has revealed a child's pattern of cognitive-perceptual-sensory strengths and weaknesses, a decision must be made: should remediation be directed to the strengths or to the weaknesses? The entire concept of individual diagnosing and selecting a method best suited for the child hinges on the recommendation to teach either to the assets or to the deficiencies.

Silver and Hagin present a highly cogent and data-derived rationale for teaching to the weaknesses. Frostig, however, suggests that teaching should favor the child's areas of strength, but not to the total neglect of his weaknesses. She also introduces the teacher to the area of perceptual disturbances and to training methods for ameliorating them.

Bateman's article reveals disenchantment with attempting to match child and method via either strengths or weaknesses. If, in fact, matching attempts were abandoned altogether, it would be necessary to put more exclusive emphasis on improvement of the method or methods used in teaching the specific subskills of the complex task called reading. The remainder of the papers expand just this emphasis.

In their article on intervention strategies, Silver and Hagin move even further toward developing a teaching methodology. They have prepared a theoretical job analysis or task analysis of the process of learning to read and suggest that one's views of the etiology of reading disorders determine where and how to intervene in the job-analysis framework. Their own view, based on clinical study and longitudinal follow-up, is that training in deficient perceptual skills is important.

Regardless of how remedial strategies are initially selected, every remedial teacher faces the problem of determining when reading retardation exists and when it has been alleviated. McLeod carefully and critically examines prevalent concepts for determining reading expectancy. His position is that a behavioral analysis of the skills relevant to the learning deficiency is necessary. Such an analysis of a learning deficiency involves diagnosis of the child having the learning problem. The effort is to find and assess the psychological abilities basic to or underlying performance of the task to be learned. Tests like the Illinois Test of Psycholinguistic Abilities, used by McLeod, are designed to be useful in analyzing the *child's* learning deficiencies. This kind of analysis is substantially different from an analysis of the *task* to be learned. And both diagnosis and task analysis differ from an analysis of *learning conditions* such as that undertaken by Haring and Hauck in the final section.

Teaching

The final section—"Teaching"—extends the task-analysis concepts suggested by Silver and Hagin and introduces an analysis of learning conditions. Gibson aptly states that "An analysis of the reading task . . . tells us *what* must be learned. An analysis of the learning process tells us *how*." Engelmann has examined the *what* of learning to read and Haring and Hauck have investigated the *how,* in terms of improving learning conditions and arranging them to effectively bring about the acquisition of reading skills.

The investigations by Bliesmer and Yarborough and by Gurren and Hughes compare methodologies currently used in initial reading instruction. Their data illustrate a rapidly emerging consensus that instructional techniques based on reading as an auditory, code-breaking skill are more successful in teaching reading and preventing failure than are other approaches.

The final paper by Bateman presents the reading process as a rote, nonmeaningful, auditory process. If reading were taught as the code-breaking process it is, fewer reading failures would result. This paper was originally presented more than 5 years ago and met with substantial disfavor. The intervening years have seen the publication of Chall's LEARNING TO READ: THE GREAT DEBATE and the USOE studies of first-grade reading instruction. Now the case for a code-breaking emphasis seems quite well established and almost as well accepted. It remains to be seen whether this new emphasis in teaching methodology will result in the hoped-for decrease in reading disability. The papers in this last section implicitly agree that the evidence suggests that better teaching will reduce the frequency and severity of reading disorders.

To summarize, this collection of papers begins with the concept of reading disorders and the factors commonly held to cause them. The role of inadequate instruction as a possible major cause of poor reading has been emphasized. The characteristics of children said to be dyslexic or otherwise severely disabled in reading are discussed. The validity of diagnosing individual children's patterns of learning so that the technique selected is most appropriate to his strengths or weaknesses is questioned. And the collection concludes with a possible reformulation of the field of reading disability, in which full responsibility for teaching reading is placed on the method employed.

The task of reading must be so accurately and precisely analyzed that we can develop teaching programs totally consistent with what must be learned by anyone performing the reading task, regardless of his patterns of modality preference or perceptual strength, and so on. In addition to directing attention to the fundamental and basic nature of the task of reading, we also see a necessity for manipulating the conditions under which learning reading takes place so that those conditions maximize the learning process.

The movement away from viewing deficiencies in the child as the cause of reading disability and toward placing total responsibility on our method of teaching reading, as shown in the selection and sequencing of these papers, reflects the editor's personal journey through the field of learning disorders. Some of the authors of individual papers have traveled very different paths and do not share the editor's conviction that we must reformulate our view of reading problems as suggested. The reader is urged to treat each author's position independently and to recognize that the editor is solely responsible for selecting those papers which together tell a story much different from many of the individual selections.

Barbara D. Bateman
Professor of Education
Department of Special Education
University of Oregon

SECTION 1
CAUSES, SEVERITY AND CLASSIFICATION
OF SPECIFIC READING DISORDERS

1: READING RETARDATION: AN OVERVIEW

Jack C. Westman

Bettie Arthur

Edward P. Scheidler

Westman, Arthur, and Scheidler review the research on four major factors—physical (organ), emotional (individual), family, and school—said to be related to reading retardation. This survey and the excellent bibliography clearly convey the great variety of alleged causes and concomitants of reading problems. The role of the pediatrician, as he views it, is also presented. Educators may or may not agree with this concept of the medical role; in either case it is valuable to recognize the medical perspective.

B. D. B.

Reprinted with permission of the authors and publisher from AMERICAN JOURNAL OF DISEASES OF CHILDREN, 1965, 109, 359-369.

Literacy is essential in our society. Yet, at least 4 million school children are failing to acquire proficiency in reading. These children not only fall behind in school work but also suffer profound emotional and social repercussions. The pediatrician can play a role in reducing this sizable loss of individual potential through detecting, evaluating, and referring the retarded reader.

More than 20,000 articles and books are devoted to reading retardation. (1-7) While a vast array of information has been accumulated, noticeable gaps in interdisciplinary communication have prevented full use of what is known.

In clinical medicine signs (objective findings) are distinguished from symptoms (subjective complaints). Viewed in this framework retarded reading is a sign which can be identified with reasonable accuracy through standardized tests. Most authorities agree that reading retardation exists when a child's skill in reading falls 2 or more years below his mental age level, measured respectively by individually administered reading and intelligence tests. Associated symptoms, however, are not present in the usual form because the complaints about the reading problem ordinarily are made by teachers and parents rather than the patient, the child. During the onset of a reading problem, the child may experience anxiety or its somatic derivatives when confronted with the printed word, but later he may deny concern about his reading handicap. While most investigations are aimed at these signs and symptoms, it is clear that the underlying pathological processes must be identified.

This paper will review present knowledge about reading disabilities and highlight the complex nature of the reading process. We will follow Fabian's (8) convenient groupings: 1) organ centered studies, 2) individual centered studies, 3) family centered studies, and 4) school centered studies.

Organ Centered Studies

These studies are grouped according to body systems: visual, auditory, central nervous system, and endocrine.

Visual and Auditory Systems. Although reading takes place in the brain, not in the eyes or ears, defects of vision and hearing should be ruled out in all children with reading problems. Studies of visual factors disclose that while sensory impairment per se is not of primary etiological importance in the vast majority of cases, (9, 10) children with reading retardation do show defective integration of visual perceptions, e.g., difficulty in analyzing words, confused directional orientation of the printed word, and reversal of letters.

The phonetic method of teaching reading by associating sounds with visual symbols is widely accepted. An intact auditory apparatus is especially important in learning to read because of the important contribution audition makes to the early development of concept formation and the ability to manipulate abstract symbols. Hearing loss should, therefore, be ruled out in the evaluation of the retarded reader.

Central Nervous System. Current controversies over the etiology of reading retardation occur between the proponents of neurological and psychological theories. While both schools of thought recognize that brain injury can result in either the loss (acquired alexia) or impairment (acquired dyslexia) of the ability to read, there is disagreement about congenital alexia and dyslexia. (11-14)

The earliest documented cases of reading defects were clearly of neurological origin and followed injury to the brain. (15) More recently Kawi and Pasamanick (16) postulate minimal undetected brain damage arising from intrauterine or birth trauma as the cause of mental retardation, behavior disorders, and learning problems. They found more histories suggesting cerebral damage and more abnormal neurological signs in a group of retarded readers than in a group of children without academic problems. Mykelbust (17) reported that 5% of a public school population had "psychoneurological" learning disabilities as a result of occipital-parietal area disturbances. It is also known that adult patients with bilateral occipital-parietal atrophy can recognize letters and numbers but not words.

The neurological theory is also supported by Cohn (18), whose controlled study revealed that children with reading retardation show deficiencies in 1) language function, 2) somatic receiving and expressive functions, 3) spatial organizations, and 4) social adaptation. He postulated that generalized brain dysfunction affects the ability to recognize symbols and use graphic language.

Nonspecific electroencephalogram abnormalities have been reported in from 50% to 75% of retarded readers. (19) However, this study lacked normal control populations.

Another neurological approach springs from the word of Orton (20) who postulated that mixed cerebral dominance causes backward readers to have a higher incidence than normal readers of reversal of images, left-handedness, ambidexterity, and crossed laterality. His viewpoint is supported by the work of Silver and Hagin (21) whose controlled study led them to conclude that abnormal extension responses of the arm and foot are associated with reading disability.

On the other hand, a number of studies tend to discount the importance of mixed laterality in reading retardation. Gates (22) reported that reading disability cases show only 10% more laterality problems than normal children. Hammond (23), confirming this finding, concluded that mixed-dominance does not cause but rather accompanies reading disability. Furthermore, a high incidence of mixed dominance has been found in children from low socioeconomic groups, and in foster children, juvenile delinquents, and the mentally retarded.

A new concept appeared in the work of Prechtl (24) who identified a group of children with learning problems showing choreiform movements of the face, eye, tongue, neck, and trunk. This affectation of the eye muscles would hamper fixation of the eyes, cause instability in concentration, and lead to difficulty in learning how to read.

Rabinovitch (25, 26) classifies retarded readers on the basis of the presence and degree of neurological disease. He identifies three groups of children:

1) those, called "organic," who are unable to read because of demonstrable neurological damage; 2) those, called "primary reading disabilities," who show "soft" neurological signs and specific handicaps in the use of symbols; and 3) those, called "secondary reading disabilities," whose difficulty is based on anxiety, negativism, emotional blocking, or limited schooling opportunities. One of the values of this breakdown is that it differentiates types of reading retardation not only with regard to etiology and test performance characteristics, but also by the response of the child to remedial and therapeutic attempts.

Mention should be made of "reading epilepsy" (27), an uncommon convulsive disorder, usually of the grand mal type, precipitated by reading the printed word and sometimes interfering with educational progress.

Differences in the age at which central nervous system functions mature are often attributed to *maturation lags.* In educational parlance "reading readiness" blossoms in children between the ages of 3 and 8 when their brain matures sufficiently to permit the reading process to take place. Bender (28) points out that the phylogenetically most recently acquired functions of the brain show the greatest individual variation in the time of their appearance.

Educators and neurologists who rely upon the concept of maturation lag to explain some children's apparent lack of interest in reading during the early school years feel that further growth of the brain may correct the retardation. Some educators (29) believe that children should not be introduced to reading until the age of 7 or 8. Olson (30) also holds that many children are not ready to begin learning to read at 6 years of age. As a guide for assessing readiness for academic learning, he speaks of "organismic age," which is compounded from normative charts for dentition, height, weight, strength of grip, carpal age, mental age, and reading age. Both the concepts of maturation lag and congenital alexia include not only a delay in onset of the functions but also a stunting of the ultimate potential so that a congenital limit to the child's capacity exists.

Evidence that maturation lag does not adequately explain reading deficiencies comes from the facts that 3-year-olds can learn to read with special techniques and that some 9-year-olds who have achieved an adequate reading level still make perceptual errors said to be signs of a maturational lag.

Subtle and variable neurological signs found in some children support a number of neurologically based theories explaining reading retardation. Many of the cognitive and motor defects reported in older children with reading problems are found in children under the age of 7 who can read. (31) Our understanding of retarded reading would be simplified if minimal brain damage could be implicated as the core etiological factor. At this time, however, the evidence suggests that clearly neurologically based developmental and acquired alexias account for but a fraction of the children with reading problems.

Endocrine System. Through their influence on nerve cell metabolism the endocrine glands affect both motivation and the learning process. Park (32) postulated that homeostasis of the thyroid gland is necessary for the process of learning to read upon finding that 20% of a group of retarded readers showed hypothyroidism. Smith and Carrigan (33) associated disturbed acetylcholine metabolism and impaired ability to read.

The significance of endocrine abnormalities as causes of reading retardation has yet to be established. The reciprocal relationship of emotional state and the endocrine system permits the reasonable assumption that these changes are the result of another more basic process rather than the cause of defective learning.

Child Centered Studies

The appreciation of the effect of emotions on cognition has led to growing interest in psychological explanations of reading retardation. (34-37) An extensive literature exists detailing possible psychological factors at the levels of motivation, central integration of perceptions, and output of learned knowledge. A complicating factor is that the presence of central nervous system dysfunction may give rise to secondary psychological and emotional symptoms. It is also true that the failure caused by poor reading gives rise to anxiety and guilt. These secondary emotional reactions may be difficult to distinguish from primary psychological determinants of reading retardation.

Pearson (38, 39) extensively treats the psychology of learning and its possible neurotic distortions. He points out that learning draws heavily on the sublimation of instinctual drives. As the child progresses through the school years the open expression of sexual and aggressive impulses is modified through the development of inhibitions and of acceptable outlets for instinctual energy.

For convenience the literature can be grouped in seven categories.

1. Inhibition of Curiosity. This notion is based primarily on the work of Mahler (40), who described blunting of curiosity as a sequel to emotionally charged unpleasant discoveries. During World War II, for example, promiscuous mothers passed off their lovers as the fathers of their infant children while the real fathers were at war. When these children later found out the true identity of their fathers, they showed less open curiosity and developed learning inhibitions.

2. Inhibition of Aggressive Drives. Having reviewed the work on reading problems during the 1920's, Strachey (41) drew a parallel between the process of taking in information during reading and taking in food during eating. The incomplete repression of oral sadistic impulses was thought to lie behind reading inhibitions. In his view and that of Blanchard (42) the act of reading provokes anxiety because it threatens to bring about the release of aggressive impulses.

3. Projection of Fantasies to Letter and Word Symbols. Because of their ambiguity, letters and words may symbolize good or bad forces, depending upon the fantasies projected to them by children. Klein (43) held that letters and words may unconsciously represent food, feces, babies, breasts, and penises and suggested that the unconscious attitude of the mother plays a powerful role in determining how the symbols are distorted. It is likely that each child makes private associations to letters of the alphabet as he first encounters them. (44)

A bit of evidence from experimental psychology suggests that the threshold of recognition of a word rises in proportion to its emotional significance. (45) The more emotionally laden the symbol, the more likely it will not be recognized.

4. Faulty Development of Personality Functions. Anna Freud (46) implicates immaturity of parts of the personality as the primary cause of learning disabilities. The learning process requires intact personality functions of testing reality, storing memories, controlling impulses, and relating to other persons. An appropriately mature personality can obtain gratification from mastery of itself and the environment. A weak or immature personality cannot master complicated external stimuli because of its preoccupation with inner impulses and its diversion of psychic energy to defense mechanisms. One of the defensive maneuvers used by a weak personality is to constrict its range of activity and thereby escape painful situations. This mechanism is seen in the behavior of children who show little interest in learning in the classroom.

While Fleiss (47) supports Anna Freud's view, Rosen (48) sees the reading disability as arising from the precocious maturation of personality functions concerned with visual and auditory perception so that they become involved in the oedipal conflict at a crucial stage in their development. These perceptual processes are prevented from fusing into a completely autonomous structure which ordinarily would form the basis for reading.

5. Reading Retardation as a By-Product of a Neurotic Disorder. Freud (49) referred to a decrease in the ability of adults to learn during recovery from obsessional neuroses. In obsessional children preoccupation with obsessive thoughts and compulsive actions may also interfere with the process of learning to read.

6. Motivation to Defeat the Educational Process. Some children "need" to fail in learning. (50) Mahler (40) described "pseudo-imbecility" whereby children wear a mask of ignorance in order to mislead their parents and "innocently" gain access to parental secrets. Because the child appears to be incapable of learning, he also is excused from assuming the responsibilities of growing up. Mahler further notes that "pseudo-imbecility" satifies the mother's unconscious need to preserve her child's infantile dependency upon her.

Children may express resentment toward adults through passive-aggressive resistance to learning. This results in the stubborn refusal to absorb information and thereby affects motivation, or it may show at the output level when a child can read adequately but performs poorly on tests of reading ability.

7. **Diffuse Anxiety Interfering with Educational Routine.** Whether primarily resulting from intrapsychic conflict, personality weakness, or brain injury, anxiety is expressed in children through hyperactivity, short attention span, distractibility, impulsivity, and emotional instability. This behavior pattern (the "hyperkinetic syndrome") handicaps the child's participation in educational routines. Freed (51) found that reducing the manifestations of anxiety in children with reading disabilities by means of tranquilizers significantly improved their response to remedial tutoring.

Although the accumulating literature strongly points to the importance of intrapsychic conflict and personality factors in many cases of reading retardation, the reported studies base their conclusions on subjective data. The lack of parallel studies on control groups also leaves open the possibility that the positive findings are not specific to youngsters with reading problems.

Family Centered Studies

Interest in the psychological aspects of reading retardation has naturally led to exploring the families of children with reading disabilities. Family histories of reading problems have been frequently reported. (52-54) In addition to the possibility of genetic transmission the psychological influence of families on retarded readers has been suggested by a number of studies centered on the child. (55)

Liss (56), for example, has stressed the importance of parent-child and child-sibling, as well as the child-teacher, relationships in motivation for learning. Gyarfas (57) has shown that the broader context of the family background is an important variable. Children from lower socioeconomic backgrounds have received little stimulation to refine cognitive skills and show culturally determined deficiencies in language development. They are thereby less oriented to and prepared for reading instruction than are middle-class children.

Investigations uncovering family dynamics have shed light on the importance of the interaction between mother and child. Hammond (23) reported that the parents of retarded readers failed to make patient, realistic demands conducive to learning in their children. Instead a parent-child struggle over learning prevailed leading to a frustrated, fearful, or aggressive youngster with multiple emotional and behavioral problems.

Rank and Macnaughton (58) found that children with gross learning handicaps had failed to adequately separate their own personalities from those of their mothers. The mothers frequently treated their children as if they represented the unacceptable parts of themselves.

The mothers of children who fail in school were further described by Staver (59) who found that they preferred to view their child as mentally retarded rather than as emotionally disturbed. They unwittingly promoted the child's helplessness and ignorance because the child turned to them for protection and they could then ward off their own hostile wishes toward the child through overconcern for his safety.

Hellman (60) also found that the mothers of intellectually inhibited boys needed to keep their children passive and stupid because of the fear that they would lose their sons if they grew in independent masculinity.

In a similar study including both parents, Grunebaum, et al. (61, 62) found mothers who treated their sons with solicitude and overprotection and showed a general attitude of hostility toward men. The fathers were rigid and self-derogatory, regarding themselves as either failures or handicapped in their occupation. They viewed their sons as competitors for their wives' love and support. They were unable to take pleasure in their sons' accomplishments and tended to thwart their sons' desire for achievement.

26

Grunebaum's children equated academic achievement with the destruction of others and, therefore, were plagued with the fear that they would lose control of their aggressive drives if they applied themselves in learning. They chose, instead, to retreat into dependent love and sought roles as helpers to their fathers and teachers. Steward's (63) series confirmed these findings.

Miller and Westman (64) found that severe reading retardation in boys was one facet of a personality type necessary for maintaining the stability of the family. The child with a reading problem adopted a pseudo-stupid identity as a means of coping with pressures from the mother to remain infantile and from the father to suppress masculinity. Many of the families' activities actually reinforced rather than alleviated the reading disability. Both parents also tended to deny the child's unrealized academic potential, supporting his apparent stupidity and helplessness. Another striking observation was that improvement in the child's reading was often accompanied by deterioration in the adjustment of another family member.

Current evidence suggests that family forces operate in both the development and maintenance of reading problems in children. Unfortunately, the literature does not adequately distinguish children with general learning problems from those with reading retardation, and the question of specificity remains unanswered. The reactions of parents to neurologically handicapped children have not been adequately considered. Comparison with patterns in families stressing scholarship in small children who later become scholarly adults, such as in the Shtetl culture (65), also would be illuminating.

School Centered Studies

Since most children learn to read in school, the circumstances of reading instruction deserve close attention. Although the education literature abounds with techniques for teaching reading, there is surprisingly little information about what actually goes on in the first grade classroom as children are introduced to reading. (66, 67) The child's attitude toward the early years of school influences his receptivity to instruction and may even determine whether he remains in school. (68) An important question, therefore, is how

27

much of the children's negative attitudes toward school springs from factors in the school itself. (69-71)

Examining six aspects of the school experience may shed light on the meaning of school for the child: 1) attendance; 2) the physical plant; 3) the teacher-child relationship; 4) teaching methods; 5) administrative structure; and 6) peer relations.

1. **Attendance.** Although many children learn adequately without regular school attendance, there is considerable evidence that frequent absences due to illness or changing schools result in difficulty in learning to read.

Factors associated with getting to and from school may influence attendance. In some instances uncongenial neighborhoods or unfortunate experiences on school buses may color a child's attitude toward school and learning.

2. **Physical Plant.** The atmosphere of the school building and classroom plays a role in the child's feeling about school and the ease with which learning takes place. Several decades ago the inadequacy of school room lighting proved to be a significant deterrent to learning. Among the current architectural experiments for improving learning conditions is the classroom without windows in which the distractions and uneven lighting of large windows are eliminated. At the present time a widely accepted contribution to tranquility in the classroom is sound reduction by means of floor carpeting. The same principles used to improve working conditions in industry are pertinent in schools.

3. **Teacher-Child Relationship.** In the early grades a favorable relationship between the teacher and her pupils is far more important in determining the success of her instruction than her sophistication in teaching techniques. (72) Identification with the teacher is an important part of the process of learning. Hammond (23) supports this view by suggesting that the inability of chronically negativistic children to identify with the teachers plays an important role in their failure to learn. On the other hand, teachers may offer poor models for identification. Strongly suggestive evidence for the neurotic impairment of some teachers' effectiveness was found in Jersild's (73) survey of teachers who received psychotherapy.

4. **Teaching Methods.** Although constant experimentation takes place, institutionalization of teaching techniques often results from the natural tendency to use time-tested methods. Most instruction is carried out using reward or punishment as the motivating forces. The teaching of reading, writing, and arithmetic has traditionally relied on repetition, reinforcement, and rote memory.

Reading instruction ordinarily begins with small units which are easily handled, later proceeding through orderly steps from the simple to the more complex. Reinforcing learning through the use of several sensory pathways, especially visual, auditory, and kinesthetic, seems to foster retention of information. (74-77)

Although teaching techniques can be geared to children's receptivity, the most important recognition of children's natural inclinations has occurred in planning course content. Ideally subject matter is calculated to evoke children's interest by touching on subjects of immediate importance to them.

5. **Administrative Structure.** One time-honored tradition is grouping children according to their chronological age. Children enter school at a point determined by their birthdate. More realistic criteria for starting children in kindergarten are developing in some school systems because of the wide range of readiness encountered between the ages of 4 and 6. The arbitrary grade system is also being reevaluated because of children's varied capacities within each grade level. Merging of the first three grades permits recognition of differences in reading ability so that an advanced 6-year-old might read with 8-year-olds and a slow 8-year-old with 6-year-olds.

Cunningham (78) capitalized on a fortuitous situation in which a community eliminated kindergarten for economic reasons. Children started in the first grade at the age of 5 and were passed on to the second and third grades even though basic reading skills had not been acquired. After 3 years of this program, many children with reading disabilities and personality problems inflated the number of referrals to the local psychiatric clinic. Kindergarten was reinstituted, and a 5-year follow-up disclosed that referrals to the psychiatric clinic decreased by 90% from the inflated figure.

6. **Peer Relationships.** Competition with peers and siblings is an important incentive for learning. At the same time negative attitudes toward learning can be generated by peers. (79) This is especially true with boys among whom other values frequently take precedence over achieving in the classroom and pleasing the teacher. The distracting influence of children on each other during classroom routines often interferes with concentration.

The evidence suggests that the school plays a crucial role in the origin and aggravation of reading retardation, but its relative importance as compared with factors within the child and his family remains to be established. There is great need for sensitive, direct observation of children in the process of learning to read during the first and second grades. It is also during these early grades that the school offers society's first opportunity to take inventory of the products of families. The learning patterns of children are ordinarily established in the home and are applied and tested for the first time during the process of learning to read in school.

Commentary

The volume of literature on reading retardation testifies to the elusiveness of a problem that on the surface is enticingly simple but that underneath has the consistency of quicksand. Retarded reading is comparable to a physical sign which reflects underlying pathology and occurs in a cluster of other signs and symptoms. Some children show relatively isolated impairment of reading and others show generalized learning disability. Many children fail in academic learning, but learn with alacrity in other areas. We have reviewed segments of knowledge about reading problems accumulated by the various disciplines. Now we will consider how these diverse factors bear on the individual child as he learns to read in school. Our concern is the child who has difficulty learning to read, and we are, therefore, excluding the youngster who learns how to read before entering school.

If we think of a child encountering the printed word with his teacher and peer group in his first grade classroom, we can isolate six cardinal points for examination: 1) the classroom atmosphere; 2) the characteristics of the stimulus (the printed word); 3) the child's receptivity to the stimulus; 4) the child's perception of the stimulus; 5) the child's ability to integrate his perceptions; and 6) the child's ability to use his knowledge.

Classroom Atmosphere. In most school systems children are away from home for a full day for the first time in the first grade. Each child is assigned a space of his own in a large room filled with distracting objects, sounds, and people. The major part of his school day is spent in structured activities prescribed by an adult other than his parents. The child naturally transfers familiar wishes, feelings, and attitudes from members of his family to the teacher. In the past, spoken language was sufficient for communication with his immediate world. Now written language is necessary to permit contact with his widening world. Although it is a means for acquiring knowledge, reading often is seen by the child as an end in itself. His motivation to learn to read is enhanced by the degree to which he sees reading as a useful tool.

On entering kindergarten the child was caught up in society's busy process of transmitting culture to its individual members; in the first grade he becomes acquainted with the expectations of the role of student. In contrast to his accustomed way of living the child shifts from being physically active to being physically passive and intellectually active. As a student the child must passively receive and actively grasp information, comply with instructions, restrain his impulses, pay attention at prescribed times, accept judgments about his performance, and respond to correction with a desire to improve. All of these role requirements are based upon the assumption that the child wants to, and is able to, explore and master his own capacities and the world around him. These requirements are more naturally suited to the inclinations of girls than boys and are ordinarily promulgated by women teachers.

The Characteristics of the Stimulus. The peculiarities of the stimulus, printed English, should be recognized in any discussion of reading retardation. When compared with Oriental pictorial ideographs, the highly abstract and ambiguous nature of English letters and words becomes evident. A pertinent Japanese case report (14) disclosed tha a 12-year-old boy could read ideographs but had great difficulty learning to read Japanese written in the Latin alphabet. In contrast with other western languages, English has numerous phonetic ambiguities and grammatical exceptions because the same combinations of letters take on different sounds and meanings. For example, the child puzzles at length over the differences between "to," "too," and "two." Something he accepts in good faith once is not true at another time. The issue of trusting oneself and others is thereby injected into the reading process by these discrepancies. The ambiguity and complexity of English are ordinarily taken in stride, but there is room for the highly personalized projection of fantasies on letters and words by the small child.

Receptivity to the Stimulus. The receptivity of the child to learning depends upon the presence of certain personality capacities which can be seen emerging in the play of the preschool child. (80, 81) These necessary capacities are the willingness to passively receive, the ability to tolerate frustration (especially accepting one's own errors), the ability to postpone immediate gratification of impulses, the willingness to relinquish infantile omnipotence and omniscience, the willingness to submit to authority, the ability to permit thoughts to flow freely in the mind, the ability to concentrate attention at will and exclude the intrusion of distracting fantasies, and the ability to leave the familiar old and embrace the unfamiliar new. In addition to these personality capacities, the wellsprings of motivation for learning are from impulses to take things into the body, curiosity, the desire to master oneself and the outside world, identification with the teacher, the wish to please adults, the striving to compete with peers, and parental values supporting the desirability of learning.

Perception of the Stimulus. While an intact perceptual apparatus is needed for the smooth acquisiton of normal reading ability, vision and hearing can be defective and reading can still be learned through special techniques, e.g., braille. The child's cortical perception must be developed to a level which permits accurate recognition of form and differentiating figures from their backgrounds.

Integrations of Perceptions. At the level of integration the perceived stimulus becomes associated with stored memory traces, and a concept is formed. The concrete perception becomes a symbol and gains meaning through its connections with other ideas. Abstract thinking depends upon the ability to connect a perception with stored memory traces. Memory is required to permit the retention of an impression so that associations can be made to it. The correlation of visual, auditory, and kinesthesic perceptions enhances the learning process by making a number of simultaneously reinforcing cues available to the brain. Not only are preexisting ideas associated with the perceived mental image, but emotions are also evoked by the perceived image which includes not only the printed word but the person presenting the stimulus. If the total perception triggers anxiety, the learning process is blocked.

Ability to Use Knowledge. The ability to read is only practical if it can be used. Because customary methods of measuring reading ability depend upon his cooperation, the child's displayed ability may not accurately reflect his true ability. Through the use of reading the child reinforces his ability to read by gratifying himself or others. The mistakes he makes while reading help him to correct errors. If he does not pursue reading, his errors are not detected. With practice he shifts from auditory-visual reading to pure visual reading, which is considerably faster and more useful. The act of reading itself is then endowed with pleasure. By the same token a child who reads poorly experiences displeasure when he tries to read and, therefore, tends to avoid reading. The successful mastery of reading makes for better reading; failure in reading leads to further failure.

Summary

The pediatrician can play a valuable role in the identification, evaluation, and understanding of the retarded reader.

Any child with academic difficulties deserves an assessment of both his intelligence and his reading ability. Not infrequently children with poor reading ability escape detection until identified through survey reading testing in a physician's office, (82, 83) confirmed by more precise reading testing in the hands of a qualified psychoeducational diagnostician.

The pediatrician is in a key position to detect and evaluate visual acuity and auditory defects as contributing factors to retarded reading. The possibility of enervating chronic disease can also be ruled out.

Because of his medical orientation the pediatrician can also interpret the complex nature of reading disability to the family and the school. The initial detection of deficient reading ability by the pediatrician can be helpful in aiming school resources or remedial tutoring so as to correct the child's deficiency.

In some instances mildly retarded readers improve through exposure to teachers and classroom situations that offer them more favorable circumstances for learning. Most retarded readers with a moderate degree of deficiency respond to remedial tutoring in skilled hands. When these educational procedures are ineffective or insufficient, psychiatric referral for evaluation of the multiple individual and family factors is indicated. The severely retarded reader presents a difficult therapeutic problem which requires both psychiatric and educational measures.

It is quite apparent that defective reading is maladaptive in the process of education, but it also may serve adaptive purposes in neurosis and in the web of family pathology. Parents especially profit from an explanation that the problem often is not simply the result of faulty teaching. As a professional outside of the school system, the pediatrician can help parents recognize their own unwitting contribution to the problem.

Once identified, reading retardation clearly involves many differential diagnostic considerations. There are many points at which the process of learning to read can go awry. In essence successful mastery of reading depends upon an appropriately mature central nervous system, personality, and family.

References

1. Bond, G. L., and Tinker, M. A.: READING DIFFICULTIES: THEIR DIAGNOSIS AND CORRECTION, New York: Appleton-Century-Crofts, Inc., 1957.

2. Epheon, P., and Beulah, K.: EMOTIONAL DIFFICULTIES IN READING, New York: Julian Press, Inc., 1953.

3. Heller, T. M.: Word Blindness: Survey of Literature and Report of 28 Cases, PEDIATRICS 31:669, 1963.

4. Monroe, M.: CHILDREN WHO CANNOT READ, Chicago: University of Chicago Press, 1932.

5. Robinson, H. M.: WHY PUPILS FAIL IN READING, Chicago: University of Chicago Press, 1946.

6. Roswell, F., and Natchez, G.: READING DISABILITY, DIAGNOSIS AND TREATMENT, New York: Basic Books, Inc., Publishers, 1964.

7. Vernon, M. A.: BACKWARDNESS IN READING, New York, Cambridge Univ. Press, 1957.

8. Fabian, A. A.: Reading Disability: Index of Pathology, AMER. J. ORTHOPSYCHIAT. 25:319, 1955.

9. Eames, T. H.: Comparison of Ocular Characteristics of Unselected and Reading Disability Groups, J. EDUC. RES. 25:211, 1932.

10. Tinker, M. A.: Eye Movements in Reading, J. EDUC. RES. 30:241, 1936.

11. Betts, E. H.: Physiological Approach to Analysis of Reading Disabilities, EDUC. RES. BULL. 13:135, 1934.

12. Ettlinger, C., and Hurwitz, L.: Dyslexia and Its Associated Disturbances, NEUROLOGY 12:477, 1960.

13. Ettlinger, C., and Jackson, D.: Organic Factors in Developmental Dyslexia, PROC. ROY. SOC. MED. 48:998, 1955.

14. Money, J.: READING DISABILITY: PROGRESS AND RESEARCH NEEDS IN DYSLEXIA, Baltimore: Johns Hopkins Press, 1962.

15. Broadbent. W.: On Cerebral Mechanisms of Thought and Speech, MED. CHIR. TRANS. 55:145, 1872.

16. Kawi, A. A., and Pasamanick, B.: Prenatal and Paranatal Factors in Development of Childhood Reading Disorders, MONOGR. SOC. RES. CHILD DEVELOP. 24: 1959.

17. Mykelbust, H. R., and Bashes, B.: Psychoneurologic Learning Disorders in Children, ARCH. PEDIAT. 77:247, 1960.

18. Cohn, R.: Neurologic Study of Delayed Acquisition of Reading and Writing Abilities in Children, TRANS. AMER. NEUROL. ASSOC. 85:182, 1960.

19. Hermann, K.: READING DISABILITY: MEDICAL STUDY OF WORD-BLINDNESS AND RELATED HANDICAPS, Springfield, III: Charles C. Thomas, Publisher, 1959.

20. Orton, S. T.: READING, WRITING AND SPEECH PROBLEMS IN CHILDREN, New York: W. W. Norton & Co., Inc., 1937.

21. Silver, A., and Hagin, R.: Specific Reading Disabilities, COMP. PSYCHIAT. 1:126, 1960.

22. Gates, A. I., and Bennett, C. C.: REVERSAL TENDENCIES IN READING, New York: Columbia University Press, 1933.

23. Hammond, J.: Learning and Behavior Problems of Children, VIRGINIA MED. MONTHLY 89:379, 1962.

24. Prechtl, H. F. R.: "Reading Difficulties as Neurological Problem in Childhood," in Money, J.: READING DISABILITY, Baltimore: Johns Hopkins Press, 1962, p. 187.

25. Rabinovitch, R., et al.: Research Approach to Reading Retardation, PROC. ASSOC. RES. NEUROL. MENT. DIS. 34:363, 1956.

26. Rabinovitch, R. D.: "Reading and Learning Disabilities," in Arieti, S.: AMERICAN HANDBOOK OF PSYCHIATRY, New York: Basic Books, 1959, chap 43, p. 857.

27. Norbury, F. B., and Loeffler, J. D.: Primary Reading Epilepsy, JAMA 184:661, 1963.

28. Bender, L.: PSYCHOPATHOLOGY OF CHILDREN WITH ORGANIC BRAIN DISORDERS, Springfield, Ill.: Charles C. Thomas, Publisher, 1956.

29. French, B. L.: Psychologic Factors in Cases of Reading Difficulties, read before the Secondary Education Board, 27th Annual Conference, New York, March 7, 1953.

30. Olson, W. C.: CHILD DEVELOPMENT, Boston: D. C. Heath and Co., 1949.

31. Fabian, A. A.: Vertical Rotation in Visual Motor Performance: Its Relationships to Reading Reversals, J. EDUC. PSYCHOL. 36:129, 1945.

32. Park, G. E.: Reading Failures in Children, ARCH. PEDIAT. 76:401, 1959.

33. Smith, D., and Carrigan, C.: NATURE OF READING DISABILITIES, New York: Harcourt, Brace and World, Inc., 1959.

34. Anthony, E. J.: Learning Difficulties in Childhood, J. AMER. PSYCHOANAL. ASSOC. 9:124, 1961.

35. Harris, I.: EMOTIONAL BLOCKS TO LEARNING, New York: Free Press of Glencoe, Inc., Division of Macmillan Co., 1961.

36. Jackson, J. A.: Survey of Psychologic, Social and Environmental Differences Between Advanced and Retarded Readers, J. GENET. PSYCHOL. 65:113, 1944.

37. Switzer, J.: Genetic Approach to Understanding of Learning Problems, J. AMER. ACAD. CHILD PSYCHIAT. 2:653, 1963.

38. Pearson, G. H. T.: Survey of Learning Difficulties, PSYCHOANAL. STUD. CHILD 7:322, 1952.

39. Pearson, G. H. T.: PSYCHOANALYSIS AND THE EDUCATION OF THE CHILD New York: W. W. Norton & Co., Inc., 1954.

40. Mahler, M.: Pseudo-Imbecility: Magic Cap of Invincibility, PSYCHOANAL. QUART. 11:149, 1942.

41. Strachey, J.: Some Unconscious Factors in Reading, INT. J. PSYCHOANAL. 11:322, 1930.

42. Blanchard, P.: Psychoanalytic Contributions to Problems of Reading Disabilities, PSYCHOANAL. STUD. CHILD 2:163, 1946.

43. Klein, M.: "Contribution to a Theory of Intellectual Inhibition," in CONTRIBUTIONS TO PSYCHOANALYSIS: 1921-1945, London: Hogarth Press, 1948.

44. Jarvis, V.: Clinical Observations on Visual Problem in Reading Disability PSYCHOANAL. STUD. CHILD 13:451, 1958.

45. Brown, W. P.: CONCEPTIONS OF PERCEPTUAL DEFENCE, New York: Cambridge Univ. Press, 1961.

46. Freud, A.: PSYCHOANALYTIC TREATMENT OF CHILDREN, London: Imago Publishing Company, Ltd, 1946.

47. Fleiss, R.: Metapsychology of Analyst, PSYCHOANAL. QUART. 1:211, 1942.

48. Rosen, V. H.: Strephosymbolia: Intrasystemic Disturbance of Synthetic Function of Ego, PSYCHOANAL. STUD. CHILD 10:83, 1955.

49. Freud, S.: From History of Infantile Neuroses, in Freud, S.: COLLECTED PAPERS, vol. 3, London: Hogarth Press, 1925.

50. Rubenstein, B. O.; Falick, M. L.; and Levitt, M.: Learning Impotence: Suggested Diagnostic Category, AMER. J. ORTHOPSYCHIAT. 29:315, 1959.

51. Freed, H.; Abrams, I.; and Peifer, C.: Reading Disabilities: New Therapeutic Approach and Its Implications, J. CLIN. EXP. PSYCHOPATH. 20:251, 1959.

52. Hallgren, B.: Specific Dyslexia, ACTA. PSYCHIAT. NEUROL. 65 (Suppl): 1950.

53. Tjossen, T.; Hansen, T. G.; and Ripley, H. S.: INVESTIGATION OF READING DIFFICULTIES IN YOUNG CHILDREN, Seattle: University of Washington Press, 1957.

54. Tjossen, T.; Hansen, T. G.; and Ripley, H. S.: Investigation of Reading Difficulties in Young Children, AMER. J. PSYCHIAT. 118:1104, 1962.

55. Silverman, J. S., et al.: Clinical Findings in Reading Disability Children: Special Class of Intellectual Inhibition, AMER. J. ORTHOPSYCHIAT. 29:298, 1959.

56. Liss, E.: Motivations in Learning, PSYCHOANAL. STUD. CHILD 10:100, 1955.

57. Gyarfas, M. G.: Learning Disability in Boys: Exploration of Family Pathology, SOC. SERVICE REV. 35:397, 1961.

58. Rank, B., and Macnaughton, D.: Contribution to Early Ego Development, PSYCHOANAL. STUD. CHILD 5:53, 1950.

59. Staver, N.: Child's Learning Difficulties as Related to Emotional Problem of Mothers, AMER. J. ORTHOPSYCHIAT. 23:131, 1953.

60. Hellman, I.: Some Observations on Mothers of Children with Intellectual Inhibitions, PSYCHOANAL. STUD. CHILD 9:259-273, 1954.

61. Grunebaum, M. G., et al.: Renunciation and Denial in Learning Difficulties, AMER. J. ORTHOPSYCHIAT. 28:98, 1958.

62. Grunebaum, M. G., et al.: Fathers of Sons With Primary Neurotic Learning Inhibitions, AMER. J. ORTHOPSYCHIAT. 32:462, 1962.

63. Steward, R. S.: Personality Maladjustment and Reading Achievement, AMER. J. ORTHOPSYCHIAT. 20:410, 1950.

64. Miller, D. R., and Westman, J. C.: Reading Disability as Condition of Family Stability, FAMILY PROC. 3:66, 1964.

65. Zborowski, M.: "Place of Book-Learning in Traditional Jewish Culture," in Mead, M. (ed.): CHILDHOOD IN CONTEMPORARY CULTURES, Chicago: University of Chicago Press, 1955, p. 119.

66. Bruner, J. S.: PROCESS OF EDUCATION, Cambridge, Mass: Harvard University Press, 1961.

67. Conant, J. B.: LEARNING TO READ: REPORT OF CONFERENCE OF READING EXPERTS, Princeton, NJ: Princeton University Press, 1962.

68. Lichter, S. O., et al.: DROP OUTS, New York: Free Press of Glencoe, Inc., Division of Macmillan Co., 1962.

69. Kubie, L. S.: Fostering of Creative Scientific Productivity, DAEDELUS 91:293, 1962.

70. Mayer, M.: SCHOOLS, New York: Harper & Row, Publishers, Inc., 1961.

71. Skinner, B. F.: Science of Learning and Art of Teaching, HARVARD EDUC. REV. 24:86, 1954.

72. Brucker, M. D.: Factors in Teaching-Learning Situation and Their Effect on First Grade Reading, CATHOLIC EDUC. REV. 52:249, 1954.

73. Jersild, A. T.: MEANING OF PSYCHOTHERAPY IN TEACHER'S LIFE AND WORK, New York: Columbia University Press, 1962.

74. Anderson, I. H., and Dearborn, W. F.: PSYCHOLOGY OF TEACHING READING, New York: Ronald Press Co., 1952.

75. Gray, W. S.: TEACHING OF READING, International View, Cambridge, Mass: Harvard Press, 1957.

76. Morse, W. C.; Ballantine, F.; and Dixon, W.: STUDIES IN PSYCHOLOGY OF LEARNING, Ann Arbor, Mich.: University of Michigan Press, 1951.

77. Schonell, F. J.: PSYCHOLOGY AND TEACHING OF READING, New York: Philosophical Library, Inc., 1961.

78. Cunningham, J. M.: Psychiatric Case Work as Epidemiologic Tool, AMER. J. ORTHOPSYCHIAT. 18:650, 1948.

79. Lippitt, R., and Gold, M.: Classroom Structure as Mental Health Problem, J. SOC. ISSUES 15:40, 1959.

80. Namnum, A., and Prelinger, E.: On Psychology of Reading Process, AMER. J. ORTHOPSYCHIAT. 31:820, 1961.

81. Omwake, E. B.: "Child's Estate," in Solnit, A. J., and Provence, S. A. (eds.): MODERN PERSPECTIVES IN CHILD DEVELOPMENT, New York: International Universities Press, Inc., 1963, p. 577.

82. Solnit, A. J., and Stark, M. H.: Pediatric Management of School Learning Problems of Underachievement, NEW ENG. J. MED. 261:988, 1959.

83. Gray Oral Reading Paragraphs, the Test Division of the Bobbs-Merrill Co., Inc., 4300 W. 62nd St., Indianapolis, Ind. 46206.

STUDY QUESTIONS

1. Westman, Arthur, and Scheidler reviewed investigations and theories of reading disorders under the headings organ-centered, child-centered, family-centered, and school-centered. What terminology might they have used instead of those four headings, had they been writing primarily for teachers?

2. Match the four headings—1) organ-centered, 2) child-centered, 3) family-centered, and 4) school-centered—with the authors' conclusions regarding the role of each in reading retardation. Conclusions: A) definitely plays a crucial role, but its relative importance not yet established; B) important in only a very small number of cases; C) probably operative in a general fashion, but further research on specific effects needed; D) most of the data are subjective and uncontrolled, but this factor is strongly implicated.

3. The authors suggest that the pediatrician "not infrequently" is the first to identify poor reading, is in a key position to diagnose visual and auditory defects, and can interpret reading disability to the family and school. Do you see all three roles as equally appropriate? Why or why not?

4. What does the final sentence of the article suggest would be the job of a remedial reading teacher? Is this position consistent with the authors' view that maturation lag does not adequately explain reading deficiency? Why do they reject the maturation lag theory?

5. The bibliography provided by the authors is excellent. Suppose that you were to survey intensively the literature in each of the areas covered in this review. Find a major source in the bibliography that you would want to use in each of the areas.

6. The authors state that "it is clear that the underlying pathological processes (of reading retardation) must be identified." What data explanation, or rationale, do they offer to support this statement?

2: CONDITIONS RELATED TO SPECIFIC READING DISABILITY

Walter Hill

Hill focuses on the difficulties in our conceptualization and communication about the nature of reading disability. He proposes a broad continuum which covers the entire spectrum of reading disorders and encompasses the many divergent frameworks, definitions, and terminology offered by others. He presents an administrative program for providing services to children whose reading disability falls anywhere within this broad framework.

    B. D. B.

Reprinted with permission of the author and publisher from NEW FRONTIERS IN SPECIAL EDUCATION, SELECTED CONVENTION PAPERS, 43rd ANNUAL CEC CONVENTION, Washington, D.C.: NEA, CEC, 1965, pp. 196-205.

Concern for "specific reading disorders" has had a sporadic developmental history. Expressed as long ago as 1896 by Morgan, who likened it to the actions of individuals with brain damage, it has sputtered off and on through the periodic efforts of such individual theorists as Hinshelwood (1917) and Orton (1937). We appear to be entering a period of resurging concern about this problem. Developmentally, our present state may be likened to early adolescence with its rapid disorganized growth and its painfully ambitious and uncertain self-consciousness.

There is some reason to believe that we will make a better assault upon the problem of extreme reading disability in the next decade than we have in the previous half century. This conjecture is based partly upon the assumption that the revitalized concern for the exceptional individual in our society will extend to problems in learning the basic school skills. It is based also upon the assumption that the progress we have made in understanding the classic areas of exceptionality, the growth we have made in our understanding of the reading and learning to read processes, and the greater sophistication we have developed in gathering and using human research data, will be channeled toward a better understanding and treatment of this disability.

There can be little doubt that we have our work cut out for us. John Dewey once observed that "a problem well stated was half solved." If by "well stated" Dewey meant that the specific and functional nature of the problem had been defined, that the major related variables had been identified, and that the problem had been placed within a broad conceptual framework which squares with present evidence about the problem, and which permits the integration and application of new data as it is obtained—then, we are not yet halfway to our solution. Such progress would seem mandatory to a systematic attack on the cause-effect relationships which underlie effective diagnostic and treatment operations.

A fair start would be to recognize that general consensus about these aspects of the problem is lacking. Certain individual investigators have developed problem statements which satisfy their own criteria and within their own conceptual framework. That these individual conceptions of the problem have not met broad professional needs is evident in the growing number of such individual statements. That the problem should be attacked from divergent directions is laudable. The lamentable aspect is the professional communication difficulty which develops from the lack of common conception of the problem of specific reading disability. This communication problem deters the efforts of both researcher and teacher, and could lead to professional divisiveness concerning the proper nature of school treatment. If such should happen, it can be expected that efforts to provide programs for extreme reading disability will be confounded.

Why do we have such a problem? As students in elementary psychology, we learned that our perception, or the meaning we associated with objects and symbols, was highly dependent upon our backgrounds of knowledge; that, in effect, we "saw" with our existing store of information. When we observe the wide variety of professional backgrounds represented among those who have researched and written about reading behavior and reading disability, (e.g., psychologists of various schools and research interests, sociologists, linguists, exceptional child specialists, psychiatrists, classroom teachers, medical personnel of numerous specialties, communication theorists, even remedial reading specialists), it is surprising that we have communicated as well as we have.

As students of elementary psychology, we also learned that the phenomenon of identifying with a sub-group tends to inhibit identification with the larger class. And once having formed our perceptions within the accepted group limits, we tend to challenge and reject on emotional grounds those points of view which run contrary to these beliefs.

It may be that the phenomena of perception and identification confound our efforts to develop an operational framework of reading disability which is broad enough. For example, there may be some who will be disturbed to find that the larger body of researchers of reading problems would discount the concept of a "specific reading disorder" in favor of the concept of "extreme learning difficulty in basic reading skills." Furthermore, it shows that available evidence indicates that these cases compose a relatively small percentage of those pupils whose reading difficulty provokes serious school and life adjustment problems. Yet, such evidence, objectively considered, does not prevent the development of a broad framework in which extreme reading disability, including specific behavioral and etiological patterns, can be studied and treated within a total attack upon reading problems.

It is to this difficulty in the conceptualization and communication about the nature of reading disability that this paper is addressed. Specific attention will be directed to current patterns in conceptualization, to the differential characteristics of general and extreme reading disability, to the need for a functional school framework for treating reading disability, and to the ubiquitous problem of cause and effect.

VARIATION IN DEFINITION OF THE PROBLEM

A Priori Terminology

It is natural for a communicator to select some particular term to refer to the object or class of objects about which he wishes to make statements. An unusually wide range of descriptive terminology has been employed to refer to youngsters exhibiting unusual difficulty in learning to read. Illustrative here are such appellations as: aphasic, alexic, dyslexic, congenitally word blinded, functional illiterate, language phobic, organismically immature, culturally disadvantaged, confused in lateral dominance, chemically imbalanced, autistic, retarded reader, slow learner, strephosymbolic, and remedial case. Such terms may reflect either notable descriptive characteristics or the perceptual background of the communicator, or both. It is significant, however, that such terminology quickly takes on the overtones of *a priori* definition; thus, by associating a name with the problem we have implied major causal influence.

Specific Definitions

Concise definitions of extreme reading problems are not prevalent in the literature. This may imply that we are not confident of the nature of this area of exceptionality. The definitions available find greater agreement upon the severity of the problem than upon the function or etiology of the disability. The following are representative:

Developmental alexia; noted particularly by distortion in recognition and recall of symbols and symptoms of lateral confusion; strepho-symbolia (Orton, 1937).

Unusual difficulty with reading characterized by inadequate organismic age (Olson, 1942).

Disorder in the understanding of word forms; precipitating factors may be psychological or physiological (Fernald, 1943).

Reading difficulty accompanied by the personal conviction of such difficulty; an expression of the social and emotional maladjustment of the child (Dreikurs, 1954).

The illiterates; those unable to master even the simpler mechanics of reading; probably different in nature from general backwardness in reading in which the child reads slowly and with poor comprehension (Vernon, 1958).

Severe reading disability; the lowest two percent of readers demonstrating symptoms of deficient discrimination of symbols, severe blending deficiency, and abnormally low rate on familiar material (Smith, 1959).

Specific dyslexia; both degenerative and developmental, which is severe and which does not apply to the hearing and speaking of language (Money, 1962).

These definitions tend to imply a particular etiology or basic nature for the problem, although they do not indicate a common view of this etiology. The public schools, on the other hand, have taken a developmental, normative view of the problem of reading disability; that is, they have utilized degree of difficulty rather than specific pattern or etiology of the difficulty as their basis of operation. Thus, the schools have tended to place diagnostic and treatment emphasis upon the more frequent cases which fit the classification of general reading disability. Specific or extreme reading disability case would be included in this classification, but generally, without special or differentiated attack.

Broader Theoretical Structures

Several broader theoretical settings for reading disability have been developed from which we may gain some comparative view of specific or extreme reading disability. Smith (1959) sees severe reading disability within a total context of normative progress in reading development; i.e., the lower two percent of the school distribution. However, he includes criteria of perception and blending difficulties and resistance to traditional remedial help as further delineation. Smith's analysis of the three models or analogues which have been employed to explain severe reading disability are useful here, since they suggest three different views of causation. Two of these are classical models: 1) the Hinshelwood-Orton-Rabinovitch "brain-lesion" view of etiology, and 2) the Olson-Robinson-Park organismic malfunctioning view of causation. The third is Smith's own, and may be described as a psychophysical model which places basic causal emphasis upon malfunction of synaptic transmission— as a result of metabolic imbalance.

Rabinovitch's own framework distinguishes three patterns of reading disability: 1) *secondary reading disability,* in which the capacity to learn is intact and the causative factor may come from a variety of exogenous circumstances; 2) *brain injury with a result of reading retardation,* in which there is clear evidence of neurological deficit; and 3) *primary reading disability,* in which the disabled reader manifests behavior symptomatic of neurological disorganization, but without clear history or examination evidence of the presence of brain damage.

Another comprehensive framework is developed by Bateman in the December, 1964, issue of EXCEPTIONAL CHILDREN. Bateman's concern is with the broader issue of special learning disability, and within this, she delineates three major but overlapping subcategories: 1) reading disability or dyslexia, which includes general as well as "primary" reading retardation; 2) verbal communication disorders, or difficulty with comprehension or expression of spoken language; and 3) visual-motor integration problems, with or without accompanying dyslexia.

Between these theoretical structures, a broader framework in which we may place extreme reading disability begins to emerge. However, in them we also see a common pattern in the definition of extreme reading disability: the employment of default conceptualization. As a result of this phenomenon, the specific or extreme reading disability case becomes a negative issue: a pupil who *is not* making normal progress in reading development, who *does not* fit within the classic categories of the exceptional child, and who *is not* propitiously served by programs for general reading disability. Default conceptualization is inefficient, and it does not provide for specific control in either research or treatment. However, this tendency for default classification does emphasize the need for conceptualizing extreme reading disability in such a manner that it can be integrated into a practical school program.

The Underachievement Concept of Reading Disability

While most recent writers have accepted that reading disability necessarily implies underachievement (i.e., differential between reading performance level and mental ability level), public school personnel who are responsible for the instructional needs of large numbers of children as well as for the attendant issue of school-public relations, have utilized underachievement as the prevailing criterion of reading disability. The most frequently employed school formula of underachievement has been $MA-RA>1$, which has tended to sift out approximately fifteen percent of school children in English-speaking countries.

Owing to the problem of giving special treatment to so large a group, to the increasing variability in skills achievement at successive school levels, as well as to the obvious difficulty of classifying an extremely intelligent youngster as a case of reading disability because he reads only slightly above his grade level, many schools have developed graduated criteria for special consideration of underachievement for successive grade levels. In addition, they have assumed that such underachievement is limiting (or blocking) improvement in skill function. Thus, a typical school identification system might require 1) evidence of adequate intelligence; 2) underachievement of one year at the primary level, two years at the intermediate level, and three years at the secondary level; and 3) assumption of such limiting function that the pupil evidences little reading growth through the regular classroom program. Such a classification system nudges the selection of reading disability cases in the direction of severe malfunction.

CHARACTERISTICS OF READING DISABILITY

Systematic observation of reading disability is a prerequisite to the development of effective diagnostic and treatment modes. Some of the more prominent characteristics associated with reading disability may be seen in the following clinical and research generalizations.

Factors Associated with "General" Reading Disability

For research purposes "general" reading disability usually has been defined as underachievement in reading of one or more years at the elementary school level and two or more years at the secondary school level. On the average, such broad criteria typically identify about ten percent of school females and twenty percent of the school males. Three decades of investigation have seen substantial change in the methods of investigating reading problems. The pattern of acceptable investigation has moved from single factor studies of causation, to single factor studies of association, to multiple factor studies of association, and more recently, to multiple regression investigation. This progression reflects increasing sophistication in the study of general reading disability, and accounts, perhaps, for a growing tendency to view general reading disability as a form of total pupil behavior. It may account also for an increasing skepticism of "single" approaches and solutions to reading disability. The following generalizations, which have been derived from authoritative reviews of the research, support this skepticism:

1. Excepting the condition of decided mental retardation, no factor or group of factors has appeared as a highly significant influence in a majority of studies.

2. Prediction coefficients in large sample studies have seldom exceeded +.7, which leaves approximately 50% of the sample variance of reading achievement to be explained.

3. Most problem conditions (for example, membership in lower socioeconomic class), which have been discovered among the characteristics of poor readers, have also been identified in the make-up of good readers.

4. The present handicapping influence of an anomaly is more crucial to the treatment of current reading disability than evidence of past abnormal development.

5. A direct relationship exists between the severity of the reading disability and the degree and number of associated anomalies in the case. This observation has led some researchers to hypothesize that it is the number of anomalies rather than their specific nature which breaks down the reader's basic compensatory power and thus leads to the disability.

6. The significance of the anomaly is somewhat dependent upon the reader's instructional setting. For example, emotional hyperactivity is more likely to contribute to reading difficulty in a rigidly structured reading class. Similarly, speech and hearing defects are more significant in programs emphasizing oral reading and phonic approaches.

In the thousands of studies of reading performance on record, nearly every variable which differentiates one pupil from another has been associated with individual differences in reading ability. Those which have appeared rather consistently and significantly reflect a cross-section of human characteristics— primarily exogenous influences. In addition to general mental retardation, which is tacitly recognized in utilizing underachievement as a basic criterion for identification of disability, the following indicate factors of greater probable association with general reading disability. The intensive case study of a particular pupil may not conform to these modal expectations, of course.

Intellectual Factors: mental immaturity for initial reading instruction; inadequate meaning vocabulary; comparative depression in verbal intelligence test scores; abnormal variation in subtest scores; subculture depression of cognitive power; depression from prolonged reading or communication deficiency; and variation in associational mode.

Physical Factors: visual problems in near point acuity and binocular coordination; notable hearing loss within voice range; direct evidence of neurological difficulty; endocrine disturbance, particularly hyperthyroid and hypothyroid malfunction; and general illnesses which combine to lower drive or which produce extended absence from school during the primary grades.

Perceptual-Linguistic Factors: deficiency in visual and auditory discrimination and synthesis; deficiency in visual-auditory integration; inadequate grasp of English as a basic language; and speech defect, particularly stuttering and indistinct enunciation.

Social-Emotional Maladjustment: depressed self-concept; peer aggression; hostility toward authority; withdrawal pattern; high anxiety-tension level; and specific anxiety within the instructional reading situation.

Specific Environmental Factors: deprivation of school readiness experience; cultural isolation as a result of geographic or social circumstances;

conflict of motivation due to cultural discontinuity; masculinity; inconsistent parental patterns of rejection and overprotection; lower socioeconomic class membership; and inadequate school adjustment to individual differences.

Factors Associated with Extreme Reading Disability

Most of the characteristics associated with general reading disability are appropriately associated with extreme disability. As has been observed, both the degree and number of individual anomalies tend to increase as we concentrate upon greater severity of the reading problem. Following is an overview or composite of additional conditions associated with extreme reading disability which have been drawn from various investigations.

1. The pupil's reading performance is quite low normatively, and functionally; frequently, it is blocked at the level of illiteracy or near-illiteracy. Silent reading is so slow and meaningless that the pupil requires constant teacher aid. Oral reading of the simplest material is tedious, punctuated by strain, hesitancy, repetition, and mispronunciation.

2. Extreme learning difficulty usually is observed in other basic skills, particularly those of spelling and writing.

3. The reading disability may appear as part of a larger problem of communication disability.

4. The difficulty is evident from the earliest phases of formal instruction; except in rare cases of emotional or organic pathology, the reading ability never developed to independent operational level.

5. Lack of mastery of the essential reading readiness skills is characteristic, even for those pupils in the intermediate or upper grades.

6. The reading problem is manifested most clearly in difficulty with individual word forms, including the learning and recall of total word forms as well as the effective use of word analysis. (Investigators differ in their interpretation of this phenomena: some believe the reading problem to be the result of this basic difficulty with symbols, while others feel this word difficulty to be an artifact, since word learning is the initial phase of learning to read.)

7. Difficulty with word skills in reading appears to be global. Illustrative here are confusions in association of phonic and structural word parts, substitution, reversals, omission, and addition of words and word parts, inadequate use of context as a cue to word recognition and analysis, and difficulty in the identification or production of letter forms. In many cases, a profound dislike for working with skills frosts the word cake.

8. Deficiency in general perception has been noted by a number of investigators. This extends beyond difficulty with the reading readiness skills of discrimination and synthesis of word sounds and word forms to problems in the perception of nonword forms and perceptual-motor coordination.

9. Perceptual areas of confusion which have been associated with extreme reading disability include spatial orientation, figure-ground relationship, discrimination of size and shape, and the synthesis of parts.

10. As a behaving organism, this pupil has been described as generally immature in his development—physically, emotionally, and intellectually.

11. It has been pointed out by some clinicians and researchers that many severe reading disability cases exhibit symptoms of brain damage even though clear evidence of pathology may be lacking; e.g., unusual patterns of perseveration, poor motor coordination, hyperactivity, distractibility, catastrophic release, speech abnormality, and erratic response to stimulation.

A SCHOOL FRAMEWORK FOR READING DISABILITY

The Tenuous Position of Present School Programs

Traditionally, the elementary school teacher has been entrusted with the responsibility for reading instruction, and in this, she has been expected to consider the reading needs of all pupils. Many schools now accept that some pupils will need more than regular classroom help if they are to make adequate progress in reading. Increasingly, classroom teachers become sensitive to the needs of youngsters experiencing unusual difficulty in mastering the many subskills of reading. Special reading classes as well as the employment of remedial reading specialists to provide individual diagnosis and treatment continue in their frequency of appearance.

While private clinics and research groups have much to contribute to the treatment of reading disability, it is reasonable to assume that the regular school setting provides the optimal point of attack upon the problem. Acceptance of school responsibility for providing special diagnostic and treatment services for general reading disability has developed slowly. Lack of trained personnel, ineffective communication about the problem, and the absence of organized pressure groups contribute as much to this belated development as the more frequent rationalization of limited funds.

Acceptance of this responsibility is far from complete. Some schools provide for corrective reading classes, but not for individual remedial treatment. Most schools utilize standard group measures of achievement and aptitude, but few employ a solid program of individual diagnosis. Team case study and special treatment programs for extreme learning difficulty in reading are a rarity. The remedial reading programs in many schools hang in the balance of proving themselves with the phenomenal recovery of youngsters with every type and degree of learning anomaly and emotional maladjustment.

As the adherents for specific reading disorder treatment programs grow in number, and as we become more vociferous about the neglected needs of pupils with extreme disability in reading, we run a real risk of frightening nervous school administrators and conservative school boards out of special reading services frame of mind. Furthermore, the substitution of a specific reading disorders program for a general remedial services program is dubious and shortsighted progress, as many individual school systems already have learned, and one western statewide program of subsidy is about to learn. Extreme reading disability must be provided, but in the interests of its own success, it should be developed within a total school attack upon reading disability.

Major Elements of a Broad Consideration of Reading Disability

A total framework for considering the nature and treatment of reading disability is feasible through the integration of the basic school remedial program with recent concepts of extreme reading disability. In this, diagnostic and treatment success, while adjusted always to the individual needs of the pupil, aid in determining the classification of disability. The law of parsimony is observed; no pupil is given more expensive treatment (in terms of time and professional effort) than he needs to improve his reading skill. Thus, the pupil who profits from the semi-individual diagnosis and instruction of the corrective phase of the program is a corrective case. Similarly, those reading disability cases requiring diagnosis and treatment on a sustained daily controlled environment basis are extreme reading disability cases.

The following phases are suggested as significant elements in the total school provision for reading disability. All imply the condition of underachievement.

Phase I: Short-term, non-limiting disability. A number of different patterns occur here. Perhaps the most notable are: inadequate readiness for initial formal instruction, but without unusual confounding influences; initial learning confusions in a recently taught subskill; inefficient use of secondary reading skills such as reading rate, critical comprehension, or word-study skills; and developmental reading retardation, in which the underachieving reader, after a delayed start, now makes better than average progress with normal instruction. Major program implications are for an adequate general school testing program, and the development of general school staff ability to identify and adjust classroom instruction to these reading needs.

Phase II: Corrective reading disability of a mildly limiting nature. In this case, the pupil is having some, but not yet serious, difficulty in the learning and use of fundamental reading skills. Normatively, his underachievement will be less than a year, and he will be able to make use of his skill. However, in spite of good classroom procedures he continues to be confused in some skills. He responds to normal motivational provisions, and adjusts to group instructional circumstances. Major program implications are for individual skills diagnosis and corrective instruction within the class or in a special short-term corrective class of pupils with similar problems. Special attention should be given to identifying those pupils with a developing pattern of more severe difficulty.

Phase III: Remedial reading disability of a limiting nature. This disability case is underachieving by two or more years, and though he has demonstrated that he can learn to read he does so at a level low enough to produce school learning and adjustment problems. His disability shows a decisive tendency to become worse, and his attitude toward reading is negative to the point of blocking the usual corrective instructional efforts, especially those of a group nature. He may demonstrate ability to learn school tasks which are not highly dependent upon reading, such as arithmetic computation, but he will probably have difficulty with spelling and writing skills.

Program implications here call for intensive individual assessment or case study. Regular individual remedial treatment with special approaches to motivation and instruction directed at alleviating the fundamental skill weakness are usually required. This individual treatment should be integrated with and reinforced by appropriate adjustments in regular school instruction. The diagnostic, treatment, and consultant services of a remedial specialist with adequate time and training are essential to the program.

Phase IV: Extreme reading disability, including specific and generalized disorder patterns. The distinguishing feature of this disability is that functional reading ability is practically nonexistent in spite of evidence of general learning ability and adequate regular and remedial instruction. We have much to learn of the nature and treatment of these cases.

Further research may make it possible to develop clear subclassifications with attendant programs of instruction. It is assumed that children with clear etiologies of neurological impairment or pathological emotional disturbance will be placed in programs especially geared to their needs and not classified primarily as reading disability cases, although they will need special provision for reading development. Individual case study involving team members of varied progessional competencies will be necessary.

Perhaps the most effective step the school program could take at this time is to recognize that these pupils need a special class environment of a limited number of pupils and a remedial teacher well versed in the varied elements of specific reading disorders. The class should consist of no less than one-half of the school day, and should be free of the usual school curricular restrictions. Exploratory treatment programs of an eclectic nature guided by evidence of progress should be encouraged. From such exploration we should gain observations necessary to more controlled research.

The Argument for a Broad Consideration of Reading Disability

There are at least four major reasons why a planned total school program for treating reading disability makes better sense than the sporadic addition of specific treatment set-ups. First, it encourages an all-staff emphasis upon prevention and classroom adjustment to reading problems. Secondly, it provides for greater versatility and efficiency in diagnosis and treatment. The pattern for most general reading disability cases, if not resolved, is to move from mild limitation of skill to severe limitation of skill confounded by negative attitude and generalized maladjustment. It makes sense to get at mild difficulties when they can be diagnosed and treated with a modest effort. For the same reason, we should prevent the extreme disability program from becoming so overloaded with cases that it can't prove its usefulness.

A third argument for a total program approach is that it improves administration and communication with the larger school administration, staff, and general public. It permits the coordination of related school services. The total program attack can be presented to regular staff as a supportive service rather than a unique operation with some strange characters. Duplication of diagnosis and treatment facilities is minimized.

Since a total program is a multi-phase program, misclassification of disabled readers can be reduced. The lack of progress made by a brain-damaged child in a corrective reading class will do little good for the pupil's skill, the teacher's nerves, or the reputation of the program. Asking a slightly limiting underachiever in reading to gear himself down to the readiness activities of a class of extremely disabled readers will produce equally distasteful results.

Finally, a total school attack recognizes our cultural orientation toward the Judeo-Christian premise that one individual's problems are just as worthy of treatment as another. The esoteric nature of specific reading disorders may be intriguing, but they make the pupil no more worthy of concern or treatment expense than the child with mundane reading problems of an equally blocking nature.

NEED FOR CONTROLLED STUDIES OF CAUSE-EFFECT

Statistical association merely accounts for the beyond chance presence of two or more factors in the make-up of a disabled reader. In itself, it does not explain cause-effect relationships. A classic example of this is the contingent relationship between reading disability and emotional disturbance. While it has been deductively concluded by some theorists that emotional maladjustment would naturally lead to difficulty in reading performance, empirically derived data indicate that 1) in a larger percentage of cases, the emotional difficulty is identified after the reading disability becomes apparent, and 2) a larger percentage of disabled readers exhibit abnormal emotional and social behavior in the school-reading setting than in their general environment.

One difficulty in the investigation of extreme reading disability is the susceptibility of findings to the contamination of our research approaches. Much of our evidence has emanated from clinical settings, where we derived our generalizations from intensive "living and identifying" with the severely disabled pupil. Frequently, those involved in this work become increasingly isolated from close observation of adequate or superior readers. The possibility of a "devils horns" influence is thus increased.

However, investigations which employ a control group of adequate readers do not completely escape cause-effect contamination although they improve upon the situation. It is interesting that so many investigators tend to ignore that the learning to read process, itself, may influence the reader's attention span, ocular-motor coordination, perceptual efficiency, etc.

The writer recently checked upon this hypothesis by studying perceptual memory responses of advanced and disabled readers who were reading at the same functional reading level and who were equated for intellectual ability and school and home background. Utilizing the Memory-for-Design Test, the results indicated a slightly superior perceptual-motor memory performance for the disabled readers. More amusing was the fact that three of the superior readers met the test criteria for brain damage and seven others were classified as "borderline."

Sophistication in the scientific investigation of reading behavior has been slow to develop. It is hoped that research with extreme reading disability will profit from the experiences of those involved in the broader study of reading achievement. To this end we should be alert to the designing, controlling, and reporting of evidence—both in our own studies and those of others. Exploration is needed, but should not necessarily be interpreted as controlled research!

Bibliography

1. Bateman, Barbara. "Learning Disabilities—Yesterday, Today, and Tomorrow." EXCEPTIONAL CHILDREN, 31 (December, 1964), 167-177.

2. Cruickshank, W. M., Benton, F. A., Ratzeburg, F. H., and Tannhauser, Mirian T. A TEACHING METHOD FOR BRAIN-INJURED AND HYPERACTIVE CHILDREN. New York: Syracuse University Press, 1961.

3. Darley, Frederic L. DIAGNOSIS AND APPRAISAL OF COMMUNICATION DISORDERS. Englewood Cliffs, N.J.: Prentice-Hall, Inc., 1964.

4. Dreikurs, Rudolf. "Emotional Predispositions to Reading Difficulties," ARCHIVES OF PEDIATRICS, 71 (November, 1954), 339-353.

5. Fernald, G. REMEDIAL TECHNIQUES IN BASIC SCHOOL SUBJECTS. New York: McGraw-Hill Book Company, Inc., 1939.

6. Harris, Albert J. HOW TO INCREASE READING ABILITY. New York: Longmans Green and Co.

7. Hinshelwood, J. CONGENITAL WORD-BLINDNESS. London: H. K. Lewis, 1917.

8. Johnson, M. S. "Factors Related to Disability in Reading." JOURNAL OF EXPERIMENTAL EDUCATION, 26 (September, 1957), 1-26.

9. Money, J. (Editor). READING DISABILITY: PROGRESS IN RESEARCH NEEDS IN DYSLEXIA. Johns Hopkins University Press, 1962.

10. Orton, Samuel T. READING, WRITING, AND SPEECH PROBLEMS OF CHILDREN. New York: W. W. Norton & Co., 1937.

11. Rabinovitch, R. D. "Reading and Learning Disabilities." In S. Arieti (Editor). AMERICAN HANDBOOK OF PSYCHIATRY. Volume 1, Chapter 43. New York: Basic Books, Inc., 1959.

12. Robinson, Helen M. WHY PUPILS FAIL IN READING. Chicago: University of Chicago Press, 1946.

13. Smith, D. E. P. and Carrigan, P. THE NATURE OF READING DISABILITY. New York: Harcourt, Brace, 1959.

14. Staats, A. W. and Staats, C. K. COMPLEX HUMAN BEHAVIOR. New York: Holt, Rinehart, and Winston, 1964.

15. Strauss, A. A. and Kephart, N. C. PSYCHOPATHOLOGY AND EDUCATION OF THE BRAIN INJURED CHILD. Volume II. New York: Grune and Stratton, Inc., 1955.

16. Vernon, M. D. BACKWARDNESS IN READING. Cambridge: Cambridge University Press, 1957.

STUDY QUESTIONS

1. What two factors does Hill suggest have hindered our efforts to develop a useful and broad framework for viewing reading problems?

2. Give an example of the author's statement that some definitions imply a cause of the disorder.

3. The schools, according to Hill, have tended to use a dimension other than etiology of reader disorders as their "basis of operation." What does he suggest they have used? How satisfactory has this been?

4. What three criteria does Hill suggest schools have used in deciding whether a child is underachieving?

5. Hill lists five kinds of "factors of greater probable association with general reading disability." Compare these five headings with the four groupings used by Westman, Arthur, and Scheidler.

6. How does Hill differentiate between "extreme" and "general" reading disability?

7. What criticisms might Hill level at a study which found that slow readers had a large number of "poor eye movement patterns" and concluded that faulty eye movements caused poor reading?

3: A SUGGESTED CLASSIFICATION OF THE CAUSES OF DYSLEXIA

Alex Bannatyne

Bannatyne views dyslexia as one type of reading disability. He sub-divides dyslexia into four kinds—emotional, neurological dysfunction, genetic, and social-cultural-educational. He describes the characteristics of each and recognizes that these tentative subspecies are not mutually exclusive. Different remediation is called for in each kind of dyslexia.
B. D. B.

---

eprinted with permission of the author and publisher from WORD BLIND BULLETIN, 966, Vol. 1, No. 5, 5-14.

After twenty years' work in education and psychology and in remedial education for some of that period, for the last four years my main interest has been in reading disabilities in children of normal intelligence. Taking part in research into the nature of dyslexia has meant reading much of the vast literature on the analysis and investigation of reading disabilities and remedial techniques. At the Centre I have given diagnostic psychological examinations to over 150 children and I have discussed dyslexia with many experienced visitors. Early in 1965 I spent several days at the Word Blind Institute in Copenhagen and later toured many centres in the United States.

I have tried throughout the work to find a logical model or structural framework which would make sense of this mass of information. Keeping an unbiassed mind I have developed an eclectic but precise classification of which the main categories and their distinctive features are described here. The research evidence on which I rely is not given in detail but much is found in the incomplete but extensive bibliography. Until some current research projects are completed, the following classification and explanatory material must remain nonproven. It is published now as a collective statement of many hypotheses in the hope that others will carry out research and investigations into its validity. At the Centre only a few of the central hypotheses will be tested.

The Classification

Reading disabilities are our "universe of study." Within this universe there are several separate genera. One is a grouping of disabilities called Dyslexia, one type of reading disability which is *not* caused by low intelligence *per se,* although it can occur in children of low intelligence. In the genus dyslexia are several species, each of which has its appropriate adjectival description, shown in diagrammatic form in Figure 1.

Emotional Dyslexia is so called because it follows a poor communicative relationship between mother and child during the critical period of language development in infancy.

FIGURE 1. A CLASSIFICATION OF THE CAUSES AND TYPES OF DYSLEXIA

(Note: None of these categories is mutually exclusive.)

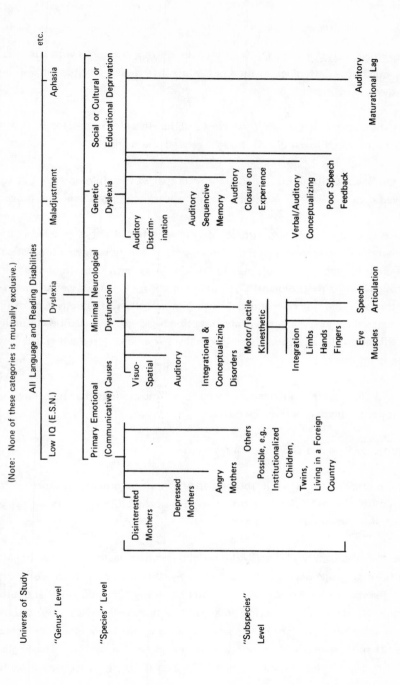

Neurological Dysfunction Dyslexia includes all those children with some *abnormal* qualitative difference of the brain which has caused a disturbance in linguistic development and functioning.

The third species is *Genetic Dyslexia* (Specific Developmental Dyslexia), the subject of much research and thought around the world.

In the Social-Cultural-Educational Dyslexia species the children have not received enough direct or indirect training to learn any given linguistic processes.

These four species are not mutually exclusive, a fact that has clouded much of the work of many investigators. A boy, who is poorly endowed linguistically speaking (Genetic Dyslexia), may in addition have been brain injured at birth through anoxia (Neurological Dysfunction group). This child could have a mother who did not communicate with him verbally to the detriment of his subsequent linguistic achievements (Emotional group), and also be culturally or educationally deprived. There are many dyslexic children where the causation is multiple.

Each of the species contains subspecies, but I must admit that my descriptions of some of them are rather tentative.

Emotional Dyslexia (Communicative)

As the original causes are in the past they cannot be directly measured. Proof would need an extensive longitudinal study. Even projective tests cannot yield much information about this group.

The three "subspecies" described have one common factor. During the critical phase of language development and differentiation, from birth to four years of age, the mother or mother surrogate, has not given her child sufficient verbal stimuli for the child to develop an accurately differentiated auditory discrimination and perhaps a clarity of speech. Each language is composed of dominant sounds and sequences of sounds, and even exclusion of sounds. The English child must learn by imitation which sounds occur in which sequential contexts, and which other sounds it need not use at all; for example, in English he usually strings together the phonemes for the word "mummy" in the right sequence fairly quickly and these along with many other sounds are reinforced by his day to day communication to and fro with his mother. English mothers do not use vocal clicks very much because the English language makes little use of clicks, therefore the clicking noises which all babies make are slowly dropped. If the mother speaks little during the child's formative years, he lacks this linguistic information and the linguistic conventions that go with it, and so he can make little use of language. His vocabulary is limited, speech development is slow, and speech defects common. The child does not *listen* properly and is disinterested in auditory stimuli. If nothing is done to alter this pattern during the early school years it may very well "congeal" in the course of a normal neurological maturation, and subsequently it may be very difficult to modify.

The "subspecies" are related to the types of mother. The first is the Disinterested Mother who, being otherwise preoccupied, neglects, among other developmental areas, the linguistic communication with her child. The second is the Depressed Mother. She has an adverse effect on her child not only because she tends not to talk very much but also because the verbal communication she does have with her child is not reinforced by such pleasurable rewards as evocative laughter, etc. The third subspecies, the Angry Mother, repeatedly slaps her child and attacks it with angry words so that language is associated in the child's mind with extremely unpleasant situations. A great deal of anxiety may be aroused, and linguistic functions are associated with these negative feelings. Such a child has great difficulty in accepting or facing language and tends to run away from it and to avoid using words.

This does not exhaust the mother-child relationships which need investigation.

Neurological Dysfunction

Under the heading of *Minimal Neurological Dysfunction Dyslexia* are included only those children whose brains are abnormal in the sense that they are qualitatively dissimilar by reason of, for example, unusable cells or malformed areas which are not found in the normal population. A "normal population" includes other types of dyslexic children. Children whose brains are malformed or damaged even when the reason is genetic are included in the M.N.D. species and excluded from the Genetic species. This subtle distinction will become clearer in the section on Genetic Dyslexia.

Different kinds of lesions can cause similar symptoms just as widely differing symptoms can result from apparently similar lesions. This may be because some brain areas are "established" and programmed by the environment and training in infancy and early childhood. Variations in the extent and the nature of cell impairment or malformation makes categorization difficult so that the subspecies appear more homogeneous, neater and more precise than is found in practice. Nevertheless a stylized map of broad highways is useful. Such a cluster map must take into account the main neurological areas of the brain in terms of sensory and motor functioning, which are well described in accounts of cerebral palsied children to which the reader is referred. The subspecies can be classified into those with visuo-spatial disorders, those with auditory disorders, those with motor-kinaesthetic disorders, those with "integrative" disorders. Presumably the last group in terms of linguistic functioning mostly results from impairment of appropriate areas of the peripheral cortex or reticular formation. As such they are disorders resulting from faulty neurological *intercommunication* on the conceptual level between particular functional areas, possibly with a poor *suppression* of extraneous input stimuli, and with the neurological "inability" to *reinforce* definite pathways as habitual channels.

The differences depend on the receptive area damaged, and these areas are not mutually exclusive in terms of malfunction. Any permutation or combination of these areas may be damaged and deficiencies may range from a tiny lesion in one particular area to a generalized impairment over the whole cortex. A brain injured dyslexic child rarely has only one narrow deficiency.

The educational techniques appropriate for training these children are many and varied. Children with a visuo-spatial deficiency must be trained with spatial techniques, reinforced with appropriate linguistic experience through the neuro-sensory channels which are intact. A child with poor auditory discrimination needs to be *taught* to listen and speak accurately, and a child with motor kinaesthetic or even tactile disabilities must have these trained while full use is being made of all the other input systems.

Genetic Dyslexia

This, the most homogeneous species of dyslexia, is also the most controversial. Although supported by much empirical observation both by myself and other people, the following hypothetical deductions require further research and observational verification.

Children suffering from Genetic Dyslexia (Specific Developmental Dyslexia) have, I suggest, not inherited the specific ability to acquire linguistic functions easily. They form the lower end of a *normal continuum* of the linguistic or verbal ability of the whole population. Almost everybody accepts that while environmental training can play a great part in the fulfilment or development of any particular talent, the talent itself with its maximum of potential is inherited. This is readily accepted for musical ability, the ability to draw, mathematical ability and even verbal ability when found to excess in a talented person. Most people are willing also to admit that a *lack* of these abilities is inherited. The tone deaf person, the incompetent artist, the poor mathematician, have not inherited the given talent even though the subsequent cultural environment be sometimes favourable or sometimes unfavourable. The tone deaf person may happily practise music for many years and not make a success of it. I suggest, then, that the "genetic" dyslexic child has not inherited those specific psychological abilities (and of course their neurological bases), necessary to the development of language functioning at a *particular level.* The concept of level of attainment is an important one. Sophisticated adult reading and writing is the equivalent in music of being able to understand and to write music. The analogy which need not be pressed helps to illustrate the level of reading attainment demanded from most children. In the last hundred years universal education has revealed a small proportion of otherwise intelligent children who are unable to learn to read and to spell easily. If everyone had to be able to draw a face accurately there would be many artistic "dyslexics," if everyone had to write a symphony there would be many musical "dyslexics" in the community; and because we demand of everybody fluency in reading there is a small proportion of children suffering from linguistic dyslexia.

Most American workers in the field, including the Orton Society, use as a synonym for genetic dyslexia the term "specific language disability," an extremely accurate and appropriate term for this group of children.

One of the most important characteristics of dyslexia is difference in sex incidence. Depending on one's "cut-off point" in terms of severity, the greater is the ratio of boys to girls. If the cut-off point is in the mild dyslexic area the ratio of boys to girls may be three or four to one. In the very severe cases the ratio may rise to ten to one, and so there seems to be little doubt that genetic dyslexia is in some way a sex-linked characteristic, though not necessarily a 100% male one. The original cause is almost certainly an extensive polygenetic one.

Dyslexic boys in this genetic group do quite well in all those spatial tests which do not demand sequencing, and their visual perception in terms of relationships in three-dimensional space is usually good. Their ability to conceptualize logically in terms of meanings is also usually quite competent. The main area in which they fail is in terms of linguistic or other types of automatic *coding fluency.* In fact arbitrary (that is "nonlogical") sequencing tests are especially difficult, and in essence learning to read and spell *are* nothing more than arbitrary, irregular, sequencing processes *mostly auditory* in nature— processes which in the average person rapidly become automatic with some training.

A good appreciation of spatial relationships demands a fairly well-coordinated motor system involving both hemispheres of the brain, and acute three-dimensional vision in *both* visual fields. This calls for the equal use of the visual areas of the brain in *both* hemispheres. This neurological state of affairs, i.e., the equality between the hemispheres, in people with a reasonable or high degree of spatial ability tends to make them ambidextrous, and to make them *scan* the whole field of vision very rapidly in *all* directions as is necessary in a three-dimensional world. (Reading calls for the discipline of scanning in one direction only.) Of course most things learned by one half of the body and its hemisphere are immediately transferred neurologically to the other half of the body presumably through the other hemisphere, although not always necessarily to the same degree. But an appreciation of space in terms of survival value, particularly in terms of vision, demands peripheral stimuli to be rapidly recognized and interpreted in both the left and right visual fields, and hence in both the right and left visual areas of the brain.

Moreover, nature probably invented the two hemispheres to work in terms of mirror images, or rather mirrored sensory and motor functions. Most external bodily functions, particularly those involving the motor and visual areas, require mirrored neurological impressions because one side of the body surface is very much a mirror image of the other. Since men have learned to read, this ancient requirement for other purposes has been a slight handicap. When we learn to read, convention demands that our eyes move from left to right, at least in the European languages. Quite apart from this fact that reading demands training the eyes to move in *one* dimension in *one visual field* and that there are many problems connected with this muscular training, only the right visual field is dominantly involved. This means that almost all the visual information during the reading process is fed into the left occipital lobe from which it is probably internally transferred in its mirror image to the right occipital lobe. But in "visuo-spatial" people, with hemispheres having an equality of dominance, these transferred mirror images (letters) in the right visual field can be fed *out* when writing or even when reading almost as easily as the correct ones in the left visual cortex. As both are almost equally associated with a particular sound *either one* can be fed out in response to that sound. The muddle is increased when the mirror image of the one letter is also the primary image of yet another letter-sound combination. Therefore the visual letters b and d and the phonemes for b and d become a four-way tangle. In short, mirror imaging and the poor lateralization of eye movements in one dimension is probably caused by a superior spatial ability which itself results from a relatively superior development of the visual and motor cortexes. Good visuo-spatial ability demands an equality of hemispheric dominance even though in most people there seems to be some kind of control centre in the right hemisphere. Verbal-auditory abilities, by contrast, seem to demand a strong dominance of one hemisphere, usually the left, for their successful and rapid processing. Using the right visual field for reading and the right hand for writing means that almost all linguistic material will be processed in the left hemisphere of the brain and within that hemisphere there will be an economy of neurological communication. During linguistic activities the right hemisphere in people with good verbal ability can thus be suppressed in terms of most interference, be it visual, motor or auditory.

The cortical and psychological associations of writing and reading processes in terms of symbols are usually written down as a triangle with the stimulus object at the apex, the sound-phoneme symbol for that object in one lower corner and the secondary visual symbol for the sound in the other corner. This is an incorrect way of looking at linguistic processes. The stimulus object (e.g., a table) in early childhood (and because of early childhood, throughout life), is always associated with an *aural sequence of phonemes* (e.g., the sounds t-a-b-l-e), and later when learning to read these aural sequences of phonemes in their turn are always associated with a series of visual symbols (e.g., the letters t-a-b-l-e) which represent them. The visual symbol *never* directly represents the stimulus object. *It must always work through the medium of auditory processes.* (This may not be true in the case of pictograph languages or with the congenitally deaf, but this does not invalidate my argument which is confined for the moment to phonetically symbolised languages.) Since blind children learn to read well using touch, vision cannot be essential to the reading process.

Genetically dyslexic boys are probably better than many others at appreciating visual stimuli and their interrelationships, and they certainly know the shapes of all letters. Their major problem lies in the *auditory area* which must mediate in all linguistic functions. There is evidence to show that these genetically dyslexic boys are unable to discriminate between arbitrary sequences of sounds, which have no logically phonetic order for them. These children also find it difficult to associate to or remember sequences of sounds even though they usually comprehend the meaning (associated concept to a given gestalt of sound). Even so, their early speech development is often delayed and their auditory discrimination is often poor. I should emphasize that there is no question of deafness or ear defect of any kind whatsoever.

Because the traditional orthography of the English language is extremely irregular, that is, the particular association of each auditory symbol to each visual symbol is only accurately identifiable in one single sequential context, the task largely becomes one of rote memory associations, each cued by several conventional contexts—the sequence of sounds, the sequence of letters in a word, the number of letters in the word, the sequence of words in the sentence and the conceptual content of the passage. The difficulty is increased when one realizes that the visual symbols must also be sequenced *separately* from the phonemes in a word-context. In short, the sequences of sounds and their multiple arbitrary associations with sequences of visual symbols must always be learned by rote, because there is no logic to them. Spatial concepts are amenable to "first principle" conceptual logic as in, for example, geometry and the spatially capable person prefers a logical structure of principles from which he can work in any applied field, for example, architecture or engineering. Spatially capable children being part of the group also prefer the logic of applied principles. On the other hand, the verbally (auditory type) able person can more easily memorise arbitrarily associated or unsystematically linked material, such as objects and their linguistic symbols. Languages are founded on a variety of arbitrary conventions, most being unsystematic in their coding conventions. There are reports that languages which are phonetically "logical" are less of a problem to dyslexic people. With this in mind, the additional burden of the eyes wanting to move in all directions and mirror images frequently cropping up, the task of reading becomes well-nigh impossible.

If the major problems for the "genetic dyslexic" are auditory sequencing, auditory discrimination and associating auditory symbols to sequences of visual symbols, the central emphasis in any training programme must be auditory sequencing, a training in careful listening, the whole approach being phonic in nature.

The evidence to hand so far suggests that fathers in highly spatial occupations, for example, surgeons, architects, engineers, farmers, tend to have more genetically dyslexic children than do fathers in other occupations. Although the mothers and daughters in these families may be linguistically superior to the males, the difference is relative because the verbal talents of these women (in the community as a whole) will also tend to be lower than they might be. In other words, the women in "genetic dyslexic" families, although nowhere near as bad as the men, will exhibit minimal symptoms. For example, their ability to learn foreign languages may be limited because of a fundamental lack of talent.

Social, Cultural and Educational Deprivation Dyslexia

These children, if they are not too maladjusted, will learn to read when the environmental conditions are made conducive to reading.

There is some confusion about emotional causes. Primary emotional dyslexia has been described and needs no further elaboration. The child who is dyslexic for any of the three main reasons (emotional, brain injury or genetic) may suffer from *secondary* emotional problems in the form of poor work attitudes and a tendency to run away from school situations. Such negative attitudes need correction before the process of training the dyslexic child can begin. A child may be backward because of emotional maladjustment for quite other reasons. The child with a reactive behavioural problem who rebels against the authority of the school will probably not learn to read well, nor will he learn anything else. Such a child would not be included in this species of "social, cultural and educational dyslexia."

Conclusion

Much research and anecdotal evidence is needed to verify the above classification, which is suggested to encourage investigation. This classificatory grouping by original causes accounts for almost all the points of view expressed by workers in the field of dyslexia. It also accounts for all the reported symptomatology, however complex.

Only hints have been given at the various types of training required for the different groups and subgroups of dyslexic children described. Both diagnosis and treatment are made extremely complex because of the fact that *the groups are not mutually exclusive,* children commonly combining two and sometimes even three. Perhaps one of the underlying causes of the number of conflicting or confused results in much of the earlier research into reading disabilities was the lumping together into one experimental group of the various aetiologically different "species" of dyslexic children.

A large number of diagnostic tests is required on almost every physiological, neurological and psychological level for accurate differential diagnoses and such tests form part of the Centre's research programme.

The following bibliography contains much of the evidence on which the classification is based:

Bibliography

Abercrombie, M. L., PERCEPTUAL AND VISUO MOTOR DISORDERS IN CERE-BRAL PALSY. The Spastics Society, Heinemann Medical Books, London, 1964.

Birch, H. C., BRAIN DAMAGE IN CHILDREN. Williams & Wilkins, Baltimore, 1964.

Bonin, G. Von, THE EVOLUTION OF THE HUMAN BRAIN. University of Chicago Press, 1963.

Burr, H. S., THE NEURAL BASIS OF HUMAN BEHAVIOUR. Charles C. Thomas, Springfield, Ill., 1963.

Clark, M. M., LEFT-HANDEDNESS. University of London Press, 1957.

Cratty, B. J., MOVEMENT BEHAVIOUR AND MOTOR LEARNING. Henry Kimpton, London, 1964.

Critchley, McD., DEVELOPMENTAL DYSLEXIA. Heinemann Medical Books, London, 1964.

Denhoff, E. and Robinault, Isabel R., CEREBRAL PALSY AND RELATED DISORDERS. McGraw-Hill, 1960.

Hebb, D. O., THE ORGANIZATION OF BEHAVIOUR. John Wiley & Sons, Inc., Canada, 1949.

Hillman, James, EMOTION. Routledge & Kegan Paul, 1962.

Kellmer Pringle, M. L., DEPRIVATION AND EDUCATION. Longmans, London, 1965.

Kirk, S. A., EDUCATING EXCEPTIONAL CHILDREN. Houghton Mifflin Co., Boston, 1962.

Klosovskii, B. N., THE DEVELOPMENT OF THE BRAIN. Pergamon Press, 1963.

Macfarlane Smith, I., SPATIAL ABILITY—ITS EDUCATIONAL AND SOCIAL SIGNIFICANCE. University of London Press, 1964.

Money, John (ed.), READING DISABILITY—PROGRESS AND RESEARCH NEEDS IN DYSLEXIA. Johns Hopkins Press, Baltimore, 1962.

Morley, M. E., THE DEVELOPMENT AND DISORDERS OF SPEECH IN CHILDHOOD. Limpingstone, London, 1957.

Mountcastle, V. B., INTERHEMISPHERIC RELATIONS AND CEREBRAL DOMINANCE. Johns Hopkins Press, Baltimore, 1962.

Orton, June L. (ed.), SPECIFIC LANGUAGE DISABILITIES—A COMPILATION OF SELECTED PAPERS. Bulletin of the Orton Society Vol. XIII, 1963.

Osgood & Miron, APPROACHES TO THE STUDY OF APHASIA. University of Illinois Press, 1963.

Pearson, G. H. J., PSYCHOANALYSIS AND THE EDUCATION OF THE CHILD. Norton, N.Y., 1954.

Penfield & Roberts, SPEECH AND BRAIN MECHANISMS. Princeton University Press, 1959.

Strauss & Kephart, THE BRAIN-INJURED CHILD. Grune and Stratton, 1955.

Vereecken, P., SPATIAL DEVELOPMENT. Wolters, Groningen, 1961.

Vernon, P. E., THE STRUCTURE OF HUMAN ABILITIES. Methuen, 1961.

White Franklin, A. (ed.), WORD BLINDNESS OR SPECIFIC DEVELOPMENTAL DYSLEXIA. Pitman Medical Publishing Co., 1962.

STUDY QUESTIONS

1. Bannatyne hypothesizes four kinds or species of dyslexia. Compare these four to the four headings used by Westman, Arthur, and Scheidler.

2. Give Bannatyne's description of reading and spelling. Notice throughout all your reading on reading how many authors define or describe it. What effect might the failure of some "authorities" to discuss the nature of reading have on their recommendations regarding teaching reading? When we say a child is unable to read, what *exactly* do we mean that he cannot do? Begin to formulate your own description of what is involved in the task of reading.

3. Bannatyne points out that vision cannot be essential to the reading process. What *is* essential to reading?

4. What must be the central focus in any reading training program for genetic dyslexics? Should this also be the central focus in *any* reading program?

5. What rationale would Bannatyne give for the sex difference in the frequency of reading disorders?

SECTION 2
SOME CHARACTERISTICS OF POOR READERS

4: READING SKILLS IN EMOTIONALLY DISTURBED, INSTITUTIONALIZED ADOLESCENTS

Helen E. Shimota

Shimota presents unusually interesting data on the characteristics
of adequate and disabled readers, all of whom are emotionally
disturbed. This study, by attempting to hold complicating emotional factors constant through inclusion rather than exclusion,
casts fascinating shadows on some long-cherished ideas about differences between good and poor readers.

B. D. B.

Reprinted with permission of the author and publisher from THE JOURNAL OF EDU-
CATIONAL RESEARCH, 1964, 58, 106-111.

The most vital academic problem facing the school-age child is the development of adequate language skills. As he progresses through school, reading skills, even more than adeptness in oral communication, become increasingly important. Upon his reading depends his acquisition of most other classroom subjects. Although ability to read adequately is no insurance that the child will do well in other academic areas, inability to read adequately acts as an almost insurmountable obstacle in his attempt at learning academic subjects.

Over the years parents have been concerned with the education of their children, but their concern appears to have increased since the advent of the space age. Examine the nearest display rack of popular magazines: one, two, three, perhaps even more, will contain an essay or two on the education of youth. Often they contain suggested remedies to cure the existing ills. Granted, a newsstand survey may discover only those topics thought by the editors to increase sales; however, a recent study by Larson and Selland (12) indicates that public concern is somewhat justified. They found 36.7% of the sixth graders in the Fargo, North Dakota, public schools to be reading one year or more below their mental age level; the major share of the retarded readers, 77%, were of, at least, average intellectual ability.

With cause and cures rampant in the outpouring of the press, a glance at the professional literature adds to one's confusion about the problem of reading disability and its solution. Miller, Margolin, and Yolles (14), for example, consider reading disability "an important reservoir of psychopathology from which a variety of disorders may emerge," but Hansburg (6) considers it to be the symptom of an existing conflict between the individual's needs and desires and his restraining superego. Definitions of reading disability and statements about its etiology can readily be found to demonstrate the absence of definitive answers and factual knowledge.

The present study was undertaken in order to provide, if possible, answers to some of the many questions about reading disability. In effect, it is an attempt at cross-validating the results of several previous studies:

1. Reading problems have been identified in 30 to 85% of the children and adolescents institutionalized for emotional disturbance or delinquency (13). Is this the incidence rate when the patient's intellectual ability is considered?

2. Several psychometric test patterns are said to be associated with reading problems. Can these patterns be used to differentiate between good and poor readers?

3. Rabinovitch and his associates (16) identified three etiological types of reading disability. Can these types be identified in the present sample?

4. Various factors have been thought to be of etiological importance in reading problems. Can the relationships be replicated?

Method

File data were available for some 360 children and adolescents admitted to Western State Hospital during the period between 1956 and 1959. All subjects of Caucasian ancestry, aged 13-0 to 15-11, and with at least dull normal intellectual ability (Wechsler FS IQ of at least 80) were selected for further study provided that they had taken both reading and intelligence tests at the Mental Health Research Institute. The 74 subjects who met these criteria are additionally described in Table 1.

The clinical record of each of the subjects was perused for certain other variables before any attempt was made to evaluate his reading ability.

The Expected Grade Placement (E.G.P.), that reading level attained by the average child with the same age and intellectual ability, was determined for each child. Norms published by the California Test Bureau (18) were used. Considered to be disabled readers were those subjects whose reading performance was 25% or more below the expected grade placement (5). Finally, the disabled readers were compared with the able readers, those who were reading at or above their E.G.P.

83

TABLE 1. CHARACTERISTICS OF TOTAL GROUP OF
74 SUBJECTS SELECTED FOR STUDY

	Mean	Range
Chronological Age	14-4	13-0 to 15-11
Actual grade placement	8.43	3.9 to 10.8
Intellectual ability		
Full Scale IQ	96.01	80 to 124
Verbal Scale IQ	91.49	70 to 129
Performance Scale IQ	101.05	77 to 132
Reading achievement	7.0	1.4 to 11.0
Sex	22 girls, 52 boys	

Results

In terms of the above definitions, 43.2% of the total group had developed adequate reading skills, and 31.1% were disabled readers. In the remainder of the study the adequate readers were compared with the definitely disabled readers; the borderline group was omitted from the comparisons.

Comparable in age, IQ, actual grade placement, and diagnosis, the two groups differed in composition by sex and by reading skills. (See Tables 2 and 5.) Boys were more likely to be disabled readers than were girls.

As seen in Table 2 the performance on three of the Wechsler-Bellevue subtests— Digit Span, Picture Arrangement, and Object Assembly—differed significantly between the two groups. The disabled readers were superior on the two performance subtests and below the able readers on Digit Span. As a group the able readers were significantly more variable on Picture Completion and Object Assembly and significantly less variable on Information and Similarities than were the disabled readers.

TABLE 2. COMPARISON OF DISABLED AND ADEQUATE READERS ON AGE, GRADE PLACEMENT, READING LEVEL, AND WECHSLER-BELLEVUE TEST SCORES

Variable	Disabled N=22 $\bar{x}$	Disabled N=22 SD	Adequate N=31 $\bar{x}$	Adequate N=31 SD	t	F
Chronological age	14.28	0.75	14.00	0.62	0.26	1.47
Actual grade placement	8.12	1.32	8.35	0.89	0.67	2.18*
Reading grade level	3.60	1.86	8.75	1.20	11.20‡	2.40*
Wechsler—Bellevue, Form II						
Full scale IQ	94.45	10.22	94.19	9.31	0.09	1.20
Verbal scale IQ	87.23	11.90	91.87	8.97	1.51	1.76
Performance scale IQ	103.59	12.27	97.13	12.12	1.86	1.03
Subtests[a]						
Information	6.24	2.28	6.63	1.52	0.67	2.25*
Comprehension	8.71	2.22	9.00	2.69	0.41	1.47
Digit Span	6.71	2.76	8.33	2.17	2.20*	1.62
Arithmetic	5.86	2.42	6.50	2.27	0.93	1.09
Similarities	7.95	2.48	8.53	1.68	0.91	2.19*
Vocabulary	8.33	1.59	8.27	1.58	0.13	1.02
Picture Arrangement	11.14	2.39	9.47	2.08	2.53*	1.32
Picture Completion	9.43	1.91	9.17	2.68	0.40	1.96
Block Design	10.14	2.46	9.03	2.79	1.47	1.29
Object Assembly	12.86	1.49	11.43	2.16	2.74†	2.09*
Digit Symbol	7.90	2.51	8.13	1.94	0.35	1.67

*p= .05
†p= .01
‡p= .001
[a]N disabled = 21; N adequate = 30

Burks and Bruce (2) report that poor readers obtain relatively high scores on the Picture Arrangement, Block Design, and Comprehension subtests while doing poorly on the Information, Arithmetic, and Coding subtests. In the current study the disabled readers as a group follow the subtest pattern reported by Burks and Bruce; however, the adequate readers also display the same intertest variations. When the pattern was applied to the individual subjects (see Table 3) it failed to differentiate between the two groups. Similarly, their finding that the good readers were superior on the similarities subtest was unconfirmed in the present study.

Further attempts were made at differentiating the adequate and the disabled reader by applying the results reported by Altus (1) to the individual subject's test profile. As shown in Table 3 none of the patterns could be used successfully to identify the reading level of the subjects. Stroud and Bloomers (1917) found the subtests best correlated with achievement to be Arithmetic, Vocabulary, Block Design and Object Assembly. If so, the disabled readers, poor achievers by definition, should do less well on these tests than their overall performance, while adequate readers should have scores on the four subtests equal to or above the level of their overall performance. This prediction, however, was not borne out by the data.

Koppitz (10), Harriman and Harriman (7), and Lachmann (11) have used the Bender-Gestalt to study learning ability in children. As seen in Table 3 their findings could not be successfully replicated with the adolescent subjects in the present study.

Rabinovitch (16) has reported three etiologically distinct types of reading disability: a) reading disability associated with frank organic damage as shown by gross neurological deficit; b) primary reading retardation associated with defect in that basic capacity necessary to associate concepts with symbols and to integrate written material; c) secondary reading retardation associated with either emotional disturbance or an inadequate learning situation. Table 4 compares the adequate and the disabled readers on those variables reported by Rabinovitch to be symptomatic or causal factors. For the most part these factors occurred with comparable frequency in the two groups. No greater

TABLE 3. COMPARISON OF DISABLED AND ADEQUATE READERS ON SEVERAL PSYCHOLOGICAL TEST VARIABLES

Variable	Number with variable listed		Chi square[a] (df=1)
	Disabled N=21	Adequate N=30	
Wechsler—Bellevue Scale			
Altus			
1) D Sym and Arith < Voc, Simil, PC, OA, PA	5	9	0.238
2) Info < PC, Voc, D Sp	15	19	0.406
Burks and Bruce			
1) Info, Arith, D Sym < PA, BD, Comp			
Marked agreement with pattern	9	7	
Moderate similarity	8	14	
Chance agreement with pattern	4	9	2.288[b]
2) Sim > Mdn subtest	4	8	
= Mdn	8	6	
< Mdn	9	16	2.063[b]
Stround and Blommers			
(A, V, BD and OA)/4 < Mdn	7	9	0.064
Bender—Gestalt			
Pascall—Suttell score > Mdn (82)	10	17	0.453
Koppitz			
Rotation (+2)[c]	21	26	0.760[*]
Distortion of shape	0	3	0.829[*]
Failure to integrate parts and wholes (Sep. +2)	0	0	0.000
Angulation difficulties, Figures 7 and 8	8	10	0.097
Angles used, Figure 6	4	8	0.103[*]
Circle, dash or dot substitute	19	22	0.973[*]
Perseveration	9	7	2.051
Harriman and Harriman			
Lack of orderliness	10	9	1.509
Elaboration	8	10	0.097
Overlapping designs	8	7	1.205
Variability in size	15	15	0.958

[*]Yates correction used.
[a]None significant at .05 level.
[b]df=2.
[c]Peek and Quast (15) scoring system used.

TABLE 4. COMPARISON OF DISABLED READERS AND ADEQUATE READERS ON VARIABLES RELATING TO RABINOVITCH'S CLASSIFICATION OF READING DISABILITY

| | Number with variable listed | | | |
| | Disabled | Adequate | Chi square | |
Variable	N=22	N=31	(df=1)	p
A. Frank organic damage				
Diagnosis positive or probable	5	9	0.263	---
Abnormal EEG	5	13	2.117	---
History of head injury and/or high fever	9	15	0.290	---
B. Primary reading deficit				
1. Diagnostic signs				
a) Male sex[a]	20	15	7.639	.01
b) Gross verbal incapacity				
Performance IQ–Verbal IQ $\leq$ 20	8	5		
Perf. IQ–Verbal IQ = 10–19	8	6	7.182[b]	.05
c) Mixed eye-hand dominance	8	5	2.846	.10
d) Anxiety about reading	6	1	4.563[*]	.05
e) "Soft" neurological signs	4	8	0.103[*]	---
f) Difficulty with abstract concepts	7	4	1.694[*]	---
g) Perceptual difficulties–auditory or visual	4	2	0.789[*]	---
2. Ability of signs to differentiate groups				
a) Considering all 7:				
One or None	7	7		
Two	7	9		
Three or more	8	5	3.679[b]	---
b) Considering all but sex				
None	5	14		
One	8	11		
Two or more	9	6	3.937[b]	---
c) Considering all but sex and anxiety				
None	7	14		
One	7	12		
Two or more	8	5	2.886[b]	---

[*]Yates correction applied.
[a]Disabled, N=23; Adequate, N=32.
[b]df=2.

incidence of organic brain damage was found in the disabled readers. Only three of the variables thought by Rabinovitch to be related to primary reading retardation differentiated the adequate from the disabled readers.

One of these, anxiety about reading, could easily be predicted; successful readers ordinarily would show little or no anxiety about their reading performance.

As, for the most part, the symptoms alone did not differentiate between the two groups, so also did the symptoms in combination fail to distinguish between them. In examining the individual cases of reading disability only four boys could be identified as approximating the primary reading defect described by Rabinovitch. Yet in none of the four cases was there marked agreement with his description. In general, the subjects showing the greatest agreement with the primary reading defect syndrome were those subjects with abnormal EEG's, with neurological evidence of a cerebral lesion, or with a history of head injury or high fever; these factors would contraindicate the diagnosis of primary reading defect.

Gross general verbal incapacity demonstrated by a performance IQ markedly higher than the verbal IQ, occurs significantly more often among the disabled readers. However, learning to read is by no means contraindicated by a discrepancy between performance and verbal scale IQs. Among the adequate readers 40% of the girls but none of the boys had performance scale IQs 15 points or more above their verbal scale score.

Crisp (3) and Eames (4), among others, consider visual handicaps important in the development of reading problems, though by no means does either of them consider them the most important causal factor. As seen in Table 5, significantly more of the adequate readers had visual problems.

Table 5 reveals other data frequently gathered in the study of severe reading problems. In a group of elementary school children with reading problems, Tjossem (20) and Kawi and Pasamanick (9) found a high incidence of atypical birth history in disabled readers. This finding, however, is reversed in the

TABLE 5. COMPARISON OF DISABLED AND ADEQUATE READERS ON VARIABLES THOUGHT RELATED TO READING DISABILITY

Variable	Number with variable listed Disabled $N=22$	Number with variable listed Adequate $N=31$	Chi square $(df=1)$	p
Psychiatric diagnosis[a]				
Psychosis or neurosis	8	6		
Personality disorder	6	10		
Transient situational dist.	7	13	1.852[b]	...
Reaction to stress:				
Aggressive, impulsive	15	22		
Repression, withdrawal, projection	7	9	0.047	...
Id vs. Super Ego conflict	6	8	0.029	...
Atypical birth (abnormal pregnancy, premature, birth injury, O_2 given at birth)	1	13	7.431*	.01
Speech disturbance (currently or during development)	4	3	0.239*	...
Coordination disturbance (current or developmental)	6	4	0.924*	...
Eneuresis (currently or delayed training)	7	11	0.077	...
History of allergies	3	9	0.973*	...
Visual problems (with or without correction)	6	17	3.981	.05

*Yates correction applied.
[a]Disabled, $N=21$; Adequate, $N=29$.
[b]$df = 2$.

current study; significantly more adequate readers (41.9%) had atypical birth histories than did the disabled readers (4.5%).

The groups did not differ on such variables as eye-hand coordination, speech problems, postnatal head injury, or dominance.

A number of authors (6, 8) consider reading problems symptomatic of or resulting from intrapsychic problems. In the present study there was essentially no difference between the two reading groups in diagnosis, reaction to stress, or reported id-superego conflict. Eneuresis and allergies, often considered the result of psychological problems, also did not differ significantly.

Discussion

This study by no means defines the etiology of reading disability. In effect the results reported above contradict or question those of studies published earlier. Neither brain damage nor mixed dominance, neither emotional problems nor physical handicaps loom as the important causal agents that some have claimed them to be. Almost every factor studied could be shown to occur as frequently in the able readers as it did in the disabled readers when both reading groups are emotionally disturbed and hospitalized.

In Tables 3, 4 and 5, chi-square values have been calculated for 39 variables. Three of these are significant at the .05 level, and two at the .01 level. However, two of these, birth injury and visual problems, are in the opposite direction than that predicted by earlier research, and a third difference, anxiety about reading, would be more surprising if it did not occur. Remaining, then, are two variables reliably different between the groups: The higher incidence of boys among the disabled readers and the discrepancy between performance and verbal scale IQs. Stated in another way, verbal ability is needed for the acquisition of reading skills; girls, perhaps because they have a developmental superiority in verbal behavior, are less likely to have reading difficulties.

But one question remains: Is there any reasonable explanation for the marked discrepancy between these results and those reported by others? It is possible that these results reflect errors of the beta-type, but the erroneous acceptance of the null hypothesis can be detected only by replicating the study.

An alternative explanation is lent support by the work of Thorpe and James (19) and Lachmann (11). Thorpe and James measured the effect of the testing situation context on the test scores of normal and neurotic school children. When all children were tested in a mobile caravan on the school playground, most of the differences found in earlier studies disappeared. Lachmann's use of three groups—retarded readers, emotionally disturbed but normal readers, and normal children—demonstrates that the development of reading disturbances is not simply the result of a single factor. In the present study both adequate and disabled readers were tested routinely at the Research Institute after their admission to a psychiatric hospital. Reading tests were only a part of the battery administered during the examination.

Contrasting disabled, emotionally disturbed readers with adequate, but also emotionally disturbed readers, permitted closer examination of reading disability as it relates to certain other variables. Previously several research studies demonstrated the relationship of a specific pattern of Wechsler—Bellevue subtest scores to reading disability; while the pattern reappears in this study, it occurs in both groups and is not specific to reading disability. Instead emotional disturbance, adolescence, the test structure itself—all or none of these may be related to the subtest pattern.

Obviously further research is necessary. It will be done, if for no other reason, because the magazine editors and newspaper publishers will demand it. But perhaps the conflicting results already obtained are evidence that our research efforts are misdirected. Perhaps reading disability occurs as a result of the teaching methods used. Perhaps the interaction of some teachers and some methods and some pupils produces reading disability. If so, new teaching methods should be devised and utilized. The time-worn controversy of sight reading versus phonics may be only a debate about the lesser of two evils. Teaching machines with well-constructed programs may prevent or inhibit the development of reading disabilities. If so, their use would provide much more definitive knowledge about the etiology of reading problems.

References

1. Altus, Grace T. "A WISC Profile for Retarded Readers," JOURNAL OF CONSULTING PSYCHOLOGY, XX (1956), pp. 155-156.

2. Burks, H. F., and Bruce, P. "Characteristics of Poor and Good Readers as Disclosed by the Wechsler Intelligence Scale for Children," JOURNAL OF EDUCATIONAL PSYCHOLOGY, XLVI (1955), pp. 488-493.

3. Crisp, W. H. "The Psychology of the Poor Reader," AMERICAN JOURNAL OF OPHTHALMOLOGY, XXXIII (1950), pp. 235-242. Also in ROCKY MOUNTAIN MEDICAL JOURNAL, XLVI (1959), pp. 833-836.

4. Eames, T. H. Reading Failures and Nonfailures in Children with Brain Damage. AMERICAN JOURNAL OF OPHTHALMOLOGY, XLVII (1959), pp. 74-77.

5. Fabian, E. I. "Reading Disability: An Index of Pathology," AMERICAN JOURNAL OF ORTHOPSYCHIATRY, XXV (1955), 25, 319-329.

6. Hansburg, H. G. "A Reformulation of the Problem of Reading Disability," JOURNAL OF CHILD PSYCHIATRY, III (1956), pp. 137-148.

7. Harriman, Mildred, and Harriman, P. L. "The Bender Visual Motor Gestalt Test as a Measure of School Readiness," JOURNAL OF CLINICAL PSYCHOLOGY, VI (1950), pp. 175-177.

8. Jarvis, V. "Clinical Observations on the Visual Problems in Reading Disability," in R. Eissler, et al., Editors, THE PSYCHOANALYTIC STUDY OF THE CHILD, XIII (New York: Inter University Press, 1958).

9. Kawi, A. A., and Pasamanick, B. "Prenatal and Paranatal Factors in the Development of Childhood Reading Disorders," MONOGRAPHS OF SOCIAL RESEARCH CHILD DEVELOPMENT, XXIV (1959), No. 4 (Whole No. 73).

10. Koppitz, Elizabeth M. "The Bender Gestalt Test and Learning Disturbances in Young Children," JOURNAL OF CLINICAL PSYCHOLOGY, XIV (1958), pp. 292-295.

11. Lachmann, F. M. "Perceptual-Motor Development in Children Retarded in Reading Ability," JOURNAL OF CONSULTING PSYCHOLOGY, XXIV (1960), pp. 427-431.

12. Larson, R. E., and Selland, Cynthia T. "A Comparison of Reading Ages with Mental Ages," JOURNAL OF EDUCATIONAL RESEARCH, LII (1953), pp. 55-59.

13. Millar, T. P. "Reading Retardation," NORTHWEST MEDICINE, LIX (1960), pp. 1385-1390.

14. Miller, A. D., Margolin, J. B., and Yolles, S. F. "Epidemiology of Reading Disabilities; Some Methodologic Considerations and Early Findings," AMERICAN JOURNAL OF PUBLIC HEALTH., XLVII (1957), pp. 1250-1256.

15. Peek, R. M., and Quast, W. A SCORING SYSTEM FOR THE BENDER-GESTALT TEST (1951).

16. Rabinovitch, R. D., et al. "A Research Approach to Reading Retardation," in NEUROLOGY AND PSYCHIATRY IN CHILDHOOD, XXXIV (Baltimore: William and Wilkins Co., 1954), Chap. 15.

17. Stroud, J. B., and Blommers, P. "Correlation Analysis of WISC and Achievement Tests," JOURNAL OF EDUCATIONAL PSYCHOLOGY, XLVIII (1957), pp. 18-26.

18. Sullivan, Elizabeth T., Clark, W. W., and Tiegs, E. W. CALIFORNIA TEST OF MENTAL MATURITY, MANUAL (Los Angeles: California Test Bureau, 1957).

19. Thorpe, J. G., and James, D. R. "Neuroticism in Children: I. An Investigation of Normal and Neurotic Group Differences," BRITISH JOURNAL OF PSYCHOLOGY, XLVIII (1957), pp. 86-135.

20. Tjossem, T. D., Hansen, T. J., and Ripley, H. S. AN INVESTIGATION OF READING DIFFICULTY IN YOUNG CHILDREN, paper read at the American Psychiatric Association Annual Meeting, Chicago, May 12, 1961.

STUDY QUESTIONS

1. Describe carefully the two groups compared by Shimota. What major factor did Shimota control in this unusual study? What are some other factors, usually not controlled, which might be held constant by using Shimota's design? What would you predict might be found if one started with a brain-injured population and compared the good readers in that group with the poor readers in the same group?

2. The disabled readers were inferior to the adequate readers on only one Wechsler subtest. Which one? How does this finding relate to Bannatyne's description of the reading process?

3. Name several factors which other studies suggest would differentiate the disabled from the adequate readers, but which failed to do so in Shimota's study.

4. What factor, not investigated in this study, does Shimota suggest might actually be the cause of reading disability? What recommendations does she make regarding the possibility?

5: PSYCHOLINGUISTIC DISABILITIES OF CHILDREN WITH READING PROBLEMS

Corrine E. Kass

Kass administered a battery of carefully selected tests, including the Illinois Test of Psycholinguistic Abilities (ITPA) to disabled readers. This study represents a search for correlated, rather than causal, factors. The disabled readers had deficiencies in tests of integrative functions, suggesting decoding rather than comprehension problems. This study is included here both because of the important deficiencies revealed in the testing and because of its excellent presentation of the ITPA.

B. D. B.

Reprinted with permission of the author and publisher from EXCEPTIONAL CHILDREN, 1966, 32, 533-539.

Reading disability, or dyslexia, has been the subject of much research and popular discussion over the years. Despite this interest, a comprehensive theory has not yet appeared in the literature. While there are some reading problems which are undoubtedly caused by poor teaching methods, lack of intelligence, sensory defects, or excessive absence from school, most reading problems defy such explanations and are enigmas to teachers, parents, and clinicians. There seem to be two positions regarding causation:

1. Some researchers, primarily neurologists and physiologists, seek to link inability to read with a primary cause, such as brain dysfunction. This view leads to a narrowed remedial approach or none at all.

2. Some experts, primarily clinical psychologists, view reading disability from the comfortable position of multifactored causation. This belief leads to a potpourri of trial and error remedial measures.

A more fruitful approach for the educator at this time seems to be one in which causation is minimized and an effort is made to discover psychological correlates of reading disability. Hopefully, this should lead to more specific remedial procedures.

This article is a report of the results of an experiment which had as its purpose the examination of some psycholinguistic correlates of reading disability. Reading disability (dyslexia) was defined in this study as a retardation in reading which occurs after adequate instruction and which is not due to mental retardation or sensory defects (blindness or deafness).

This article is based on the author's doctoral dissertation completed under the direction of Samuel A. Kirk at the University of Illinois. This investigation was supported in part by a grant from the Psychiatric Training and Research Fund of the Illinois Department of Public Welfare.

Theoretical Basis for a Study of Reading Disability

An analysis of the existing theories led this investigator to take a close look at the process of reading and to logically relate this to the developmental process within the child. The reading process was considered to be primarily a communication process. If we consider reading to be a communication process (i.e., the development of a system of informational input, integration, and output), then it should be possible to develop a theoretical structure which would account for deviations from normal development. The model upon which the Illinois Test of Psycholinguistic Abilities (Kirk and McCarthy, 1961) is based suggested a way of approaching this task.

As the basis for a study of reading, however, the ITPA model appears to be incomplete in measuring all the facets of psycholinguistic functioning. Although the ITPA has six tests at the representational level, it has only three at the automatic sequential level. For example, the automatic sequential level contains a test of auditory closure, but not one of visual closure. The literature on reading suggests perceptual factors, such as closure and rate of perception, which are generally referred to as integrational in nature. The ITPA model has been extended by the investigator to allow for the assessment of additional psycholinguistic abilities. The proposed model is presented in Figure 1.

This diagram represents tests at two levels of psycholinguistic organization. Tests at the representational level assess the child's ability in the meaningful aspects of language. The psycholinguistic processes which are tapped are decoding, association, and encoding. Decoding is the ability to understand the meaning of symbols, association is the ability to relate symbols on the basis of their meaning, and encoding is the ability to express ideas in symbols. Each process is tested through one of the channels of communication. The numbers one through six in the figure correspond to the subtests of the ITPA at the representational level and indicate the process and channel.

Tests at the integrational level (called automatic sequential by Kirk and McCarthy, 1961) assess the child's ability in less meaningful, more automatic

FIGURE 1. CLINICAL MODEL OF READING PROCESSES INDICAT-
ING AREAS OF STRENGTH, NO DEFICIT, MARGINAL
DEFICIT, AND DEFICIT.

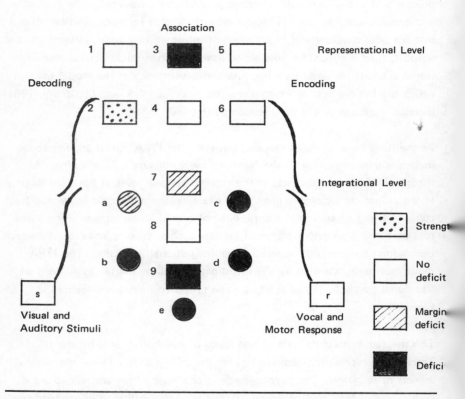

Representational Level

1. Auditory Decoding
2. Visual Decoding
3. Auditory-Vocal Association
4. Visual-Motor Association
5. Vocal Encoding
6. Motor Encoding

Integrational Level

7. Auditory-Vocal Automatic
8. Auditory-Vocal Sequential
9. Visual-Motor Sequential
a. Visual Automatic
b. Sound Blending (Monroe)
c. Mazes
d. Memory-for-Designs (Graham-Kendall)
e. Perceptual Speed (PMA)

use of symbols. The use of grammar and rote memory (both short and long range) is the type of task at this level. The numbers seven through nine in the figure correspond to the ITPA subtests at this level and are divided according to channel.

In addition to the above subtests of the ITPA, a test was devised and some standardized tests were used to gain more information regarding communication processes at the integrational level. These tests have been lettered (a) through (e) and are pictured in Figure 1 as part of the integrational or automatic sequential level. The following discussion of each subtest should clarify its inclusion at this level.

Test a—Visual Automatic. This test was devised by the writer (Kass, 1962) and involves a closure task in the visual area. It assesses the child's ability to automatically predict a whole from a part. A factor analytic study by Goins (1958) suggested that visual closure as a perceptual ability is related to success in first grade reading. This test comprises a short fifteen minute task in which the child is shown a series of unfinished pictures and asked to guess what the completed picture will be. Figure 2 shows some test items.

Test b—Sound Blending (Monroe, 1932). Reading involves the blending of sounds into words as well as the visual closure phenomenon. In this test, the child is presented with a series of separated sounds which form a word and is asked to tell what word the sounds make.

Test c—Mazes (Wechsler, 1949). This test seems to test a type of visual motor predictive process and may bear some relationship to eye-hand coordination.

Test d—Memory-for-Designs (Graham and Kendall, 1960). This test assesses the child's ability to represent a visual image through motor means and appears to be related to spelling or writing words from memory. In this test, the child is shown simple geometric designs which he is asked to reproduce from memory.

FIGURE 2. VISUAL AUTOMATIC TEST ITEMS

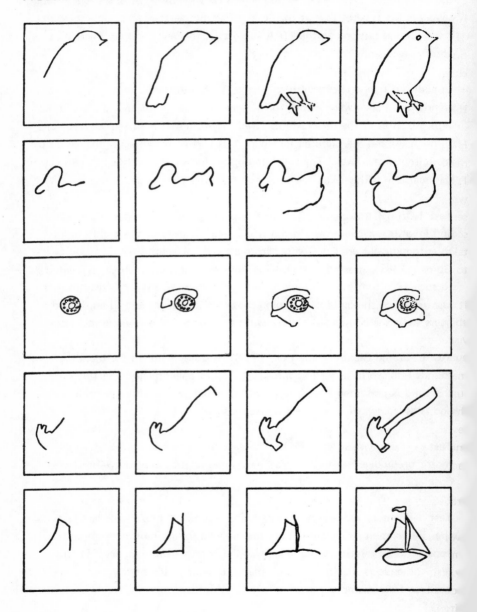

Test e—Perceptual Speed (Thurstone and Thurstone, 1954). Perceptual speed is reported to be one of the perceptual factors found in factorial studies by Thurstone. It was chosen because it may be one of the bases for discrimination of details which differentiate words. It requires the ability to visually compare detailed figures as rapidly as possible.

Hypotheses

Hypotheses regarding the performance of children with reading disability in relation to the norms for each subtest (called normative group) were made. It was predicted that children with normal intelligence with reading disability would be like the normative group in the auditory vocal subtests at the representational level. This prediction follows the assumption that children who score within the normal range on Binet type intelligence tests show that they take in information through the auditory channel, can relate this information to past experience, and can respond adequately through the vocal channel.

It was further predicted that children of normal intelligence with reading disability would not be like the normative group and would be deficient in the visual motor subtests at the representational level, in the sequencing (both auditory and visual) subtests at the integrational level, in the Visual Automatic, the Sound Blending, the Mazes, the Memory-for-Designs, and the Perceptual Speed subtests at the integrational level. This prediction was made on the basis that reading is primarily visual motor at the beginning stages and research suggests that auditory and visual sequencing (or memory), auditory and visual closure, eye-hand coordination, and discrimination are important factors in beginning reading.

Procedure

Twenty-one elementary school children from the Decatur, Illinois, school system were used for this study. The subjects were selected from referrals made by school principals through the office of the assistant superintendent. In order to qualify as having reading disability, each subject met the following criteria:

1. Chronological age between 7-0 and 9-11.

2. IQ at least normal on the Stanford-Binet, Form L-M (85 or above).

3. In the second, third, or fourth year in the primary grades (including the repeaters).

4. Retarded in reading on a battery of diagnostic reading tests (Monroe 1932): one-half year retarded if in second year in school; one and one-half if in third year; and two and one-half if in fourth year.

5. No known defects in visual and auditory acuity (determined from school records).

The selection tests included an intelligence test and a battery of diagnostic reading tests. The psychological measures included the nine subtests of the ITPA, plus the five supplementary measures.

Results

The nine experimental hypotheses of this study were tested by comparing the standard scores for the sample subjects with the population norms for each subtest. The z test was used except where the sample deviation was significantly different from one, in which case a t test was made. The means and standard deviations of the sample group standard scores are presented in Table 1, along with their z or t values and the probabilities of occurrence by chance.

The hypotheses that children with reading disability would not be deficient in the auditory vocal subtests at the representational level nor in the Auditory Vocal Automatic subtest at the integrational level were confirmed for Auditory Decoding and Vocal Encoding, but not for Auditory-Vocal Association and Auditory-Vocal Automatic.

TABLE 1. COMPARISON OF MEANS AND STANDARD DEVIATIONS OF SAMPLE STANDARD SCORES WITH THE NORMAL DISTRIBUTION.

$(\mu = 0 \quad \sigma = 1)$

	Mean	SD	$z(t)$[a]	χ^2[b]	p
Auditory Decoding	−.04	.51	− .34(t)		.75
Visual Decoding	.56	.90	2.56		.01
Auditory-Vocal Association	−.47	1.08	−2.15		.03
Visual-Motor Association	−.32	.76	−1.47		.14
Vocal Encoding	.00	.95	.00		1.00
Motor Encoding	−.05	.99	− .23		.82
Auditory-Vocal Automatic	−.38	.85	−1.74		.08
Auditory-Vocal Sequential	−.19	.99	− .87		.38
Visual-Motor Sequential	−.50	.90	−2.29		.02
Visual Automatic	−.56	1.45	−1.77(t)		.09
Sound Blending				47.84	.001
Mazes	9.14[c]	1.32	−2.35(t)		.05
Memory-for-Designs	−.59	1.22	−2.70		.01
Perceptual Speed	−.65	1.02	−2.98		.002

[a] Where $\sigma = 1$ could not be assumed, t values are given as indicated.

[b] The norms for Sound Blending permitted only crude classification into approximate percentiles.

[c] The norms for Mazes are given in scaled scores with a mean of 10 and a standard deviation of 3.

The hypothesis that children with reading disability would be deficient in the visual motor subtests at the representational level was not confirmed. In the case of Visual Decoding, the results were in the opposite direction. The sample showed a strength in the ability to understand the significance of what is seen.

However, the predictions that they would be deficient in the Auditory and Visual Sequencing, Visual Automatic, Sound Blending, Mazes, Memory-for-Designs, and Perceptual Speed subtests were confirmed, except for Auditory-Vocal Sequencing.

These results have been incorporated into the clinical model of reading processes through differential shading (Figure 1).

Discussion of Results

From the analysis of results, it can be stated that this sample of children with reading disability tended to have certain psycholinguistic disabilities, especially at the integrational level. A correlative relationship between these disabilities and lack of reading achievement is therefore supported. While not all children with reading disability will have these particular psycholinguistic disabilities, it is suggested that such areas of psycholinguistic dysfunction are ones which might be considered in planning for remediation of a reading problem.

Because of the small number of cases in this study, however, the reader is cautioned against indiscriminate generalization from the results. With this limitation in mind, the writer makes some postulates regarding the results:

1. It is posited that children with normal intelligence who have difficulty in handling the symbols in reading compensate by garnering information from pictures, as shown by their superior performance in the ability to interpret pictures (Visual Decoding). Visual Decoding includes visual recognition and understanding of an image which is presented from outside stimuli and is probably quite different from the recognition and understanding of a mental image which must be generated

and/or reproduced from within. This is borne out by the subjects' poorer performance in closure type tasks (Auditory-Vocal Automatic, Visual Automatic, and Sound Blending), in which the whole must be predicted from its parts.

2. It is further suggested that Auditory-Vocal Association, in which the sample subjects performed less well than they did in the other tests at the representational level, involves closure and may actually belong at the integrational level.

3. Another speculation regarding the results is that the integrational level of the communication process is more closely related to the acquisition of reading skill than is the representational level. Studies of intelligence (Gallagher and Lucito, 1961; Serra, 1953) have indicated that the factor which appears to differentiate giftedness from low intelligence is conceptualization ability. The fact that the sample subjects were children with normal intelligence suggests that they are able to conceptualize to some extent, whereas the fact that they cannot read suggests that they are not able to integrate elements into meaningful wholes.

Theoretical Implications

Psychological research, mainly clinical, on certain mental processes involved in the acquisition of reading skill seems to point toward the necessity of adequate auditory and visual integration. These perceptual factors have a number of different labels. Some of these terms are auditory and visual discrimination, auditory and visual memory, auditory and visual perception, sound blending and visualization, and auditory and visual closure. These are all related, it is believed, to central nervous system processes of an integrative nature.

It is suggested that the data of the present investigation of psycholinguistic correlates of reading disability may be related to the above constructs (and it is assumed that they all mean approximately the same thing). The psycholinguistic deficits noted in the study sample are those which appear to involve auditory and visual integration within the mental system.

Some theorists have embodied ideas within their theoretical structures on cognition which the writer feels correspond rather well to this notion of the auditory and visual integrative aspects of the central nervous system.

Kirk (1959) has repeatedly made the clinical observation that two key concerns in reading diagnosis are the child's performance in sound blending and in visualization, both of which refer to central processes.

Osgood (1957) places an integration level within his communication model. By integration he means that "certain patterns and sequences of responses are more readily executed than others and that certain patterns and sequences of stimuli have priority over others. Apparently, both motor and sensory signals are capable of becoming structured or organized" (p. 79).

Mowrer (1960) stresses the "cognitive or mnemonic aspect" of learning in his concept of the "image." That this is related to integration is thought by this investigator to be exemplified in the following quotation from Mowrer:

> An image, in common parlance, is some object which an individual "sees" or otherwise "perceives" without the object being objectively present. By a word, another image, or some other stimulus, the individual is reminded of the object and reacts somewhat as if it were actually present. In other words, a part of the total experience produced by the object itself is here being aroused as a learned, conditioned response; and this response we call an image . . . (p. 166).

Wepman (1961), in a paper given at a Dyslexia Conference at Johns Hopkins University, presents the concept that "reading is not a visual skill alone for all children, but for some it may be the integration of many skills . . . ." He postulates "intense interrelationships between the factors underlying the development of cognition." He arrived at this idea from his own studies of auditory discrimination abilities in children and from studies of others which concerned visual discrimination abilities.

Inhelder, in a lecture at the University of Illinois, 1962, discussed the difference between "operative" and "figurative" symbolic behavior. According to Inhelder, the term operative thinking refers to a transformation or classification of concepts, and the term figurative thinking means the process of imitating reality or the approximate correspondence between copying and reality. The operative kind of symbolism seems to be related to the representational level of psycholinguistic functioning as it appears in the ITPA, while the figurative seems to be comparable to the integrational level. Inhelder suggested that symbolic storage may be lower in figurative disability.

Penfield and Roberts (1959) suggest a reflexive connection between the speech mechanism, which is said to be located in the cortex, and the concept mechanism, which they locate in the brain stem ("centrencephalic system"). This latter mechanism is thought to be responsible for the integration of the functions of both hemispheres. The association process of our reading model seems to be related to Penfield's centrencephalic system. Perhaps psycholinguistic functioning at the integrational level also is dependent upon such a system of concepts. For example, in order to recognize a whole from a part, one must be able to call forth the concept of the whole as well as its label.

Vernon (1952) seems to be discussing this same sort of mechanism from a psychological point of view when she suggests that awareness of an idea or experience must come before awareness of structure; in other words, imagery must come before meaning. She cites evidence for and against this notion.

It appears possible, then, that a deficiency in the brain stem may limit the symbolic storage of children with reading disabilities, and this in turn may create deficits in integrational functions, such as closure, sequential memory, and rate of recognition. Future neurological research may reveal whether this is a tenable assumption.

Practical Implications

Practical implications, as well as theoretical, for the diagnosis and remediation of reading disability can be extracted from the data gathered for this study.

As a diagnostic instrument, the ITPA seems to be valuable in some respects and not in others. Given a child of normal intelligence who has not learned to read after at least one year in school, the subtests which might be used to some advantage are those at the integrational level (tests 7 through 9) and Auditory-Vocal Association (test 3) at the representational level. In addition, tests which are measures of the integrative aspects of mental functioning would appear to be suitable. Tests (a) through (e) used in this study are examples of such measures.

Remediation following the use of the above measures should relate to the specific cognitive process which is defective. For example, a disability in Visual-Motor Sequential (test 9) might be ameliorated through the use of exercises in imitating a series of gestures, completing visual patterns, or reproducing a series of visual symbols.

The clinical use of these diagnostic instruments should be emphasized because not all children with reading problems will display all of the psycholinguistic deficits found in this study. Each child must be diagnosed according to his own deficits which require remediation.

From the practical point of view, then, determination of psychological correlates of reading disability should lead to research in methods of training the integrational, rather than the representational, processes.

References

Gallagher, J. J., and Lucito, L. J. Intellectual pattern of gifted compared with average and retarded. EXCEPTIONAL CHILDREN, 1961, 28, 479-482.

Goins, Jean T. Visual perceptual abilities and early reading process. SUPPLE-MENTARY EDUCATIONAL MONOGRAPH, University of Chicago Press, 1958, Number 87.

Graham, Frances K., and Kendall, Barbara S. Memory-for-Designs test: re-vised general manual. PERCEPTUAL MOTOR SKILLS. Missoula, Montana: Psychological Test Specialists, 1960.

Kass, Corrine. Some psychological correlates of severe reading disability. Un-published doctoral dissertation, University of Illinois, 1962.

Kirk, S. A. Remedial work in the elementary school. MICHIGAN EDUCATION ASSOCIATION JOURNAL, 1959, 48, 24-25.

Kirk, S. A,. and McCarthy, J. J. THE ILLINOIS TEST OF PSYCHOLINGUISTIC ABILITIES: EXPERIMENTAL EDITION. Urbana: Institute for Research on Ex-ceptional Children, University of Illinois, 1961.

Monroe, Marion. CHILDREN WHO CANNOT READ. Chicago: University of Chicago Press, 1932.

Mowrer, O. H. LEARNING THEORY AND THE SYMBOLIC PROCESSES. New York: John Wiley and Sons, 1960.

Osgood, C. E. In J. S. Bruner (Editor), CONTEMPORARY APPROACHES TO COGNITION, A BEHAVIORISTIC ANALYSIS. Cambridge, Massachusetts: Har-vard University Press, 1957.

Penfield, W., and Roberts, L. SPEECH AND BRAIN MECHANISMS. Princeton, New Jersey: Princeton University Press, 1959.

Serra, Mary C. A study of fourth grade children's comprehension of certain verbal abstractions. JOURNAL OF EXPERIMENTAL EDUCATION, 1953, 22, 103-118.

Thurstone, L. L., and Thurstone, Thelma G. SCIENCE RESEARCH ASSOCIATES PRIMARY MENTAL ABILITIES FOR AGES 7-11. Chicago: Science Research Associates, 1954.

Vernon, Magdalen D. A FURTHER STUDY OF VISUAL PERCEPTION. Cambridge, Massachusetts: Harvard University Press, 1952.

Wechsler, D. WECHSLER INTELLIGENCE SCALE FOR CHILDREN, MANUAL. New York: Psychological Corporation, 1949.

Wepman, J. M. Dyslexia: its relationship to language acquisition and concept formation. Paper read at Dyslexia Conference, Johns Hopkins University, Baltimore, November, 1961.

STUDY QUESTIONS

1. Kass points out a limitation (to educators) of the "primary cause" approach to reading problems. What is this limitation? What limitation of the "multi-factored causation" approach is cited? What approach does she recommend to educators?

2. What does Kass recommend should be done about a psycholinguistic deficit revealed by the ITPA profile of a youngster with a reading disability?

3. In your own words, what does this statement mean: Reading is basically an automatic-sequential or integrational process rather than a representational process.

6: CHARACTERISTICS OF DYSLEXIA AND THEIR REMEDIAL IMPLICATION

N. Dale Bryant

Bryant describes the characteristics of dyslexic children as they are manifest in the reading situation. The experienced teacher will readily recognize these difficulties as she has seen them in the classroom and in tutoring sessions. The remedial strategies to overcome these problems will be appreciated by all those who struggle to improve reading instruction.

B. D. B.

Reprinted with permission of the author and publisher from EXCEPTIONAL CHILDREN, 1964, 31, 195-199.

Remedial procedures for dyslexia are implicit in the general characteristics of the reading disability as those characteristics are revealed through diagnostic measurements, including errors made in reading and difficulty in accomplishing certain simple learning. Dyslexia is not a simple entity since there is considerable variability in degree and nature of the impairment. However, much of this variability arises from associated and secondary factors, and there are certain common characteristics that form the core of the disability. This paper will attempt to outline some of these characteristics and point out a few remedial cues to be gained from them.

Dyslexia must be differentiated from other reading difficulties, such as problems of reading comprehension, lack of adequate reading instruction, attentional problems, or "emotional blocking," even though in some cases these may also be present, thus complicating the symptom picture. Dyslexia is concerned with word recognition, and the term "word-blindness" used by some neurologists to popularly identify the dysfunctioning is descriptive of the extreme difficulty in learning to recognize words. The term dyslexia implies a neurological dysfunctioning if only because of its similarity to the neurological condition alexia, which represents a loss of ability to read resulting from damage to the association areas and connections in and around the angular gyrus of the dominant cerebral hemisphere. However, while alexia is a traumatic disruption of existing skills and memories, dyslexia represents a developmental inefficiency in functioning that handicaps learning. Certainly, in some cases, damage, prenatal complications or genetic factors have been causally associated with dyslexia. In most cases, however, a neurological disorder is merely inferred from the nature of the dysfunctioning and associated symptoms. In many cases, it is also apparent that emotional and educational factors are contributing to the learning problems of the child, regardless of whether or not neurological factors are primary.

This study was supported in part by a grant from the Association for the Aid of Crippled Children.

Associated Characteristics

Dyslexia first becomes evident as a child reaches kindergarten and first grade, though it is often not recognized until much later and, indeed, is frequently never recognized for what it is.

The child is usually a boy although the reason for this is not unquestionably established. Explanations include: a) greater vulnerability of males to prenatal and other sources of brain damage; b) sex linked or sex influenced genetic factors; c) slower maturation of males; d) different social expectations and activity levels for males. It is probable that, at least in some cases, each of these factors contribute individually or in combination to the higher frequency of dyslexia in males.

Dyslexia is not a broad defect in general intelligence; IQ's tend to be in the normal range and occasionally reflect very superior ability. However, certain indices of intellectual performance are usually found to be relatively low, e.g., the Coding subtest of the Wechsler Intelligence Scale for Children.

While the primary symptoms are not apparent until school age, many associated symptoms occur with much greater frequency than in the normal population. Usually associated with reading difficulties is confusion when quickly identifying left or right. There is a good chance that the dyslexic boy has some confusion about months, seasons, and judgment of time, direction, distance, and size. On a test of motor development and coordination, he is likely to score low, frequently below the norms for his age. He is much more likely than a normal child to have had speech difficulties and some difficulties may still remain. Similarly, he may have poor auditory discrimination in spite of his adequate auditory acuity. He is more likely than the normal child to have male relatives with similar difficulties in learning to read, and he is also more likely to have been premature or to have survived some complication of pregnancy. The dyslexic child will probably not show gross defects on a neurological examination and will not necessarily appear immature on pediatric examination, although both of these conditions are not infrequent. As in all cases of children with difficulties, he is likely to feel inadequate, stupid, and guilty because of his disability and his repeated failures.

Primary Characteristics

With the exposure to reading instruction, the primary characteristics of the disability become apparent. In spite of learning to recognize some words, he has extreme difficulty in associating the sounds with the visual symbols of letters. This disability is apparent in the confusion of letter sounds, particularly the vowels which have several interfering sounds. Even in the simplest situation of remedial instruction, the stability of sound association in word recognition is many times more difficult to establish than for the normal child. In the classroom situation, children are expected to abstract the common sound elements associated with letters when words containing different letters and sounds are presented. For the dyslexic child this compounds the associational problems. Either because of interference between the various associational pairs or because of a defect in the ability to abstract in this area, the dyslexic child has great difficulty in learning sound associations as they are commonly taught in the classroom. This is a key point in designing remedial instruction for dyslexia. Remediation is almost doomed to failure if it merely repeats the classroom procedure requiring the child to abstract and associate common visual and sound elements when several associations are to be learned at once.

A second primary characteristic of the dyslexic reader is his tendency to ignore the details within words and, instead, to base word recognition on initial letter, length of word, and a few other insufficient cues. This is not due to a simple defect in visual discrimination since adequate discrimination can be made when two words are presented together; rather, the defect comes in the utilization of memory of word shape wherein the details and sequences of letters within the word are often undifferentiated. Thus, a dyslexic boy is likely to accept the word "postal" and even, in an extreme case, a letter combination such as "peistad" as being the word "pasted." No other memory difficulties may be apparent though the inadequacies of most memory batteries make this very hard to determine. Lack of sound association may contribute to the dyslexic's inadequate use of details in word recognition since sound association helps identify and sequence a perception of separate letters within a word. However, the converse may also be true and poor differentiation of details in the visual

117

memory of words may contribute to the difficulty in learning to associate sounds with the letters in those visual memory images. It is evident that classroom or remedial procedures which do not focus attention on the details within words are unlikely to overcome this disability.

A third primary characteristic is a spatial confusion most obvious in the child's inability to consistently differentiate between reverse images such as letter pairs like "b" and "d." Sometimes, up and down reversals add "p" to the b-d confusion. Since this confusion of reversed images is often associated with confusion of the child's own left and right and, because proper differentiation depends entirely upon subjective cues, not merely greater discrimination of shape variations, this is one of the confusions most resistant to remediation. Since the subjective cues of left and right are based upon kinesthetic experience, remedial procedures need to use kinesthetic factors.

These three primary characteristics are probably manifestations of basic defects in neurological functioning. However, for purposes of describing the consistent symptoms of dyslexia, these characteristics may be adequate even if not all inclusive. These same characteristics are normally seen in children just beginning to read but they are rapidly overcome without special help. The dyslexic child persists in these characteristics as he grows older. It is as if dyslexia represents a massive unreadiness for reading. The maturational process, that, in conjunction with experience, produces reading readiness in beginning readers seems to lag for dyslexic youngsters even though there is some slow improvement apparent as the child grows older. Improvement with age in a dyslexic boy who had not been helped by years of remediation may reflect maturation. However, in addition, it may also reflect the fact that remedial procedures often confuse and obscure the very learning they are attempting to bring about. As he grows older, a child with moderate dyslexia may develop considerable reading ability, even though he is still far behind his agemates. His recognition of familiar words increases, but his errors in reading are likely to reflect the same characteristics described. While his reading may be at fourth grade level, most of his errors are likely to be simple ones, more typical of the reading performance of a child reading at first or second grade level. Simple words are correctly identified in one sentence and incorrectly recognized in a later one because of poor differentiation of details within the words. Vowel sounds are inconsistent if the word is the least bit unfamiliar and reversals of letters (and sometimes words or word parts) are still frequent.

Remedial Implications

First of all, it is essential to understand that the dyslexic child's inability to abstract when several associations are presented together makes it necessary to simplify tasks that he is asked to perform so that only one new discrimination or association is made at a time. Furthermore, this discrimination or association must be made repeatedly until it is automatic for the child. Thus, if a child confuses the letters "m" and "n," he needs to differentiate them alone. Once this is done, differentiation should be made in words where no other discriminations or associations are required, e.g., when he knows that one of the two words shown him will be "map" or "nap," "man" or "tan." Correct differentiation of perhaps a dozen trials for each pair of words would prepare the child for correct differentiation of "m" and "n" in pairs and then groups of words of gradually increasing complexity until the child is recognizing the "m" and "n" in words he knows but doesn't expect to be presented. In this way, a dyslexic child may learn to discriminate "m" and "n" in a matter of fifteen minutes and may never have trouble with that discrimination again. The same child might go for years having his "m" and "n" errors pointed out to him without learning to correctly and consistently differentiate between them because there were too many other discriminations and associations that he was attending to at the same time.

Similarly, the dyslexic child will probably never learn vowel sounds when they are thrown at him all together. However, practice with a single vowel and a single sound for that vowel (preferably the more common short sound) when no other discriminations or associations are required is likely to establish an association that will become automatic. Later, when another vowel or another sound for the previously learned vowel is introduced, the automatic association is likely to be retained without either interfering with the new learning or causing a loss of established association.

Thus, an essential procedure in remedial instruction for dyslexia is to simplify a confusing task to a single discrimination or association that can be correctly made by the child and then to practice it in recognition tasks of increasing complexity until it is well established as an automatic response. In this manner, the dyslexic's inability to abstract from a complex situation can be circumvented. Identifying letter-sound associations that the child confuses and working in the manner described helps overcome the difficulties in associating symbols and sounds.

There are several procedures suggested by the primary characteristic of ignoring details within words. Obviously, the child's attention needs to be called to the details. The usual teaching by the "whole word method" which is adequate for the normal child who will attend to details on his own, is not adequate for the dyslexic child. Writing a word is useful, not only because of kinesthetic feedback, but because each letter must be remembered and reproduced even when the child has to look at a copy of the word immediately before he writes it. If he cannot write it, tracing it and copying it can prepare him for writing it. Filling in missing letters in a word is another way of forcing attention to the details and, perhaps, sharpening the visual memory image. Regardless of the procedure used to call attention to the details of each word learned, once the word is learned, it should be differentiated from other words with which it is likely to be confused. For example, if a child learns the word "then," he should practice differentiating it from "thin," "there," "their," "than," etc., even though he may not be able to identify the other words except that they are not "then" which he has just learned. This child, dyslexic though he may be, is unlikely to confuse these words later but without such discrimination practice, he would be almost certain to confuse some of them.

Confusion of reversed images as in "b" and "d" particularly need to be approached in as simple a task as possible because of the great difficulty in overcoming this confusion. If the child is also confused about his own left and right, this should be worked on, perhaps by using a ring, watch, or bracelet on the dominant hand and by providing kinesthetic practice for the dominant side. An important procedure in kinesthetic practice is writing or tracing one of the confused letters. Each day a large letter (i.e., "b") should be traced

120

and words such as "bab" pronounced as it is traced. (A tracing poster on the door of the child's room at home can encourage frequent practice.) The letter should be traced or copied in various sizes on blackboard, paper, and in the air. Variations of this practice should proceed until the child can differentiate "b" from "d" when the letters are presented alone. Subsequently the same procedures can be followed that are described above for overcoming confusion between "m" and "n"; that is, from "b" and "d" presented alone, a child can go on to practice with pages of words like "dog" and "bog." These more complex words should be gradually introduced with the child tracing each of the "b's" on a page and saying the word. As he establishes correct differentiation of the letter "b," he can begin to trace the letter "d," always saying words containing that letter. The steps in increasing the complexity of the task should be so small that he is never allowed to make a mistake because a few errors can disrupt a great deal of previous learning and reinstitute confusion. Thus, the characteristic of letter reversals suggests a procedure for using kinesthetic practice and discriminating tasks of gradually increasing difficulty. Experience suggests short practice periods separate from other remedial work, very gradual steps when increasing difficulty, and massive distributed practice.

Summary

Dyslexia is a complex syndrome with considerable variability in degree of reading disability and nature of associated characteristics. Secondary factors, as well as emotional and educational factors, increase the apparent complexity of the disorder. However, there are at least three characteristics that are so consistent as to be considered primary to the disability. These are: a) difficulty in simple learning of associations between letter symbols and letter sounds (particularly multisound vowels). This difficulty is related to trouble in abstracting common elements from complex experiences; b) use of insufficient word recognition cues by attending primarily to initial letter, length, and general shape while tending to ignore cues of details within words; c) confusion of left-right reversals in letters of similar shape (i.e., "b" and "d").

These primary characteristics suggest procedures that might help overcome the disability. Each discrimination or association problem that causes repeated errors in material even below the child's reading level should be worked with by itself until the difficulty is overcome. The simplest and most basic discriminations or associations should be established first. Each new word should be taught by some procedure involving writing the word or filling in missing letters so that attention is directed to details within the word. In addition, it is essential to provide discrimination training between each new word and words of similar shape. Confusion in left and right reversals of letters requires distributed kinesthetic practice and discrimination training with materials of gradually increasing difficulty. No other discriminations should be required during the practice in discriminating left-right reversals. In contrast with the standard, but relatively ineffectual, remedial procedure (of having a dyslexic child read "at his level" with correction of errors), the above procedures consistently work to improve the dyslexic's reading ability because they help overcome specific disability characteristics.

References

Bryant, N. D. Reading Disability: Part of a syndrome of neurological dysfunctioning. In J. A. Figurel (Ed.) CHALLENGE AND EXPERIMENT IN READING. 1962 Yearbook of the International Reading Association, New York: Scholastic Magazine Press, 1962, 7, 139-143.

Bryant, N. D. Learning disabilities in reading. In J. A. Figurel (Ed.) READING AS AN INTELLECTUAL ACTIVITY. 1963 Yearbook of the International Reading Association, New York: Scholastic Magazine Press, 1963, 8, 142-146.

Bryant, N. D. Some principles for remedial instruction for dyslexia. READING TEACHER. In press.

Hermann, K. READING DISABILITY. Springfield, Illinois: Charles C. Thomas, 1959.

Money, J. (Editor) READING DISABILITY. Baltimore, Maryland: Johns Hopkins Press, 1962.

Pasamanick, B. and Knobloch, H. Epidemiologic studies on the complications of pregnancies and the birth process. In G. Kaplan (Ed.) PREVENTION OF MENTAL DISORDERS IN CHILDREN. New York: Basic Books, 1961. Pp. 74-94.

Rabinovitch, R. Reading and learning disabilities. In Sylvano Arieti (Ed.) AMERICAN HANDBOOK OF PSYCHIATRY. New York: Basic Books, 1959. Pp. 857-869.

STUDY QUESTIONS

1. Remedial reading sometimes consists of giving the child "more of the same," but more slowly. Why does Bryant say this approach is doomed to failure?

2. Bryant makes a distinction between dyslexia and reading difficulties due to poor instruction. How is it determined whether a child's tendency to ignore details in a word is due to dyslexia or to poor instruction?

3. Bryant makes certain remedial suggestions. If a child did not differentiate *m* from *n*, would it be reasonable to try the suggested teaching technique, regardless of *why* the child didn't make the differentiation?

4. Make a brief list of "do's" and "don'ts" for new teachers of reading based on Bryant's remedial recommendations. Illustrate each "don't" with a common violation.

7: DYSLEXIA IN YOUNG CHILDREN

John McLeod

McLeod's article—subtitled "A Factorial Study, with Special Reference
to the Illinois Test of Psycholinguistic Abilities"—is of a statistical nature,
and a precise understanding of all the terminology is beyond many of us.
However, his findings are of utmost importance to all concerned with the
nature of the reading process and with the nature of disabilities in reading.
Therefore, the study is presented here in full. His findings substantiate
those of Kass and others who hold that reading disability is related to
automatic, nonmeaningful language functions. McLeod also presents a
brief questionnaire which appears highly useful in identifying preschool
children who show a proneness to dyslexia.

B. D. B.

Reprinted with permission of the author and publisher from IREC PAPERS, Vol. 2,
Urbana, III.: University of Illinois, Institute for Research on Exceptional Children, 1967
(revised and reprinted, 1968).

125

The data whose analysis is described in the present paper were obtained during the course of experiments which were carried out in Brisbane, Australia. These experiments were designed to compare the performance of 23 dyslexic children on several psychological and psycholinguistic tests with that of a similar number of controls.

In the present paper, the original experiments are briefly described, the findings summarised and there then follows a factor analysis of the data which was carried out with the facilities of the SSUPAC program of the Statistical Services Unit of the University of Illinois.[1]

Situational Background of the Research

In some quarters, there is still dispute as to whether there exists an identifiable subgroup of backward readers who may legitimately be termed "dyslexic" (Vernon 1965), while it is clear from the published writings of those workers who accept the concept of dyslexia that its symptoms are not invariant and unidimensional. Myklebust and Johnson (1962), for instance, point out that "it should not be construed that all facets of this syndrome of childhood dyslexia will be present in a given child," while Rabinovitch (1959) ascribed to children with what he terms *primary reading retardation* "a characteristic pattern with much variability from patient to patient." From the clinical reports of workers in the field, a "characteristic pattern" *can* be sensed, even though the pattern is blurred by "much variability from patient to patient." One approach toward a deeper understanding of the nature of dyslexia is to examine the characteristics of group of backward readers where there is a reasonable probability that the reading disability does not result from exogenous causes and which can, therefore, be described with some confidence as "dyslexia-enriched."

Brisbane appears to be an eminently suitable location for such an inquiry. Surveys which were carried out in 1965 at the Grade Two and Grade Four

[1]This research was partially supported by a grant from the National Science Foundation, no. NSFGP700.

levels, indicated that the incidence of reading retardation in the metropolitan area was remarkably low. For instance, the survey of Grade Four children showed that in a representative sample of approximately 400 children, only about three and a quarter percent had reading quotients of 80 or less, compared with at least 21 to 25 percent in Britain (Ministry of Education 1957). In the Grade Two survey, the reading performance of Brisbane children was compared with that of children in the English i.t.a. experiment (Downing 1964). The Neale Analysis of Reading was administered to a representative sample, again consisting of some 400 Brisbane children under exactly the same conditions as those in the English experiment. It can be observed from Table 1 that every Brisbane child who was examined achieved some score on the test, whereas 38.95 percent of the English control group and 14.45 of the English i.t.a. group failed to score. Furthermore, while two-thirds of the English control group and nearly a third of the English i.t.a. group scored 10 or fewer, the corresponding incidence in Brisbane was less than 6 percent.

TABLE 1. READING ACCURACY OF BRISBANE CHILDREN AND CHILDREN IN THE ENGLISH I.T.A. EXPERIMENT, AFTER 1½ YEARS IN SCHOOL.

	Percentage of children		
Neale Test Score	English i.t.a.	English t.o.	Brisbane
0	14.45	38.95	0.0
1-10	17.8	28.4	5.7
11-20	11.65	16.85	31.0
21-30	26.7	9.45	46.1
31-40	13.0	3.7	10.2
41-50	8.2	1.05	3.9
51-60	6.15	1.6	3.1
61-	2.05	0.0	0.0

If dyslexia is a function, or a partial function, of neurological or genetic factors, it would be reasonable to expect that its incidence should be relatively constant from culture to culture, at any rate in English-speaking communities. On the basis of probability alone therefore, the chances of a case of reading failure in Brisbane being dyslexic ought to be greater than in places where the incidence of reading failure is several times higher. If, in addition, attention is confined to those children in respect of whom there are no detectable exogenous factors which might account for their reading failure, confidence that the group's reading disability is of a more inherent nature is reinforced.

The Grade Two Study of Dyslexia

The selection of the dyslexic group and controls, and the experimental materials and procedure have been fully described elsewhere (McLeod 1967). The tests which were administered are set out in Table 2 of the Appendix to the present article. The Dyslexia Schedule referred to is a questionnaire that had been developed at the Remedial Education Centre of the University of Queensland (McLeod 1968). In an earlier validatory study, a number of its items had been shown to discriminate significantly between children who had been referred to the Centre on account of reading disability, and controls. The items which discriminated significantly are set out in the appendix to this paper. In the experiment under discussion, the number of adverse responses to these critical items was termed the child's AR score.

Summary of Experimental Findings

1. In the Wechsler Intelligence Scale for Children, the Information and Digit Span subtests differentiated significantly between the two groups ($p = .01$) in favour of the control group after adjustment had been made for Full Scale IQ. Arithmetic discriminated in favour of the control group at the .05 level of confidence. The Coding test too discriminated at the .05 level, but in favour of the dyslexic group. This result appears at first glance to run counter to those of a number of other researches, including one by the present author (McLeod 1965). However, the children who were concerned in the present experiment were only seven years old, and therefore had been given the WISC Coding Form A, which has five geometrical symbols. All the experiments in which Coding has been found to discriminate in favour of nonretarded

readers have been concerned with older children who have completed the Coding Form B, which has nine geometrical symbols and associated digits. It seems therefore that the relationship to reading disability of skills which are tapped by tests such as WISC Coding depends upon the number and/or type of symbols, and upon the chronological age of the child. If, for instance, the dyslexic child may be thought of as a communication channel capable of processing more than five signs in a Coding-type task, but incapable of processing nine signs (Miller's "magic number seven, plus or minus two"?), then the apparent inconsistency of experimental results can be reconciled. Exploration of this phenomenon is beyond the immediate scope of the present study, but is one that will probably repay further research.

2. The Illinois Test of Psycholinguistic Abilities discriminated significantly ($p = .01$) between the dyslexic and control groups, over and above the WISC. That is, there was still a significant difference between the two groups' scores on the ITPA after adjustment had been made for differences in IQ.

3. Within the ITPA itself, the Auditory-Vocal Automatic, the Auditory-Vocal Sequential and the Auditory Decoding tests discriminated in favour of the control group, and Motor Encoding discriminated in favour of the dyslexic group, after adjustment had been made for the difference between the two groups on overall ITPA Language Age. Because of a significant heterogeneity of variance of the groups' scores on the Visual-Motor Sequential test, data on this test could not validly be analysed.

4. The dyslexic group was consistently inferior in reproducing visual letter sequences at all levels of approximation to English. That is, their inferiority was neither more nor less marked when zero-order approximations to English words were displayed than when second-order approximation words were used.

5. The Wepman test discriminated significantly ($p = .001$) between the dyslexic and control groups, but the N.U.4 Auditory Test did not, suggesting a weakness on the part of the dyslexics in the perception of phonemes. An alternative, but equivalent, way of expressing this interpretation would be to say that the dyslexics exploited redundancy within a word to a relatively greater extent than did the controls.

6. The dyslexic group was significantly inferior in their vocal reproduction of words that had been auditorily presented in context. This was true for both first- and for third-order contexts. However, the deficiency was significantly less marked in the case of words that were preceded by third-order context, suggesting that the dyslexics took advantage of redundancy *between* spoken words, or conversely, that the dyslexics' performance deteriorated as the information rate of the material increased. As their deficiency in auditory-vocal processing of spoken language signals had been particularly pronounced when redundancy between and within words was minimal, the dyslexic group's performance on the auditory perception tests was as if they were acting like communication channels of particularly limited capacity.

7. Defining each child's AR score on the Dyslexia Schedule as the number of adverse responses to items which the earlier validatory study had shown to be effective discriminators, twenty of the 23 members of the dyslexic group received an AR score of six or higher, whereas only a single child of the control group attracted such a high AR score.

FACTORIAL ANALYSIS OF DATA

Summary of the Analytical Design

In the course of the experimental studies, 29 separate quantitative assessments had been recorded for each of the 46 children in the investigation. Product-moment correlations between the 29 variables were computed and these were factor analysed. No definitive test data were included in the correlational matrix; that is, no data such as reading ages which had been used as one of the criteria to determine whether or not a child should be included in the dyslexic group. The 29 tests are listed in Table 2 (Appendix).

Principal Axis factor analysis was employed, and factors were extracted until the criterion of eigen value equal to unity was reached. The element of largest absolute magnitude in each row was used for the estimation of communalities and the principal axis factors were subjected to Varimax rotation, thus yielding an orthogonal solution.

The factor scores of each of the 46 children on the rotated factors were computed and these factor scores were then used in order to predict whether a child belonged to the dyslexic group or the control group. Prediction was achieved by multiple regression, the scores on the rotated factors being the independent predictive variables.

The multiple regression equation was built up stepwise, introducing the independent variables (i.e., rotated factors) one at a time. The most significant factor was identified first and correlated with the criterion, then other factors were introduced one by one in order of the significance of their correlation with the criterion until no further significant gain accrued in the multiple correlation coefficient.

Results

The matrix of intercorrelations between the 29 tests are set out in Table 6 in the Appendix. The factor analysis proceeded until an eigen value of unity was reached, at which stage five factors had been extracted, accounting for 62.00 percent of the variance. The variance accounted for by each of the unrotated factors is recorded in Table 7 of the Appendix.

Table 3 in the Appendix depicts the rotated factor matrix with all loadings deleted whose rounded absolute value is less than 0.4. The actual values of factor loadings higher than a rounded 0.6 are reproduced to two places of decimals; loadings which are at least 0.5 are represented by a single plus sign and loadings of 0.4 or higher by a plus sign in parentheses.

Interpretation of Factors

All the Automatic-Sequential level tests of the ITPA have significant loadings on Factor 1 and the test which has the heaviest loading is the WISC Digit Span. The reproduction of tachistoscopically presented letter sequences also has a heavy loading on this factor, which is interpreted as a Sequencing-Integrative factor.

131

The factor is characterised by skills at the integrative level of the Osgood (1957a) theoretical model, where response is a function of frequency and contiguity, rather than a consequence of representational or semantic mediation. Sequencing has been specifically emphasised in the labelling of this factor because of the particularly heavy loadings of tests where the response involved some sequential element.

Two tests which loaded moderately on Factor 1 and which might appear to be representational in nature rather than integrative are the ITPA Auditory-Vocal Association test and the WISC Information test. However, many of the responses to the Auditory-Vocal Association test are such as might be expected to be elicited spontaneously, for example in a word association test, by the operative word in the initial sentence. Comprehension of the whole item "Soup is *hot*; ice cream is _____?" is, to some extent at any rate, unnecessary. The stimulus "hot" alone would have been sufficient to arouse the response "cold," as has been confirmed informally on many occasions in the clinical training situation. Similarly, items in the WISC Information test which require the number of days in a week or pounds in a ton, the discoverer of America or the capital of Greece, etc., call for responses that are of a rote nature in that they have been frequently associated and do not solely depend upon cognitive synthesis.

The tests which had loadings on Factor 2 were the ITPA Visual Decoding, Motor Encoding, Vocal Encoding, WISC Similarities, Vocabulary and, to a smaller extent, Information. Each of these five tests are characterised by being response-oriented; that is, they require the subject to have a prior mental set which is vocally or subvocally mediated. In the case of Similarities, which had the heaviest loading on Factor 2, the subject awaits the two stimulus word with the preceding directive of "How alike?" With Vocal Encoding, he is pre pared to "tell all about this," his response being elicited by the presentation of the stimulus object. Again, in the Vocabulary test, he awaits the stimulus wo to trigger off a response that has been oriented toward "telling the meaning o . . . ." As Osgood (1957) has described intention (s_m) as the essential charac teristic of the encoding process, and has further defined encoding as "the asso ciation of mediated self-stimulation with overt instrumental sequences," it seems reasonable to regard Factor 2 as an Encoding Factor. It might be noted incidentally that Comprehension and Arithmetic of the WISC Verbal Scale, where there is no preliminary set by the subject, do not load on this factor.

The loading of the ITPA Visual Decoding on Factor 2 appears to pose a problem, but perhaps the nomenclature of this test is misleading. The relationship between Visual Decoding and Encoding tests is not a finding unique to the present study. McCarthy and Kirk (1963, p. 61) themselves report that in their statistical analysis of the ITPA standardization data, "half the correlations between Motor Encoding and Visual Decoding are significantly different from zero," and for their seven-year-old sample, Vocal Encoding, Motor Encoding and Visual Decoding were the three tests which loaded significantly on the second factor of their analysis, the factor being interpreted as Encoding.

The test procedure which is followed in the Visual Decoding test is that the subject is first shown a single illustration of, say, a table. Then he is shown a page which contained four illustrations and he is required to "find one there." It *is* conceivable that the child examines each picture in turn, assesses their respective similarities to the previously presented picture, and selects the most appropriate. Observation of children in the actual test situation, however, suggests that after an initial visual decoding of the first picture, they are again response-oriented when they examine the second card and that they approach the pictures looking for "tableness." Although nominally a test of decoding skill, therefore, it is plausible to argue that there is, as the factor analysis suggests, a substantial element of encoding involved also.

Block Design, Object Assembly and Picture Completion from the WISC, and Visual-Motor with smaller loadings on the WISC Picture Arrangement, ITPA Motor Encoding and Visual-Motor Association constituted the tests which identified Factor 3. This was termed a Visual-Motor factor.

The tests which loaded significantly on the fourth factor were those which involved the reproduction of, or discrimination between, auditorily presented words, and the ITPA Auditory Decoding. Moreover, although it is doubtful how much significance should be attached to the fact, the loadings of the tests which involved less redundant stimuli were greater than those of tests whose stimuli were more redundant. That is, the Wepman test loaded more heavily than did the N.U.4 test, and of the tests requiring the vocal reproduction of auditorily presented words in context, the first-order context test loaded more heavily than did the third-order context, while the Auditory Decoding test, which involves highly redundant material, had the least of the significant loadings. Factor 4 was therefore interpreted as an Auditory Language Input Capacity factor, the word "capacity" being included because of the heavier loadings of the tests whose items had a higher information rate.

Arithmetic, Mazes and to a lesser extent Comprehension, all from the WISC, loaded on Factor 5. Each of these tests requires some degree of planning ahead, of anticipating the consequences of particular responses or chain of responses, or, in the language of the Osgood model, a multistage mediational process. Factor 5 was designated a Planning factor.

In summary, the five rotated factors were interpreted as follows:

1. Sequencing-Integrative
2. Vocal Encoding
3. Visual-Motor
4. Auditory Language Input Capacity
5. Planning

Derivation of Multiple Regression Equation

Each child's factor scores on the five rotated orthogonal factors were computed. The five factors were then treated as independent variables from which, through multiple regression, was to be predicted whether the child was a member of the dyslexic or control group. As a criterion, or dependent variable, each member of the dyslexic group was arbitrarily assigned a score of 1.0 and each member of the control group a score of 2.0. Factors were entered in to the multiple regression equation until no further significant improvement in multiple correlation was achieved. The criterion for a variable to be entered in the multiple regression equation was that it should have an F value of more than 2.0. The factors which were found to contribute significantly to the multiple regression, listed in the order in which they were entered, are shown in Table 4, together with the coefficient of multiple correlation between the criterion and the weighted factors as they had been included in the regression equation.

TABLE 4. FACTORS INCLUDED IN REGRESSION EQUATION TO PRE-DICT MEMBERSHIP OF DYSLEXIC OR CONTROL GROUP

	Factor	Cumulative Multiple correlation with
No.	Name	criterion
1.	Sequencing-Integrative	0.622
4.	Auditory Language Input Capacity	0.791
2.	Encoding	0.820
5.	Planning	0.845

Table 5 records the standardised regression coefficients of each factor, together with their respective t-ratios. Standard errors of the coefficients were of the order of 0.08.

TABLE 5. STANDARDISED REGRESSION COEFFICIENTS

Factor	Standardised regression coefficient	t-ratio
Sequencing-Integrative (1)	0.586	7.006
Auditory Language Input Capacity (4)	0.483	5.776
Encoding (2)	0.215	2.577
Planning (5)	0.204	2.436

Discussion of Results

The results of the present factorial study reinforce, in a single consolidated analysis, the general picture which had been synthesised from the separate experiments from which the data had been gathered. For example, the experimental approach had indicated the greater sensitivity of the ITPA, compared with the WISC, in discriminating dyslexics; the importance within the ITPA of the Automatic-Sequential tests; and the relative competence of dyslexics on the WISC Coding and ITPA Motor Encoding tests. These findings were reflected in the factorial study in that the most significant factor which emerged had substantial loadings on four of the nine ITPA subtests but only two—both verbal—of the twelve WISC subtests. Of the four ITPA subtests which loaded on this factor, all three Automatic-Sequential level tests were in evidence, while one of the WISC subtests was the Digit Span.

The significance of the Dyslexia Schedule and of the tests which involved the reproduction of tachistoscopically presented letter sequences, and the reproduction or discrimination of auditorily presented words, had emerged from the experimental studies. These findings were paralleled in the factorial analysis where all of the measures were found to have substantial loadings on one or both of the two most significant factors in the regression equation.

As far as the sample of seven-year-old children used in the present study is concerned, it would appear that severe reading disability can be inferred—and, hopefully, predicted—from measurable correlates, with a satisfactorily high degree of reliability. What might be somewhat surprising is the factorial nature of these correlates. Examination of Table 4 reveals that a multiple correlation coefficient of 0.791 was achieved by Factors 1 and 4, both of which involve integrative or automatic-sequential level skills only. Further, there was no factor in the final regression equation which could be linked *specifically* with visual perception.

CONCLUSIONS

The ITPA Model

The present analysis affords some support for the validity of the subtests of the ITPA and of the theoretical model on which the test is based.

The ITPA subtests loaded on four factors that were definable by reference to tests other than those of the ITPA itself.

Of the four factors, the first supported the theoretical and clinical postulate of an automatic-sequential level of perceptual organization which involves skills that transcend sense modality, are pertinent to psycholinguistic behaviour, and yet whose characteristics are distinctive from cognitive skills where semantic mediation and meaningful manipulation of verbal concepts are predominant. Factors 2 and 4 lent support to the ITPA's classification of decoding and encoding processes, while Factor 3 was consistent with the classification according to psycholinguistic modal channel.

Psycholinguistic Correlates of Severe Reading Disability

From the present investigation, there would appear to be grounds for some optimism that severe reading disability can be inferred with a fair amount of accuracy from the assessment of correlated skills such as those measured in the experiments which underlie the analysis.

In particular, more than a half of the total variance was accounted for by the two factors which were shown to have the most significant regression coefficients in the multiple regression equation. The first of these factors was associated with automatic-sequential or integrative skills which involved both visual and auditory input. The second factor was associated with the discrimination between, and vocal reproduction of, auditorily presented words, and which therefore appears to be related to auditory receptivity.

The findings thus provide still further support for the numerous researches, summarised by Bateman (1965), which have reported weaknesses in the automatic-sequential area in children who have learning disabilities.

Diagnosis of Dyslexia

The ideal at which to aim in the treatment of dyslexia is to *predict* those children who are "dyslexia-prone," rather than to confirm that a child presents certain characteristic symptoms after severe reading disability has manifested itself.

The present study indicates that more attention needs to be focused on skills at the automatic-sequential level of perceptual organization if accurate prognosis is to be achieved rather than to rely almost exclusively on measures of general mental development and visual perception as has so often been the case in the past. As a screening device, an instrument such as the Dyslexia Schedule appears to hold some promise of value. Being composed of items which are based on symptoms which are observable in the preschool child, it can be completed by parents and does not require any prolonged individual testing. The Dyslexia Schedule had a substantial loading on the first, predominant factor in the multiple regression equation and a smaller, but significant, loading on the fourth factor. Thus the Dyslexia Schedule achieved loadings on the two factors that had the most significant predictive coefficients.

APPENDIX

TABLE 2. TEST VARIABLES INCLUDED IN FACTOR ANALYSIS

	Name of test	Abbreviation
1.	ITPA Auditory-Vocal Automatic	AVAut
2.	Visual Decoding	VD
3.	Motor Encoding	ME
4.	Auditory-Vocal Association	AVAss
5.	Visual-Motor Sequential	VMS
6.	Vocal Encoding	VE
7.	Auditory-Vocal Sequential	AVS
8.	Visual-Motor Association	VMA
9.	Auditory Decoding	AD
10.	WISC Information	I
11.	Comprehension	C
12.	Arithmetic	A
13.	Similarities	S
14.	Vocabulary	V
15.	Digit Span	D
16.	Picture Completion	PC
17.	Picture Arrangement	PA
18.	Block Design	BD
19.	Object Assembly	OA
20.	Coding	CO
21.	Mazes	MZ
22.	Tachistoscopic Letter Sequences (Zero-order)	TLS(0)
23.	Tachistoscopic Letter Sequences (2nd-order)	TLS(2)
24.	Words in spoken context (1st-order)	WiC(1)
25.	Words in spoken context (3rd-order)	WiC(3)
26.	Wepman Test in Phonemic Discrimination	WEP
27.	N.U.4 Auditory Test	NU4
28.	Dyslexia Schedule Adverse Responses	DSAR
29.	Chronological Age	CA

TABLE 3. ROTATED FACTOR LOADINGS

Test	1	2	3	4	5
			Factors		
AVAut	.70				
VD		.58			
ME		.55	(+)		
AVAss	.61	(+)			
VMS	.58				
VE		+			
AVS	.78				
VMA			+		
AD				(+)	
I	.59	+			
C		+			(+)
A	(+)				.56
S		.66			
V		.61			
D	.84				
PC			.61		
PA	+		(+)		
BD			.75		
OA			.66		
CO					(+)
MZ					.63
TLS(0)	.80				
TLS(2)	.73				
WiC(1)				.73	
WiC(3)				.69	
WEP				.57	
NU4		(+)		+	
DSAR	+			(+)	
CA					

TABLE 6. TEST INTERCORRELATIONS (DECIMAL POINTS OMITTED)

Test No.	Title	1	2	3	4	5	6	7	8	9	10
1	AVAut	1000									
2	VD	371	1000								
3	ME	152	498	1000							
4	AVAss	660	340	362	1000						
5	VMS	512	408	277	482	1000					
6	VE	447	520	259	290	294	1000				
7	AVS	510	166	301	528	471	182	1000			
8	VMA	112	153	266	117	228	260	166	1000		
9	AD	242	167	-004	152	211	080	028	007	1000	
10	I	520	458	295	579	605	427	454	153	154	1000
11	C	095	316	337	162	239	207	055	221	045	364
12	A	358	337	098	281	456	272	454	170	159	470
13	S	427	454	370	415	230	462	266	361	065	489
14	V	350	458	272	294	416	497	352	398	070	577
15	D	635	252	194	509	612	267	799	268	126	586
16	PC	264	230	177	281	268	249	157	236	216	155
17	PA	309	412	379	513	341	412	446	287	089	464
18	BD	148	283	385	298	425	170	044	330	255	254
19	OA	307	235	490	272	298	197	244	512	109	254
20	CO	-135	211	294	061	226	-051	074	-161	-287	147
21	MZ	230	198	078	092	451	108	315	141	040	229
22	TLS(0)	686	386	197	565	596	334	627	335	218	547
23	TLS(2)	526	333	070	452	555	311	556	295	271	561
24	WiC(1)	368	248	-103	258	049	206	194	086	186	149
25	WiC(3)	178	049	-360	044	043	-016	065	-168	326	044
26	WEP	275	089	042	235	221	227	284	165	092	353
27	NU4	106	225	083	202	067	147	020	014	199	100
28	DSAR	599	394	125	529	388	314	425	182	295	566
29	CA	-037	040	348	197	-066	-093	-096	044	-070	-179

TABLE 6. (CONT.)

Test No.	Title	11	12	13	14	15	16	17	18	19	20
11	C	1000									
12	A	380	1000								
13	S	250	214	1000							
14	V	412	425	598	1000						
15	D	018	468	325	378	1000					
16	PC	-076	088	115	122	368	1000				
17	PA	156	357	365	384	438	477	1000			
18	BD	314	257	062	258	268	516	462	1000		
19	OA	263	216	286	254	344	347	373	549	1000	
20	CO	262	209	-066	109	-112	-076	184	017	-092	1000
21	MZ	334	442	-019	220	352	196	336	416	329	219
22	TLS(0)	189	444	410	504	699	355	540	298	265	009
23	TLS(2)	166	515	307	439	662	367	550	380	194	-059
24	WiC(1)	072	230	145	213	293	057	141	068	193	-324
25	WiC(3)	-082	025	-117	027	170	-028	-174	-175	-225	-077
26	WEP	221	105	188	382	331	-171	199	157	270	-162
27	NU4	352	268	185	142	-097	-214	085	089	148	-030
28	DSAR	199	418	371	282	494	005	409	175	151	-155
29	CA	-181	-460	045	-068	-137	024	-054	035	086	-134

Test No.	Title	21	22	23	24	25	26	27	28	29
21	MZ	1000								
22	TLS(0)	344	1000							
23	TLS(2)	455	840	1000						
24	WiC(1)	257	304	372	1000					
25	WiC(3)	153	076	178	543	1000				
26	WEP	296	265	305	507	445	1000			
27	NU4	289	035	114	427	276	417	1000		
28	DSAR	275	556	606	432	248	368	291	1000	
29	CA	-408	-006	-180	060	-138	-120	-093	-070	1000

TABLE 7. VARIANCE ACCOUNTED FOR BY UNROTATED
PRINCIPAL AXIS FACTORS

Factor	Variance	Percent variance
1	8.95	30.85
2	2.94	10.15
3	2.19	7.57
4	2.05	7.07
5	1.84	6.36
		62.00

TABLE 8. VARIMAX ROTATED FACTOR MATRIX

Test	Factors (decimal points omitted)				
	1	2	3	4	5
AVAut	.6978	.2587	.0775	.2842	-.0689
VD	.2572	.5817	.1960	.0522	.0854
ME	.1061	.5506	.3902	-.2787	-.0973
AVAss	.6072	.3729	.1606	.1091	-.1372
VMS	.5814	.2239	.2678	-.0210	.3014
VE	.2826	.5068	.1397	.1126	-.0068
AVS	.7772	.1157	.0164	-.0043	.1335
VMA	.1152	.2727	.4823	.0462	-.0326
AD	.1462	-.0567	.2029	.3825	.0034
I	.5892	.4829	.0539	.0466	.2173
C	-.0566	.5153	.1539	.0208	.4299
A	.4154	.2406	.0869	.0659	.5614
S	.3222	.6551	.0671	.0500	-.1694
V	.3414	.6064	.1120	.0556	.1868
D	.8434	.0345	.2125	.1383	.0966
PC	.3347	-.1252	.6145	-.0579	-.0949
PA	.4620	.3069	.4313	-.0566	.1245
BD	.1113	.1379	.7543	.0316	.2028
OA	.1062	.2936	.6631	.0859	.0218
CO	-.0004	.1972	-.0771	-.4957	.3771
MZ	.2167	.0365	.3049	.1736	.6271
TLS(0)	.7977	.2056	.2435	.1428	.0868
TLS(2)	.7262	.0817	.2735	.2704	.2718
WiC(1)	.1818	.1427	.0483	.7281	.0170
WiC(3)	.1120	-.1600	-.2364	.6910	.0942
WEP	.1525	.2839	.0144	.5674	.1838
NU4	-.1438	.3737	-.0160	.4835	.2697
DSAR	.5361	.3180	.0136	.4182	.0955
CA	-.0886	.1228	.1373	-.0550	-.6302

DYSLEXIA SCHEDULE
LIST OF ITEMS DISCRIMINATING DYSLEXIC CHILDREN

1.   (a) Have you ever suspected that S may have defective eyesight?
       (b) If so, has S ever been seen by an optometrist or by an eye specialist?
       (c) (If yes) What was the result of the examination?

                                                                                                  (AR : n.a.d.)

2.   (a) Have you ever suspected that S may have defective hearing?
       (b) If so, has S ever had his hearing tested?
       (c) (If yes) What was the result of the examination?

                                                                                                  (AR : n.a.d.)

3.   Was S ever in hospital *at all* before he was 3 years old?

                                                                                                  (AR : yes)

4   If S has been separated at all from one or both parents, did he seem different in any way after separation? (e.g., more clinging, affectionate, indifferent to parents)

                                                                                                  (AR : yes)

5.   Has S any nervous tendencies?

(a) bedwetting		(AR : yes)
(b) excessive story-telling (lies or fantasy)		(AR : yes)
(c) fear of dark		(AR : yes)
(d) fear of making mistakes		(AR : yes)

6.   Does S show anxiety and/or depression?   (AR : yes)

7.   Is S over-active?   (AR : yes)

8.   Was S over-active in infancy?   (AR : yes)

9.   Was S over-active before he was born?   (AR : yes)

10.   Does S vary rapidly between moods? (e.g., from timidity to **aggressiveness**)

                                                                                                  (AR : yes)

11. At what age did S speak? (apart from "da" and "ma")

(AR : 24 months +)

12. At what age was S's speech (i.e., 2 or more continuous words) intelligible to persons *other than mother*?

(AR : 30 months +)

13. Was S's talk still immature at age 4 or 5, i.e., at or just prior to commencing school? (e.g., "fink" for "think," "dat" for "that," reference to himself by name rather than by "I" or "me")

(AR : yes)

14. Has S ever tended to mix up the order of words in a sentence or to mix up parts of words? (e.g., "flutterby" for "butterfly," or "hopgrasser" for "grasshopper," "Did you lawn the mow?" for "Did you mow the lawn?" etc.)

(AR : yes)

15. (a) Can S write his name?
(b) If so, does he jumble or reverse any letters?

(AR : yes)

16. Has S had any difficulty in distinguishing right from left? (e.g., in following directions, performing actions involving turning handles to right or left, etc.)

(AR : yes)

17. Have any members of S's family experienced difficulties with reading and/or spelling?

(AR : Mother, Father,
Grandparent,
or sibling)
(Only 1 counted)

References

Bateman, Barbara D. THE ILLINOIS TEST OF PSYCHOLINGUISTIC ABILITIES IN CURRENT RESEARCH. Urbana, Illinois. Institute for Research on Exceptional Children, 1965.

Downing, J. A. THE I.T.A. READING EXPERIMENT. London, Evans Bros., 1964.

McCarthy, J. J. and Kirk, S. A. THE CONSTRUCTION, STANDARDIZATION AND STATISTICAL CHARACTERISTICS OF THE ILLINOIS TEST OF PSYCHOLINGUISTIC ABILITIES. Madison, Wisconsin. Photopress Inc., 1963.

McLeod, J. A Comparison of WISC Sub-test Scores of Pre-adolescent Successful and Unsuccessful Readers. AUSTRAL. J. PSYCHOL. 1965, 17, 3, 220-228.

McLeod, J. Prediction of Childhood Dyslexia. SLOW LEARNING CHILD. 1966, 12, 3, 143-154.

McLeod, J. The Perceptual Bases of Reading. PROCEEDINGS OF THE FIRST INTERNATIONAL CONGRESS ON READING, PARIS 1966. Newark, Delaware, International Reading Association. (1966a)

McLeod, J. Some Psycholinguistic Correlates of Reading Disability in Young Children. READING RES. QUART. 1967, 2, 3, 5-32.

McLeod, J. DYSLEXIA SCHEDULE, SCHOOL ENTRANCE CHECK LIST AND MANUAL. Educators Publishing Service. Cambridge, Mass. 1968.

Miller, G. A., Bruner, J. S. and Postman, L. Familiarity of Letter Sequences and Tachistoscopic Identification. J. GENERAL PSYCHOL. 1954, 50, 129-139.

Miller, G. A., Heise, G. A. and Lichten, W. The Intelligibility of Speech as a function of the Context of the Test Materials. J. EXP. PSYCHOL. 1951, 41, 329-335.

Miller, G. A. and Selfridge, J. A. Verbal Context and the Recall of Meaningful Material. AMER. J. PSYCHOL. 1950, 63, 176-185.

Ministry of Education. STANDARDS OF READING. London, H.M.S.O., 1957.

Myklebust, H. and Johnson, Doris. Dyslexia in Children. EXCEPTIONAL CHILDREN, 1962, 29, 1, 14-26.

Neale, Marie D. NEALE ANALYSIS OF READING ABILITY. London, Macmillan, 1958.

Osgood, C. E. A Behavioristic Analysis of Perception and Language as Cognitive Phenomena, 1957. (In CONTEMPORARY APPROACHES TO COGNITION, THE COLORADO SYMPOSIUM. Cambridge, Mass., Harvard Univ. Press. 1957).

Osgood, C. E. Motivational Dynamics of Language Behavior, 1957a. (In NEBRASKA SYMPOSIUM ON MOTIVATION. Lincoln, Univ. of Nebraska Press, 1957.)

Rabinovitch, R. Reading and Learning Disabilities. AMER. HANDBOOK PSYCHIAT., N.Y. Basic Books, 1959, 857-869.

Radford, W. C. A WORD LIST FOR AUSTRALIAN SCHOOLS. Melbourne, A.C.E.R., 1960.

Southgate, Vera. SOUTHGATE GROUP READING TESTS. London, U.L.P., 195

Stowe, A. N., Harris, W. P. and Hampton, D. B. Signal and Context Components of Word-Recognition Behaviour. J. ACOUST. SOC. AMER. 1963, 35, 5, 639-644.

Thorndike, E. L. and Lorge, I. THE TEACHER'S WORD BOOK OF 30,000 WORD N.Y. Bureau of Publications, Teachers' College, Columbia University, 1964.

Tillman, T., Carhart, R. and Wilber, Laura. A TEST FOR SPEECH DISCRIMINA-
TION COMPOSED OF CNC MONOSYLLABIC WORDS (N.U. AUDITORY TEST NO. 4).
U. S. Dept. of Commerce, Office of Tech. Services, 1963.

Vernon, M. S. Specific Dyslexia. THE SLOW LEARNING CHILD. 1965, 12, 2,
71-75.

Voelker, C. H. The One-Thousand Most Frequent-Spoken Words. QUART. J.
SPEECH, 1942, 28, 189-197.

Wepman, J. M. AUDITORY DISCRIMINATION TEST. J. M. Wepman, 950 E.
59th St., Chicago 37, 1958.

STUDY QUESTIONS

1. Complete understanding of all the procedures described in this article requires more statistical knowledge than many of us possess. Nevertheless the important results, conclusions, and discussions are clearly presented.

    a. McLeod found dyslexics inferior to controls on the WISC information and digit span tests, and superior on coding. Compare these findings with Shimota's results.

    b. What does McLeod conclude about the usefulness of the ITPA in cases of reading disorders? Which subtests are most useful?

2. What is the Dyslexia Schedule? What is it used for?

3. Compare McLeod's finding that weaknesses in the automatic and sequential (rote) aspects of language are associated with reading problems to Kass' finding regarding this area.

4. If automatic, sequential, rote, and integrative skills are highly correlated with reading abilities, does this necessarily say anything about the nature of reading itself?

8: EARLY PREDICTION OF READING FAILURE

Katrina de Hirsch
Jeanette J. Jansky
William S. Langford

De Hirsch, Jansky, and Langford describe the construction and preliminary data on the Predictive Index, a test battery which can be administered to 5-year-olds and which appears very useful in finding those
children who are likely to fail in reading unless we provide better-than-
usual instructional procedures. Transition classes are urged in which a
"match" can be made between the child's developmental readiness and
the type of teaching offered.

B. D. B

Reprinted with permission of the authors and publisher from BULLETIN OF THE
ORTON SOCIETY, 1966, 16, 1-13.

Prediction of reading success or failure has been the objective of a number of both clinical and more formal studies. Among the statistical investigations, some have taken single variables, such as auditory discrimination, visuo-motor competence, anxiety level or self-concept as measured in kindergarten or early first grade, in order to predict reading competence 9-12 months later. A few have constructed a battery of predictive tests—one of the best was Monroe's.

Our own investigation differs from others in three important respects: it explores a far larger section of the child's perceptuo-motor and linguistic organization than do other studies, it predicts spelling and writing in addition to reading achievement, and finally the interval between prediction and outcome is more than twice as long as it is in most other studies.

Schools have, of course, informally assessed children's readiness for years and they have by and large relied on three types of evaluation: on reading-readiness tests, on determination of IQ and on informal sizing up of the child by the kindergarten teacher. All of these techniques are legitimate, but all have certain disadvantages: reading-readiness tests do not always reveal enough about a child's specific weakness and strength to assist the teacher in the planning of educational strategies; most, moreover, fail to predict for writing and spelling. Reliance on intelligence tests has been challenged first because severe reading disabilities are known to occur on practically all intellectual levels, secondly because an intelligence quotient represents at best a global rather than a differentiated evaluation of a child's potential, and finally because IQ does not sufficiently take into account important perceptual factors which, we feel, are significant for reading success and failure. The developmentally oriented teacher's assessment of a child, finally, though often remarkably accurate, cannot be easily duplicated. Such a teacher will often say that a given child is "immature" without being able to state what went into her judgment.

The project was supported by the Health Research Council of the City of New York. The study was published in its entirety by Harper & Row, Oct., 1966, under the title of Prediction of Reading Failure.
This paper, essentially in its present form, was presented by Mrs. de Hirsch at the Sixteenth Annual Meeting of The Orton Society, Inc., held at the Academy of Sciences, New York City, October 29, 1965.

Our own attempts at prediction in the Pediatric Language Disorder Clinic, Columbia-Presbyterian Medical Center, go back over nearly 20 years. They were largely informal and stemmed from our experience with pre-school youngsters referred for a variety of oral language deficits. An extraordinarily large proportion of these children developed reading, writing and spelling difficulties several years later. The clinical impression of these youngsters was one of striking immaturity. In spite of adequate intelligence their performance on a variety of perceptuo-motor and language tasks resembled that of subjects of chronologically younger ages. Our original predictions were based primarily on a clinical evaluation of the child's developmental level and only secondarily on his performance on a battery of tests which we had assembled over the years. By and large our predictions were successful, but they raised a number of new questions. We were dealing with a speech defective, that is to say, with a clinical group—other clinicians deal with disturbed children or brain-injured ones—and we were by no means sure (looking at the discrepancies between research results based on clinical as against school populations) whether our predictions would hold for an unselected group of children. Above all we did not know in how far our predictions relied on clinical judgment and in how far on the children's objective scores on tests. Finally it became clear that whatever it was we based our judgment on could not necessarily be handed on to someone else.

In order to shape an instrument for the use of schools which would enable them to identify at early ages what we call "academic high risk" children, we felt we would have 1) to use tools relatively untainted by subjective clinical judgment and 2) to use in addition to a clinical group, one which would be representative of a school population.

We used two groups of children: a sample of 53 youngsters from the general population and a sample of 53 prematurely born subjects. The investigation of the children from the general sample was designed to assist us in our practical goal: to shape a predictive instrument for the use of schools. The study of the prematurely born youngsters, who can be assumed to have started life with neurophysiological lags would, we hoped, teach us something about the relationship between neurophysiological immaturity and language disabilities.

Criteria for excluding certain children were: bilingual home, sensory deficit severe enough to interfere with learning, IQ beyond the range of one standard deviation above and below 100 and significant psychopathology, as judged clinically.

The heart of the investigation consisted of an attempt to determine which of our 37 perceptuo-motor and linguistic tests would prove to be potential predictors of reading, writing and spelling ability two and a half years later. A further goal was to combine the best potential predictors in a way which would yield an instrument of widespread applicability.

We fully realize that a multiplicity of social, environmental and psychological factors enters significantly into the acquisition of reading skills and we agree with Fabian that learning to read requires the developmental timing of both neurophysiological and psychological aspects of readiness. If nevertheless we limited ourselves to perceptuo-motor and linguistic facets of readiness, it was not only because we are impressed with their significance, but also because until recently they have been largely neglected.

Development proceeds from a state of relative globality and undifferentiation in the direction of increasing articulation and hierarchic organizations. Our tests, some of them a standardized variety, some adapted by us, some fashioned by ourselves, reflect our theoretical position derived from Piaget, Gesell and Werner who postulate evolving stages in sensori-motor and linguistic functioning. Since development is by and large a consistent and lawful process we assumed that a kindergarten child's perceptuo-motor and linguistic status would forecast his performance on such highly integrated tasks as are reading, writing and spelling. The tests covered several broad aspects of development: behavior and motility patterning, large and fine motor coordination, figure-ground discrimination, visuo-motor organization, auditory and visual perceptual competence, ability to comprehend and use language and, more specifically, reading-readiness. After the administration of the large test battery we wrote a short profile on each child in which we summarized our impression of his overall functioning, of his learning style, as well as of his specific weakness and strength.

Administered two and a half years later at the end of second grade were standardized reading, writing and spelling tests. We also visited each school to get the teacher's assessment of the youngsters and an impression of the teaching methods used in each classroom.

Computation of a coefficient of association between the 37 tests, on the one hand, and end of second grade performance scores on the other, provided a basis for ascertaining which kindergarten tests might be strongly enough associated with end of second grade reading, spelling and writing achievement to have predictive value. Those tests for which the coefficient of association with subsequent performance scores were statistically significant at the .05 level of confidence or less were considered potential predictors.

Using these criteria we found that 22 out of the 37 tests administered at kindergarten age had predictive possibilities. The following performances were found to be pertinent for later functioning:

To begin with, a marked degree of hyperactivity, distractibility and disinhibition appeared to be a poor prognostic sign, since at kindergarten age it denoted a lack of behavioral control which was bound to interfere with academic functioning.

It was of interest that pegboard speed which is a relatively sensitive test of finer motor control was significantly associated not only with writing, which could have been expected, but with spelling as well. This lends support to various statements by Orton who drew attention to psycho-motor lags in children with difficulties in the language area. Grapho-motor control—the way a child held the pencil at kindergarten age—showed a high correlation not only with writing, but also with the remaining achievement scores, probably because verbal symbolic behavior is involved both in the handling of the pencil and in reading and spelling.

A child's ability to draw a human figure showed a weak, but statistically significant association with reading and spelling 30 months later. It did not correlate with writing, which means that motor competence plays a relatively small role in the ability to project graphically the image of the human body. This image, according to Bender, is a Gestalt, determined by laws of growth and development; it reflects the degree to which a child has integrated information about his body, its parts and their relationships to each other. Appreciation of these relationships is basic to a child's orientation in space and enters into his awareness of right and left. It is this awareness, according to recent research, rather than the establishing of hand dominance, that discriminates between good and poor readers.

The Bender Visuo-Motor Gestalt Test, which better than most others measures spatial organization and integrative competence, ranked near the top of the predictive tests in that its correlation with end of second grade achievement was very high indeed. It is a particularly sensitive test at this age because certain of its features—such as crossing wavy lines and the drawing of a diamond—seem to mature at the very time the child enters first grade.

We administered a heavy battery of oral language tests—14 of them. The literature is filled with statements referring to the close relationship between organization in *time*—as reflected in oral language—and organization in *space*—as reflected in printed and written language. Lashley says the two are interchangeable and, in fact, in reading, space is used to express time; the printed word is a time chart of sounds. When we inquired into the extent to which certain temporal dimensions *predict* scholastic performance several years later, we found, for instance, that the ability to imitate tapped-out patterns—the ability, in other words, to retain and reproduce a non-verbal auditory Gestalt—was a surprisingly good predictor of later reading achievement. This was true also for auditory discrimination, not surprising when one considers the large number of poor spellers whose auditory discrimination is extremely diffuse. Among the *expressive* language tests, the number of words used by a child in the telling of a story was by far the best predictor; in telling the story of the Three Bears, the number of words used ranged from 54 to 594. Beyond factors related to environmental stimulation, the richness of a child's verbal output undoubtedly reflects his inherent linguistic endowment.

Organization of a story which requires ability to integrate details into a meaningful whole was another test that showed a statistically significant association with end of second grade reading achievement, as did the capacity to verbally group objects or events in terms of their common denominator.

As could be expected, a number of specific reading readiness tests were significantly associated with later achievement. A reversal test was one of them; the Gates Matching test was another. Name Writing and Letter Naming have long been known to be predictive, but they are, of course, largely dependent on previous training. Two tests designed by Mrs. Jansky which involved the practice teaching of words, were others.

In summary, 22 out of 37 tests administered at kindergarten age showed significant correlations of varying degrees with second grade reading, writing and spelling scores.

We furthermore examined IQ, as obtained on Form L of the Stanford Binet Test of Intelligence, 1937 Revision, administered at kindergarten age and, treating it as one among other possible predictors, found that it correlated to a statistically significant degree with second grade performance. However, IQ ranked only 12th as a predictor; in other words, 11 other tests in our battery were better predictors than was IQ. Moreover, the correlation between intelligence quotients as measured at kindergarten age and end of second grade *spelling* was non-significant, which confirmed our clinical impression that spelling disabilities are highly specific and are not determined by intelligence.

Ambiguous lateralization at the age between 5½ and 6½ years, on the other hand, was *not* significantly correlated with end of second grade performance. Two thirds of our youngsters had settled on a preferred hand in kindergarten; those who had did not read or spell better than those whose handedness had been undetermined. At this early age, and probably considerably later as shown by Birch and Deutsch for general populations, ill-defined laterality does not discriminate between good and poor readers. It probably is, in combination with other phenomena, nevertheless a pathognomic sign in youngsters over 11 years because it seems to reflect ambiguous cerebral dominance which, in turn, may point to a generalized lag in central nervous system maturation. I refer here to Subirana's findings which show that the EEGs of strongly right-handed children are more mature than those of ambidextrous or left-handed ones.

Not even in our group of Failing Readers who had not scored at all at end of second grade was the failure to establish a functional superiority of one hand over the other a distinguishing feature. If one were to summarize the characteristics of these eight failing children whose IQs were comparable to those of the remaining youngsters in the study and ranged from 94-116, one would say the following: as a group—for what it is worth—they were unusually small in size, they were largely boys, they were disorganized, hyperkinetic, impulsive and infantile. Their motoric ability was inferior, their Bender Gestalten primitive and spatially deviating, their human figure drawings were crude and undifferentiated and their language tools were very poor. They missed out on comprehension of parts of a simple story, in particular on time concepts. The stories they told were barren and did not hang together, they had severe difficulties with word-finding and they were nowhere on reading-readiness tests. It was, however, not failure on *single* performances which characterized this group. The superior readers group *also* showed one or another dysfunction at kindergarten age. It was the *accumulation* of deficits and their severity, the pervasive diffuseness and primitivity of their performance which in these failing children pointed to a profound and basic maturational deficit, a deficit occasionally so severe that it seemed rooted in the very biological matrix of the child.

Gesell maintains that maturation is by and large related to chronological age. If this is so, if chronological age does, in fact, reflect maturational level, then those kindergarten tests on which performance was most closely related to age, should have been the ones most sensitive to maturational differences. If then, as we believe, a child's maturational status at kindergarten age forecasts his subsequent achievement, those tests that are most sensitive to differences in maturation should have been the ones that best *predicted* reading and spelling at end of second grade. On the basis of this reasoning we classified all kindergarten tests according to the degree to which they discriminated between the oldest and the youngest kindergarten children. Tests on which the oldest kindergarten children did best and the youngest children did least well were considered to be "maturation sensitive." Those that did not differentiate the children in terms of age were assumed to be "non-maturational."

Of our 37 tests 25 could, according to these criteria, be considered "maturation-sensitive." The expectation that these particular tests would better predict later achievement than the non-maturation-sensitive ones was upheld by the findings. Of the maturation-sensitive tests 76% were significantly correlated with second grade scores, compared to only 17% of the non-maturation-sensitive tests.

For most children chronological age—to the degree that it reflects maturational status—is of course a fairly workable predictor of subsequent achievement, and schools' admission procedures are based on this fact.

However, the focus in our study was on those intelligent children in whom chronological age does *not* reflect maturational level, the children who suffer from maturational lags and who therefore present a high risk of academic failure. For these children chronological age is misleading as a predictor. There were 18 children in our study who were six and a half years or older at time of first grade entrance. On the basis of chronological age and IQ they should have done well. However, four of them failed in both reading and spelling at the end of the second grade. Our predictive tests, which assessed developmental level on the other hand, identified at kindergarten age, three out of these 4 children— the data on the fourth were incomplete. The findings thus support our contention that there is, indeed, a close link between a child's maturational status at kindergarten age and his reading and spelling achievement several years later.

Since the administration of 22 separate tests would be far too cumbersome a procedure to use in schools, we decided to construct a Predictive Index, consisting of those single predictors which, in combination, would most effectively identify "high risk" children. To begin, we established that the intercorrelations between reading and spelling at the end of second grade were very high, which enabled us to use the same index for both reading and spelling. Those of the original 22 kindergarten tests that exhibited relatively high and significant correlations with achievement at the end of second grade and that thus seemed promising were then put together for trial indices. Over one hundred of them were tried out and compared in order to determine which combination would best single out those children in our sample who subsequently failed. The index we finally chose—consisting of 10 tests—five of them in the visual-perceptual, three of them in the oral-language area, one concerned with visuo-motor organization and one with pencil grasp, was finally selected because it had provided an instrument which identified at kindergarten level 91%, that is to say 10 out of 11 students, who failed all reading and spelling tests 30 months later. A validation study involving 450 to 500 children is under way in New York City. Before it is completed, we are not justified in relying heavily on our findings. In the process of validation we may add two or three tests to the original ten to see whether we can better our results.

It is, of course, important to report also on those cases in which the Predictive Index did *not* work out. The Predictive Index did not pick out *one* boy whose performance at kindergarten level, though not outstanding, had at least been acceptable. The index moreover picked up as prospective failures four children who did, in fact, "make the grade." Two of them had been slow starters and had failed all tests at the end of the first grade. One of the two will probably fail as he gets into the higher grades; he had barely passed at the end of the second year. The vision of the second child had been poor and she had been fitted for glasses on the day before the kindergarten tests were administered. This clearly interfered with prediction. A third subject, a boy, had quite obviously made dramatic developmental spurts in the interim between kindergarten and end of second grade—his initial performance had been very immature, indeed. Such sudden spurts are probably the pitfalls in this type of undertaking. The fourth, another boy, had been quite disturbed at kindergarten age—he had vomited each day before going to school and when we saw him again at age eight he was pulling his hair to a degree which left him with a bald spot—nevertheless he did well.

It goes without saying that in the interval between kindergarten and end of second grade a number of important variables, the quality of teaching, illness, frequent change of schools, major upheavals in the home, all enter into academic achievement and are bound to influence prediction. Limitations in time and funds did not permit us to take these variables into account. It is, therefore, impressive that in spite of these limitations the Predictive Index reported here effectively identified at kindergarten age the overwhelming majority of children who failed later.

Our tests should, however, do more than simply pick out the youngsters destined to do poorly; they should reveal also in which particular area a given child is lagging, what kind of help he needs and what to do about it. Educational diagnosis is productive only if it can be translated into specific educational strategies. By comparing a given kindergarten child's performance in the auditory and in the visual-perceptual areas, it is possible to assess his strength and weakness and to determine which particular pathways facilitate learning. In our study the majority of youngsters did *not* show what we call "erratic" modality patterning. They did either well or poorly, both auditorily and visually; their integrative competence or lack of it cut through all modalities. On the other hand, 19% of our children showed bizarre modality patterning; striking discrepancies between visual-perceptual and auditory-perceptual tests. Seven children performed on a high level on audiological tasks and poorly on visual ones. Three others showed the opposite picture—excellent visual perceptual ability and failure in the entire auditory perceptual realm. The three children with superior *visual* competence did very well in reading in spite of their auditory lags; they even made the grade in spelling. Reading is after all primarily a visual perceptual task and, thus, the usual procedures offered at school were entirely adequate. The seven youngsters with *visual*-perceptual deficits clearly needed phonics and, in fact, the five youngsters who were exposed to heavy doses of it did well, while two, who were not, failed.

The child who does well in both auditory and visual perception will tend to benefit from any method; the one who does poorly in both will need heavy reinforcements and the activating of as many pathways as possible. The poor visualizer needs phonics. However, to the brain injured child for instance— and their numbers seem to be growing—phonic teaching often presents overwhelming difficulties. Such youngsters with their frequently severe integrational defects are often totally unable to analyze or synthesize and their failure to cope with phonics may lead to a catastrophic reaction—the disorganized response of the organism that is exposed to a task with which it is unable to cope. The point we want to make is this: teaching methods must be determined in terms of the individual child's inherent strength and weakness and both can be determined at kindergarten age.

Roughly 20 per cent of our children from lower middle class homes—and the number is undoubtedly far higher in those from deprived environments—showed a kind of performance at kindergarten age which clearly revealed that they would meet with total failure in second grade, an experience which may have seriously damaging effects on their self-image and may adversely affect their attitudes to learning in general.

We therefore suggest that the school system introduce "transition classes" between kindergarten and first grade for those children who according to the Predictive Index are found to be "immature."

The Index is, of course, only a formula and it would be unfortunate if it were to draw the teacher's attention away from the child's actual behavior and performance. Rather than being a substitute for observation, the Index should assist the teacher in translating her often excellent but impressionistic judgment of the youngster's readiness into a more specific assessment of his perceptuo-motor and linguistic status.

Saying that a child is not ready or is "immature" does not mean that one can afford to sit back and let maturation take its course. Schilder said that training plays a significant part even in those functions in which maturation of the CNS is of primary importance. The question is only what kind of training, and above all, training at what level. What is desirable is a "match" between a child's developmental readiness and the type of teaching offered him. It is this need for a "match" which must be met in what we call "transition," and the Swedes call "maturity," classes.

Immature children's developmental timing is atypical. At kindergarten age they are unable to benefit from pre-reading programs. Repeating the kindergarten year would give them an additional year in which to mature and would thus have certain advantages. However, it would not provide the intensive and specific training they need. Promotion into first grade would not solve their problems either, since the pace is usually too fast for the child who is ready to learn but is as yet unable to cope with organized reading and writing instruction at the conventional age.

The transition class, on the other hand, would start on the ground floor. It would aim at stabilizing the child's perceptuo-motor world and would take him, in slow motion, as it were, through a program in which each step is carefully planned. Teaching methods in such a class, unlike those in first grade which provide fairly uniform training for all children, would be tailored to the child's individual needs.

The transition class would be small and more structured than are kindergarten groups and would help the "scattered" child to function, first on a relatively simple and later on a more complex plane. The small class size would enable the teacher to give massive support to the anxious and dependent youngster who tends to be overwhelmed in a setting which does not provide individual guidance.

Needless to say, the teacher in such a transition class would have special qualifications, since immature children require a greater than usual degree of tolerance and empathy.

A variety of problems could be dealt with in this kind of setting. Seating a hyperactive youngster close to the teacher would protect him from a barrage of environmental stimuli, for instance. Large motor outlets would be provided for those children who are not as yet able to sit still for extended periods of time, and activities like throwing, ball bouncing and hopping would at the same time foster large motor patterning.

Such a class would take care of children who have trouble with orientation, those who seem to be walking around in a fog, who do not really know what is happening in the classroom, who have little awareness when important events take place or where they occur. This kind of youngster usually looks lost and

163

bewildered and his energy seems to be taken up by attempts to find his bearings. Teaching this type of child the layout of the classroom, the direction in which his home lies, the position of his desk, is often helpful in a general way. Basically however, orientation in space starts with the development of a cohesive body image; his awareness of his own body, its parts and their relationship to each other is essential for right-left discrimination and directionality.

To become oriented in time the child would participate in the planning of his daily schedule; he would be taught the changes in the seasons and the times of school opening and closing. Such temporal relationships are often surprisingly difficult for the immature child to grasp and he may need very concrete clues to remember for instance the sequence of the days of the week. Any sequence represents an organization in time and to perceive, to process, to store and to recall the serial order of information is a requisite for later reading activities. Rhythmic exercises, swinging to music, tapping out patterns all help young children with organization in time.

Difficulties with verbal communication are a central problem for children with maturational lags. Many of them neither listen nor talk; they are dependent on movement as a means to come to terms with the world around them and fail to attend to the spoken word. Their short auditory memory spans, their diffuse auditory discrimination, moreover, interferes with interpretation of what they hear. Auditory discrimination practice, therefore, is an essential part of the training in the curriculum of a transition class, and will pay off later on when it comes to spelling. The verbal output of children with maturational lags mirrors their diffuse reception. Their defective articulation, their primitive sentence construction, their immature syntax, their awkward formulations all constitute a severe handicap often long beyond the elementary grades. The teacher in a transition class will first and foremost help the child to use words as the preferred form of communication. Learning to express feelings and experiences verbally precedes instruction in articulatory patterning or syntactical forms.

That children with reading difficulties have trouble with visual perception is common knowledge. The question is only at what level? Visual perception is not a unitary process. There is, on the simplest plane, the differentiation between the familiar and the unfamiliar; to distinguish an object from its mirror image is more difficult. At the heart of most reading readiness programs is practice in identification of and discrimination between "critical features" of letters and configurations. However, the immature child has to start with a more basic perceptual experience: with figure ground discrimination. Research in Russia has shown that in subjects between four and seven visual analysis is fostered by a combination of manipulation and visual exploration. The handling of plastic and plywood letters would assist the child to make the subtle discriminations required for the recognition of individual letter shapes. Tracing, stenciling and copying letters serves to integrate the visual with the graphic Gestalt of the word.

The learning of sound equivalents and their blending into new units is a necessary but a demanding task. Some of the children do not even understand that a letter seen represents a sound heard. Here again, it is essential to determine how far down in the developmental scale teaching has to go to be effective.

The transition class would, finally, provide an opportunity to translate into educational practice the insights gained from a careful study of the child's weakness and strength in the various modalities. Instruction would be geared differentially to children with auditory-perceptual deficits and to those with gaps in visual perception. During certain times of the day children with receptive and expressive language deficits would receive specific linguistic and phonic training. Others would get assistance with visual discrimination and configurational techniques. A third group would work on directional and grapho-motor patterning. In short, this class would be geared to fill in specific gaps in some areas and to utilize assets in others.

Marie van Hoosan has called the interval between kindergarten and first grade the "twilight zone" of learning. It is the twilight period which would be served by the transition class.

A few children in such a class would be integrated into the regular first grade after a few weeks or months of such intensive training. Most others would be ready to cope with first grade the next year. A small number of children suffering from severe and persisting lags might require continuing help for at least two or three years.

At present most public schools do not provide remedial help until the end of the third grade. This is unfortunate, because the development of perceptual and language functions probably follows a sequence analogous to that in organic morphological development. There are according to McGraw specific "critical" times in the child's life when he is especially susceptible to certain kinds of stimulation. The basic perceptuo-motor functions that underlie reading may be harder to train at the end of third grade than they are earlier. By the end of third grade, moreover, emotional problems and phobic responses may have so complicated the original problems that they may no longer be reversible.

The earliest possible identification of "high risk" children was the goal of our study. Identification is, however, only a first step towards reversing a situation that now results in an unjustifiable waste of educational opportunities. A second step is equally essential: "high risk" children must be provided with teaching techniques that will enable them to realize their potential and to become productive members of the community.

References

Birch, H. and Belmont, Lillian. Lateral dominance, lateral awareness, and reading disability. CHILD DEVELOPMENT, 1965, 36, 57-71.

Coleman, R. and Deutsch, Cynthia. Lateral dominance and right-left discrimination: A comparison of normal and retarded readers. PERCEPTUAL & MOTOR SKILLS, 1964, 19, 43-50.

Deutsch, M. The role of social class in language development and cognition. AMERICAN JOURNAL OF ORTHOPSYCHIATRY, 1965, 35, 78-88.

Fabian, A. Clinical and experimental studies of school children who are retarded in reading. QUARTERLY JOURNAL OF CHILD BEHAVIOR, 1951, 3, 15-37.

Gesell, A. THE FIRST FIVE YEARS OF LIFE. New York: Harper & Bros., 1940.

Gesell, A. THE EMBRYOLOGY OF BEHAVIOR—THE BEGINNING OF THE HUMAN MIND. New York: Harper & Bros., 1945.

McGraw, Mildred B. THE NEUROMUSCULAR MATURATION OF THE HUMAN INFANT. New York: Columbia University Press, 1943.

Monroe, Marion. Reading aptitude tests for the prediction of success and failure in beginning reading. EDUCATION, 1935, 56, 7-14.

Piaget, J. THE ORIGINS OF INTELLIGENCE IN CHILDREN. New York: International University Press, 1952.

Schilder, P. CONTRIBUTIONS TO DEVELOPMENTAL NEUROPSYCHIATRY. New York: International University Press, 1964.

Terman, Lewis M. and Merrill, Maud A. MEASURING INTELLIGENCE. New York: Houghton Mifflin, 1937.

Van Hoosan, Marie. Just enough English. READING TEACHER, 1965, 18, 507.

Werner, H. The concept of development from a comparative and organismic point of view. In D. B. Harris (Ed.), THE CONCEPT OF DEVELOPMENT. Minneapolis: University of Minnesota Press, 1957.

STUDY QUESTIONS

1. Analyze carefully de Hirsch's position on teaching to a child's weakness or to his strengths.

2. What would be the purpose of a "transition class?" What advantages and disadvantages do you see if such classes were widely instigated?

3. What objections are raised to delaying remedial instruction until 3rd grade?

4. How would de Hirsch defend the "maturational lag" theory against objections raised by Westman, Arthur, and Scheidler (and in later chapters implied by Engelmann and by Haring and Hauck)?

5. Can you think of any possible objections to the earliest possible identification of "high risk" children?

9: RESEARCH IN VISUAL TRAINING
AND READING DISABILITY

Stanley Krippner

Krippner reviews thoroughly some of the research on the relationship between visual training and reading performance. Readers who have puzzled over the differences which exist between the positions of optometry and ophthalmology will especially appreciate the candid light shed by Krippner on this area.

B. D. B.

Reading disability is generally defined in terms of a level of reading skill which is significantly below expectancy for a child in terms of his mental ability (1). Surveys indicate that in typical elementary schools one out of three children reads one or more years below grade level. Harris (2) states that "the majority are dull children whose reading is on a par with their other abilities. A substantial minority, comprising about 10 to 15 per cent of all the children, are cases of mild or severe reading disability."

It is generally agreed that there is no one cause of reading disability. The 10 to 15 per cent of children who are reading below their potential capacity may be suffering from one or several handicaps, but there is little agreement as to what the major handicap may be.

A simplistic approach to reading disability is proposed by Walcutt (3) who claims that a lack of training in phonics is the major cause of poor reading. Several writers take issue with Walcutt's notion but concede that educational factors outweigh any other etiological consideration. Bond and Tinker (4) demonstrate this point of view, stating that "the vast majority of our disability cases are brought about through faulty learning or lack of educational adjustment of one sort or another." Specifically, Bond and Tinker cite ineffective school administrative policies, lack of readiness programs, poor teaching methods, inadequate teacher preparation, and failure to consider individual differences, concluding that "reading disability is largely due to educational factors" (5).

A radically different approach is taken by Brandon (6) who feels that reading disability is "a psychological problem" and by Blackhurst (7) who maintains that "most poor readers . . . have psychological problems." For Delacato (8) a lack of cerebral dominance accounts for the bulk of severely disabled readers; Rosborough (9) cites faulty skeletal and autonomic nervous system development. Smith and Carragan (10) postulate the theory that much reading disability is due to an inadequate balance between acetylcholine and cholinesterase

Invited address, 21st Annual School Vision Forum and Reading Conference, Cleveland, Ohio, 1968.

at the nerve cell synapses. Other writers have given prominence to auditory processes, to hereditary factors, and to sociological forces.

In an attempt to examine etiological factors in reading disability, Krippner (11) made an intensive study of 146 poor readers with WISC IQs between 87 and 112 referred to a reading clinic. Using the Bond-Tinker formula (12), the Wechsler Intelligence Scale for Children, and the Durrell Analysis (13), it was discovered that the mean level of reading disability for the group was 1.99 years.

Following a series of diagnostic tests, a number of clinicians determined the major and the contributing etiological factors for each child. Table 1 presents the etiological factors for the 146 disabled readers studied; major and contributory factors are combined for the purposes of the table.

It can be seen that poor visual-perceptual skills were the most common etiological factor in cases of reading disability, in the opinion of the clinicians making judgments. The criteria for classification in this category included a score on the visual memory section of the Durrell Analysis a year or more below the pupil's expected reading grade (as computed by the Bond-Tinker formula) and/ or a rating of "unsatisfactory" on the Perceptual Forms Test (14). Three out of every five pupils fell into the category of poor visual-perceptual skills when these criteria were used.

A number of criticisms could be made of this study. The data represent pupils referred to a reading clinic rather than a random sampling of poor readers in the classroom. The usefulness of the Bond-Tinker formula for estimating reading disability has been called into question by McLeod (15). Furthermore, the two criteria tests do not cover the entire range of visual-perceptual skills. Nevertheless, these data resemble those of Coleman (16) who studied 87 disabled readers in grades one through six, using tests of visual acuity, ocular motility, hand-eye-foot dominance, refractive errors, ophthalmological pathology, form perception, handwriting ability, number construction, visual memory, spatial orientation, laterality, body image, hand-eye coordination, and the visual skills which produce satisfactory performance on the Keystone Telebinocular.

TABLE 1. ETIOLOGICAL FACTORS IN THE READING DISABILITIES OF 146 PUPILS OF AVERAGE INTELLIGENCE REFERRED TO A READING CLINIC

Impaired Acuity of Sight	28.1%
Impaired Acuity of Hearing	8.9
Poor Visual-Perceptual Skills	62.3
Poor Auditory-Perceptual Skills	35.6
Defective Speech	18.5
Brain Injury	20.5
Disturbed Neurological Organization	20.5
Directional Confusion (Left and Right)	26.0
Endocrinal Malfunctioning	11.6
Social Immaturity	17.1
Neurotic Tendencies	34.2
Psychotic Tendencies	2.1
Sociopathic Tendencies	5.5
Unfavorable Educational Experiences	56.8
Cultural Deprivation	6.2

Coleman discovered that 49.5 per cent of the pupils tested "had visual, visual-perceptual or refractive errors severe enough to handicap them in their approach to education."

In the Coleman study, 70.1 per cent of the disabled readers were boys. In the Krippner study, 89.0 per cent of the disabled readers were boys. Of Coleman's pupils, 20 per cent manifested impaired sight acuity and refractive errors—a proportion which is similar to the 28.1 per cent noted in the Krippner study.

Krippner emphasized the multi-causality nature of reading disabilities and the overlapping which occurs in arbitrarily drawn etiological categories. However, the importance of properly functioning vision was demonstrated by his study as well as by the more intensive investigation by Coleman.

SIGHT AND VISION

In both the Krippner and the Coleman studies, a differentiation was made between sight and vision—the former referring to sensory acuity and freedom from refractive errors, the latter referring to perceptual skills involving central nervous system functioning. This differentiation assumes importance when one considers the divergent points of view held by the two professions most intimately connected with the eyes, ophthalmology and optometry.

An ophthalmologist (or oculist) is a physician who specializes in the care of the eye and its related structures. He has completed a full course of general medical studies, received an M.D. degree, and served an internship in general medicine and surgery. He has then taken additional specialized training in ophthalmology—the branch of medical science dealing with the structure, functions, and diseases of the eye. He is the only person legally qualified to diagnose and treat all eye disorders. He may prescribe eyeglasses and contact lenses.

An optometrist also specializes in the care of the eyes and its structures. Following a general undergraduate course of study in college, he enters optometric school and eventually receives an O.D. degree. He is licensed to prescribe refractive lenses (e.g., eyeglasses, contact lenses) and to treat the functional aspects of vision. Not being a physician, he cannot treat eye diseases or prescribe medicinal agents for the eyes (17).

Many optometrists take advanced study in "developmental vision" through the Optometric Extension Program and become proficient in visual training. The concept of developmental vision was originally put forward by A. M. Skeffington who maintained that proper vision for complex skills such as reading is a learned activity which involves the central nervous system (i.e., the brain and spinal cord) as well as the eyes themselves. (18) Skeffington maintained that there were certain visual disorders that could not be ameliorated by glasses but which would respond to specific types of training. The Optometric Extension Program was organized to promulgate this point of view and to train optometrists who were interested in working with children having developmental vision problems.

A few ophthalmologists are favorably disposed toward Skeffington's concept of developmental vision and many optometrists reject it. However, the most severe criticism of Skeffington's point of view has come from prominent ophthalmologists rather than from optometrists. For example, Goldberg (19) holds that "eye exercises are not the answer" to reading disability. He further states that visual training "may increase motivation and help to provide a sympathetic atmosphere," but it has no value beyond this psychological benefit.

Gordon (20) calls visual training "worthless," adding that "optometrists are seizing on this field of therapy as a means of widening their participation and enhancing their reputation with the lay public as surveyors of 'eye care.' "

Blackhurst (21) accuses optometrists of misunderstanding the problem of reading disability, adding that an optometrist who prescribes visual training "is trying to pad his office practice." A similar position is taken by Hardesty (22), Haffley (23) and Goldberg. (24) Apt (25) notes that orthoptics—a procedure for correcting strabismus by the use of eye exercises—sometimes assists a child in overcoming his reading difficulty, but mainly because of the personal interest someone takes in the child. Apt, unlike most of his fellow ophthalmologists, does concede that "the cerebral aspect of seeing" can be improved by eye exercises.

Hardesty (26) holds that there is no research study that establishes a relationship between eye function and reading disability, or between visual training and reading improvement. Therefore, it is necessary to review the research literature and examine the pertinent data.

THE OLSON-MITCHELL-WESTBERG STUDY

Contemporary practitioners of visual training utilize techniques advocated by the Optometric Extension Program which was founded by A. M. Skeffington and E. B. Alexander in 1928. These methods have been further refined and developed at the Gesell Institute of Child Development in New Haven, Connecticut.[1] A number of early research studies were carried out by Apperson (31), Peters (32), Lyons and Lyons (33), and Worcester (34). Most of the results were favorable but the studies were criticized because they lacked control groups. In addition, it was pointed out that personal attention and motivation may have accounted for much of the improvement in reading ability.

Olson, Mitchell, and Westberg (35) attempted to determine the effect of visual training upon the reading ability of college students. They also investigated its effect upon mental ability and personality test patterns. Visual training was defined as:

> . . . a technique for improving visual skills. The basic assumption in such training is that the seeing process is a learned skill and therefore is amenable to improvement through proper development of the functions involved, reorganization of the visual skills pattern, and, in certain cases, subjecting the individual to visual phenomena never before experienced . . . . The consensus seems to be that visual training should be considered as a process for improving the innervation at synaptic and

---

[1]Gesell (27) believed that vision "is not a separate, independent function. It is profoundly integrated with the total action system of the child—his posture, his manual skills, his motor demeanors, his intelligence, and even his personality traits. When viewed in terms of the action system, the mechanisms of vision become a key to the understanding of reading behavior, both normal and deviate. Developmental optics in theory and in practice, is concerned with the growth and organization of visual functions in their dynamic relation to the total action system." Gesell utilized optometrists to administer tests of visual skills to children seen at his clinic. He was severely criticized for this practice by several members of the medical profession. However, optometric examinations are still a standard part of the test battery at the Gesell Institute. Furthermore, disabled readers do more poorly on these tests than do satisfactory readers (28, 29); and a 1967 study by Snyder and Freud (30) demonstrated significantly poorer performance on visual-perceptual tests (e.g., the Spiral Aftereffect) on the part of low-scorers on reading readiness tests than high-scorers.

neuromuscular junctions and for providing a new fund of information by which one may better interpret his visual impressions.

The subjects for this study were principally college sophomores; nearly all of the 49 students had a *C* average. All were essentially normal in terms of sight; optometric examination disclosed no significant uncorrected refractive errors or any indication of pathology. Pretest and posttests were administered of the Otis Test of Mental Ability, the Iowa Silent Reading Test, the Bernreuter Personality Inventory, and the 21-point Optometric Extension Program scale. Four subject groups were created, having been equated in terms of the Otis, Iowa, and O.E.P. scores:

1. Visual training (15 students)
2. Visual training plus counseling (14 students)
3. Counseling (13 students)
4. Neither visual training nor counseling (7 students)

Subjects reported for training on alternate days, 3 days per week over an 8 week period. The training periods were 45 minutes in length. The instruments utilized included the Arneson Korector, the Keystone Ophthalmic Telebinocular, the Keystone Ortho-trainer, the Keystone Correct-Eye Scope, the Keystone Overhead Projector, the Keystone Tele-Rater Control Unit for the Ophthalmic Telebinocular, and (for the last six sessions only) the Science Research Associates Reading Accelerator.

An analysis of covariance design was used to evaluate the posttest results. No statistically significant changes were noted for any of the groups on the Bernreuter Personality Inventory. There were no statistically significant changes for any group on the Otis Test of Mental Ability.

When the students' scores on the Iowa Silent Reading Test were examined, no significant changes in reading comprehension were noted although the mean scores were considerably higher for those groups which had received visual training. The two groups which had received visual training made a statistically significant improvement in reading rate. The group which received visual training plus counseling made a mean gain of 13.28 points in reading speed while the group receiving visual training only made a mean gain of 16.74 points. Four months after the program terminated, 14 students who had received visual training were again tested on the Iowa; there were no significant declines in their reading rate scores.

This study is an important one because of its utilization of four subject groups. In addition, it included a counseling program for two of the groups to investigate whether personal attention and motivation alone could be responsible for changes in reading test scores. The data indicated that attention and motivation did not lead to an automatic increase in reading improvement.

Although reading comprehension scores improved somewhat under visual training, the improvement was not statistically significant. This indicates that, in a college population, reading rate may be the skill most amenable to change through visual training procedures.

THE KHAN STUDY

Out of 18 children admitted at Emma Pendleton Bradley Hospital, a residential treatment center, 15 were selected as subjects for a study by Khan (36). (Of the other three, two were psychotic and one was only five years of age.) The ages of those selected ranged between 7 and 11. All of the children had severe behavior problems of many years duration. All were within the average range of intelligence.

The subjects for the study were tested by an optometrist on the following psychophysical measures: visual acuity, binocular functions (accommodation/ convergence and fusion at far and near points, macular discrimination, stereoscopic discrimination), ocular motility, form perception, digit span, and dominance. Eight subjects were identified who had visual-motor difficulty, e.g., severe difficulty in one or more of the measures of binocular functions, ocular motility, form perception, or digit span.

For the eight subjects identified as having visual-motor difficulty, visual training was inaugurated by an optometrist. The training was given 1 hour per day, 5 days per week, for 10 weeks. The outline of the training program follows:

1. Beginning exercises with gross motor coordination followed by body space relationship relating to kinesthetic sense, followed by eye coordination exercises and oculomotor routine with time factors.

2. Exercises for form perception through hand-eye coordination and exercises for laterality. Techniques were used in which the child corrected his own errors.

3. Exercises directed toward the solution of geometric form puzzles.

4. Discussion of perceptual problems with the child and coordinating this discussion with visual imagery exercises.

5. Exercises for increasing limits of the eye span; developing efficient eye movements related to reading concepts through the use of slide projections of digits and forms.

Reading tests were administered at the beginning of the academic year and at the end of the academic year. Visual training began immediately after the initial reading tests were given.

Five children, who were extremely poor readers, were given the Durrell Analysis of Reading Difficulty. All five children were 2 to 3 years behind expectancy in reading achievement, reading at the first or beginning second grade level. When the Durrell was again administered (at the end of the school year), these five subjects showed none or less than half a grade improvement in their reading.

Three children, who were on third or fourth grade levels of reading achievement, were administered the Stanford Achievement Test. All three of these subjects were from 1 to 1½ years behind expectancy in reading achievement. When the Stanford test (word meaning and paragraph meaning sections) was again administered, the three children showed more than one grade level improvement, virtually improving their reading to its expected level.

The improvement in the emotional status of these eight children over the school year was rated "mild to moderate."

Khan stressed the need for more research with larger samples that would enable statistical tests to be made. Few conclusions can be drawn on the basis of his preliminary study because the number of subjects was so small and because two different reading tests were utilized. However, visual training appeared to be more useful for the moderately disabled readers than for the severely disabled readers, at least among the severely disturbed subjects of this study.

GETMAN AND KEPHART

The lack of basic research in the area of visual training is puzzling when one considers the emphasis placed on visual-perceptual skills by Getman (37), Kephart (38), and their followers.

Gesell (39) was frequently criticized for his assertion that "minimal cerebral injuries are more common than is ordinarily supposed, and they sometimes account for certain persisting visual defects and even for personality deviations." Recent investigations, however, have confirmed Gesell's statement; Myklebust and Boshes (40), utilizing both medical and psychological measures, discovered that 5 per cent of a large sample of Chicago public school children suffered from some type of psychoneurological learning disorder.

Getman, an optometrist, has long been associated with the Optometric Extension Program. His program stresses the attainment of proficiency in six basic developmental processes:
1. General movement, e.g., crawling and creeping.
2. Special movement, e.g., manipulative skills.
3. Eye movement, e.g., visual tracking of an object.
4. Communication, e.g., speech and gestures.
5. Visual-perceptual organization, e.g., reading.

Getman's procedures were employed in a 15-week study of four first grade classes studied by McKee (41) and his associates. The experimental group's gains in reading comprehension were significantly greater than those of the control group at the end of the program.

Kephart, a psychologist, has worked closely with a number of optometrists and utilizes visual training procedures with disabled readers. Kephart attempts to orient the child more fully to his environment in order that he will make successful perceptual-motor matches, the absence of which retards learning. According to Kephart, reading disabilities often result from learning disorders because of two factors:

1. There is an incomplete integration of present and past stimuli.
2. There is an incomplete feedback from the muscle system to the brain to compensate for errors in perception.

Kephart's procedures were utilized in an experimental study reported by Halgren (42). The increase in reading scores for the experimental group was almost twice as great as that for a control group receiving orthodox remedial reading instruction and an upward shift of seven IQ points was noted for the experimental group. A study undertaken by Rutherford (43) also used Kephart's procedures; again the experimental group did significantly better on learning tasks than the control group.

Not all attempts to improve reading ability by means of visual-perceptual exercises meet with success. Cohen (44) gave 10 weeks of training, utilizing the Frostig program (45), to an experimental group and gave no special training to a control group of first grade pupils. The experimental group made a significantly greater gain in visual-perceptual skills at the end of the 10 weeks. However, it did not make significantly greater gains on the reading achievemer tests. Cohen concluded that the significant gains in visual perception of the experimental group were not reflected in gains in reading.[2]

The opinion of most medical specialists toward visual training is concisely stated by Money (47), a pediatrician who has done some significant work wit disabled readers. Specifically referring to Getman's approach, Money describe

[2]Frostig's own research reports (46) support the effectiveness of her material.

visual training as "a faddist therapy that is currently enjoying considerable vogue, generally under optometric auspices." He continues:

> This therapy is derived from a doctrine of the interrelatedness of motor, auditory, linguistic and visual maturation—with particular emphasis on visuomotor or visuopostural relatedness. The fallacy of this faddism is that it takes hypotheses which, quite conceivably, are valid principles of development and applies them, prematurely and untested, as principles of training and treatment, with unjustified reliance on disproved assumptions concerning that old psychological war horse, the transfer of training. What is needed in the place of prematurely applied visual theories is more basic investigation of vision and seeing as developmental processes prerequisite to reading.

This point of view about developmental vision pervades most of the medical profession. It is not uncommon for parents to enroll a child in a program of visual training only to have the family ophthalmologist threaten to discontinue his service to the child unless the visual training is discontinued. Physicians will often counsel parents against visual training for a disabled reader, presenting the alternatives of hiring a remedial tutor, seeing a psychiatrist, or simply having patience in the hopes that their child will outgrow his reading problem. Garvin (48) attests that many disabled readers improve simply because "time has passed" while Rabinovitch (49) admits a preference for telling parents "to do nothing" to prescribing a series of "regressive" exercises for the child.

THE KERSHNER STUDY

Although most optometrists are extremely skeptical about the procedures employed by Delacato with disabled readers, Money (50) criticizes Delacato with the same terminology he uses for Getman. Referring to Delacato's approach as one of the "current faddist therapies," he asserts that "it is far too premature to be applying hypotheses of cerebral dominance to methods of treatment."

Delacato's approach (51) is controversial because of claims to alter neurological organization through physical activity. The evidence mustered by Delacato (52) in support of his approach has been criticized by Glass and Robbins (53) who maintain that the 12 studies completed to date were "poorly designed and executed." Following the Glass-Robbins critique, an investigation was reported by Kershner (54) which overcomes several of the methodological shortcomings of the previous studies.

The purpose of Kershner's investigation was to determine the effects of a structured program of physical activities, including certain eye exercises, upon the physical and intellectual development of trainable mentally retarded children. Subjects consisted of 30 pupils from special education classes in Lehigh County, Pennsylvania. There were 14 subjects in the experimental group and 16 subjects in the control group. The programs extended for 74 consecutive teaching days and were administered by the teacher and teacher aides of the respective schools. A pretest, posttest design was employed.

For the experimental group, the activities were structured according to neurological stages of development. Each child was taught to master his lowest functional level within each stage before going on to the next higher level. The entire school curriculum involved activities consistent with Delacato's theory of neurological organization. A typical daily schedule follows:

9:00 to 9:15. . .Near point dominance eye exercises.
9:15 to 9:30. . .Far point dominance eye exercises; auditory discrimination.
9:30 to 9:40. . .Break.
9:40 to 10:40. . .Homolateral coordination; cross pattern coordination; cross pattern crawling, cross pattern creeping; tactual stimulation; bilateral reinforcement; kicking with dominant foot; throwing with dominant hand
10:40 to 11:10. . .Break.
11:10 to 11:50. . .Tactual stimulation and discrimination; auditory stimulatio and discrimination; olfactory stimulation and discrimination; gustatory stimulation and discrimination.
11:50 to 12:00. . .Break.
12:00 to 12:45. . .Lunch.
12:45 to 1:30. . . .Unilateral sleep pattern reinforcement.
1:30 to 2:30. . . . .Bilateral and unilateral group activities; cross pattern walki

For the control group, the activities also involved the entire school day. The children were given attention which equaled that of the experimental group; for example, while the experimental group was visually occluded on the non-dominant side, the control group wore an eye occluder on the back of their heads. (This was done to compensate for any possible effect that mere ownership of an eyepatch may have had on the children in the experimental group.) Nonspecific activities were introduced to achieve better rhythm, balance, and coordination. A typical daily schedule follows:

9:00 to 9:15. . . .Table play (e.g., building block towers).

9:15 to 9:30. . . ."Show and Tell" activities.

9:30 to 9:40. . . .Break.

9:40 to 10:40. . .Jumping jacks; jumping rope; marching; swinging arms; follow the leader to music; carrying rhythm sticks; stopping when the music stops; rolling balls; catching balls; playing dodge ball; hopping; jumping; galloping; skipping; duck walk; elephant walk; "flying" like a moth to recorded music.

10:40 to 11:10. .Break.

11:10 to 11:20. .Writing numbers and the alphabet to music.

11:20 to 11:30. .Break.

11:30 to 12:30. .Lunch.

12:30 to 1:30. . .Rest period; listening to music.

1:30 to 2:30. . . .Movies; group singing; dancing games; musical chairs; rhythm band.

The Revised Oseretsky Test of Motor Development was used to investigate changes in motor proficiency. Pretest and posttest data indicated that both the experimental and control groups had made statistically significant improvements. However, it could not be determined how much of the gain was due to physical maturation and how much was due to the physical activities.

The Peabody Picture Vocabulary Test was utilized to measure changes in intelligence. The data indicated that the experimental group had made significant gains but that the control group had not. The 12 point mean IQ gain of the experimental group was dramatic but Kershner noted that the two groups represented two populations rather than representing a randomization of one school population. Therefore, initial group differences may have contributed to the effect.

A 47-point crawling and creeping scale was devised to measure changes in perceptual-motor performance. The data indicated that the experimental group had made significant improvement, as measured by this scale, while the control group had not. Kershner pointed out that the results supported Delacato's theory, noting that the experimental group jumped from a mean score of 51.64 to one of 84.74 on the crawling and creeping scale. The control group improved only slightly, from 43.53 to 44.94. Once again, however, the fact remains that the two classes represented two somewhat different school populations.[3]

Kershner called for more rigorous investigations, but concluded, "Within the stated limitations, these findings suggest that the procedures may prove beneficial in application with retarded children in public schools."

THREE SUGGESTIONS

If professionals cannot agree upon the role of visual training in reading disability, one can sympathize with the confusion and conflict experienced by many parents. Not only will an optometrist and an ophthalmologist often give two entirely different prescriptions to the same child for glasses, but the two professionals will often disagree violently on the advisability of visual training to ameliorate a case of reading disability. The classroom teacher or reading clinician is often caught in the middle of the disagreement, besieged by equally imposing opinions from the opposite sides. Three suggestions are in order for those professionals who are involved in the treatment of reading disability and/or the care of the eyes.

[3]An earlier study reported by Robbins (55) failed to support the Delacato theory. Robbins used second grade pupils in Chicago parochial schools. The experimental group underwent a 3 month program emphasizing cross pattern creeping and walking, avoidance of music, and use of the specific writing positions advocated by Delacato. However, the Robbins program did not stress the visual training activities found in the Kershner program. There are many other reasons which may account for the differential results of these two experiments but the visual factor may be one of the most important.

In the first place, a great deal of semantic obscurity characterizes the entire area of visual training. Flax (56) points out that this situation has obscured the significance of visual training and has "delayed its more widespread application and acceptance by psychologists and educators." Flax continues:

> This confusion is compounded because clinicians in the eye care field utilize differing conceptual frameworks. Some tend to emphasize optical and anatomical consideration while others are more concerned with functional aspects of vision. Even the concept of visual function has differing interpretations. Some consider peripheral function while others consider inter-sensory integration to be part of the visual process.

One critical semantic problem involves whether both the peripheral nervous system (PNS) and the central nervous system (CNS) should be considered when speaking of vision or whether one should think basically in terms of PNS end organ reception. Flax (57) makes a useful distinction between PNS and CNS disorders which would at least clarify the issue even if all professionals did not agree on the definitions. To Flax, PNS disorders refer to deficiencies of the end-organ system of vision (i.e., the eye); they include visual acuity, refractive error, fusion, convergence, and accommodation, all of which involve the eye mechanism and which are responsible for producing clear, single, binocular vision. CNS disorders involve deficiencies in organizing and interpreting images received by the eyes and sent to the brain. In CNS disorders, a clear, single visual image may be present but the child still cannot decode the printed word because of problems in organization and interpretation of what is seen.

The general public has a vague understanding of PNS disorders such as myopia (near-sightedness), hyperopia (far-sightedness), astigmatism, etc. However, the parent who is told that his child may have a visual-perceptual problem is likely to respond, "Well, can't it be corrected with glasses?" At this point, the professional worker must educate the parent as to the nature of CNS disorders, pointing out that it is not the eye that reads the printed page but the brain.

A second need in the field of visual training is for communication among professional workers. Ophthalmologists and optometrists usually go their separate ways, each condemning the other and refusing to admit that the rival profession has anything unique to offer in working with reading disability cases. Most meetings on vision and school achievement sponsored by optometrists are conspicuous for the absence of ophthalmologists, or of anyone else with an M.D. degree. On the other hand, it is a rare occasion when an individual with an O.D. degree is invited to speak at an ophthalmological conference.

In 1961, the Johns Hopkins Conference on Research Needs and Prospects in Dyslexia and Related Aphasic Disorders was held. Among the 13 participants, only one had a background in optometry. His paper was notable for its lack of any mention of optometric testing or visual training. (58) In 1968, the Fifth Annual International Conference for Children with Learning Disabilities featured a panel discussion on vision and reading. (59) It was concluded that disabled readers do not have significantly more visual problems than other youngsters. The three panelists were all ophthalmologists; a more productive session—and a livelier one—would have been guaranteed had a member of the Optometric Extension Program been invited as a discussant.[4]

A third difficulty is the paucity of basic research on the validity of visual training. Even those studies which have been reported do not answer such questions as:

1. How many times per week should appointments be scheduled for optimum results?
2. Which aspects of visual training are most therapeutic in overcoming reading disabilities?
3. Are expensive machines and elaborate equipment needed in a visual training program?
4. What is the efficacy of supplementary exercises done at home?
5. For what types of reading disability is visual training best suited and for which, if any, is it worthless?

---

[4]The American Medical Association recently lifted its ban which prevented ophthalmologists from working with optometrists. This action may lead to greater interdisciplinary effort.

A professional program which charges parents fairly substantial amounts of money for its services must eventually owe its clients answers to these questions—answers which can be supported by specific facts and figures.

In conclusion, it appears as if the cold war between the supporters and the detractors of visual training will continue for some time. However, the protagonists—at the very least—ought to define their terms, communicate with each other, and engage in research projects. The data resulting from these research projects may not end the cold war, but they might at least raise the battle from the level of dogmatic assertion to that of intelligent discussion.

APPENDIX

The conflict between ophthalmologists and optometrists has been brought into sharp focus by two recent studies, one by Lancaster (60) and his associates, the other by Blum, Peters, and Bettman. (61) Both studies attempted to determine what type of visual acuity disorder, identified by public school screening tests on the Snellen Chart, should be followed by complete visual examinations.

Lancaster obtained replies from 149 ophthalmologists. Blum, Peters, and Bettman received replies from 279 optometrists and 261 ophthalmologists. Of the optometrists in these two studies, 22 per cent would agree that a child with 20/25 visual acuity on the Snellen Chart should be referred for a more extensive examination; however, only 6 per cent of the ophthalmologists would agree. A child with 20/30 visual acuity would be recommended by 75 per cent of the optometrists and 50 per cent of the ophthalmologists. A child with 20/40 visual acuity would be referred by 98 per cent of the optometrists and 95 per cent of the ophthalmologists.

Another aspect of the conflict over visual training involves the work of Woolf (62) in the Optometric Extension Program. Woolf uses the term "dysdiopia" to refer to a syndrome for which visual training, in his opinion, is especially useful. Woolf has extensively described this syndrome. He has also described the methods which can be used to detect it and the therapeutic measures best suited to correct it. Although Woolf's conceptualization of this syndrome would not be well received by anyone who ignores the role of the central nervous system in reading disability, the "dysdiopia" syndrome presents a useful model for both therapy and research. Especially pertinent, also, to therapy programs is the work with children with visual perceptual problems carried out in Winter Haven, Florida. These materials are now available to the public schools (63), as are methods compiled by Van Witsen (64) and the screening tests used in Euclid, Ohio (65), one of the few communities with a school wide visual screening program organized by a committee of both ophthalmologists and optometrists. A program in San Diego (66) includes vision screening, referrals of failures, and evaluation with followup once the examination has been completed.

References

1. Harris, A. J. HOW TO INCREASE READING ABILITY. Fourth Edition. New York: Longmans Green, 1961. Page 18.

2. Ibid. Page 18.

3. Walcutt, C. C. "The Reading Problem in America," in TOMORROW'S ILLITERATES, edited by C. C. Walcutt. Boston: Little, Brown, 1961.

4. Bond, G. L., and Tinker, M. A. READING DIFFICULTIES: THEIR DIAGNOSIS AND CORRECTION. New York: Appleton-Century-Crofts, 1957. Page 113.

5. Ibid. Page 121.

6. Hardesty, H. H., et al. "Eye Exercises," THE COLLECTED LETTERS OF THE INTERNATIONAL CORRESPONDENCE SOCIETY OF OPHTHALMOLOGISTS AND OTOLARYNGOLOGISTS, Series 4, November, 1959.

7. Ibid.

8. Delacato, C. H. THE DIAGNOSIS AND TREATMENT OF SPEECH AND READING PROBLEMS. Springfield, Ill.: Charles C Thomas, 1963.

9. Rosborough, P. M. PHYSICAL FITNESS AND THE CHILD'S READING PROBLEM. New York: Exposition Press, 1963. Page 18.

10. Smith, D. E. P., and Carragan, P. THE NATURE OF READING DISABILITY. New York: Harcourt, Brace, 1960.

11. Krippner, S. Etiological Factors in Reading Disability of the Academically Talented in Comparison to Pupils of Average and Slow-Learning Ability, JOURNAL OF EDUCATIONAL RESEARCH. 1968, 61:275-279.

12. Bond and Tinker, op. cit.

13. Durrell, D. D. MANUAL OF DIRECTIONS FOR THE DURRELL ANALYSIS OF READING DIFFICULTY. Yonkers-on-Hudson, N. Y.: World Book, 1955.

14. PERCEPTUAL FORMS AND INCOMPLETE COPY FORMS: TEACHER'S TEST MANUAL. Winter Haven, Fla.: Lions Publication Committee, 1963.

15. McLeod, J. "Reading Expectancy from Disabled Learners," JOURNAL OF LEARNING DISABILITIES, 1968, 1:97-105.

16. Coleman, H. M. "Visual Perception and Reading Dysfunction," JOURNAL OF LEARNING DISABILITIES, 1968, 1:116-123.

17. Kolson, C. J., and Kaluger, G. CLINICAL ASPECTS OF REMEDIAL READING. Springfield, Ill.: Charles C Thomas, 1963. Page 140.

18. Betts, C. A. "Leaders in Education XI: The One Who Established the Importance of Vision to Children," EDUCATION, 1958, 79:1-3.

19. Hardesty et al., op. cit.

20. Ibid.

21. Ibid.

22. Ibid.

23. Ibid.

24. Goldberg, F. "An Ophthalmologist Looks at the Reading Problem," AMERICAN JOURNAL OF OPHTHALMOLOGY, 1959, 47-67.

25. Hardesty et al., op. cit.

26. Ibid.

27. Gesell, A. "Vision and Reading from the Standpoint of Child Development," in CLINICAL STUDIES IN READING II, edited by H. M. Robinson. Chicago: University of Chicago Press, 1953. Page 133.

28. Kagerer, R. L. "The Relationship of Visual Perceptual Performance in Early Grades to Reading Level in Grade Four." Winter Haven, Fla.: Star Press, 1960. (Mimeographed.)

29. Simpson, D. M. "Perceptual Readiness and Beginning Reading." Unpublished doctoral dissertation, Purdue University, 1960.

30. Snyder, R. T., and Freud, S. L. "Reading Readiness and Its Relation to Maturational Unreadiness as Measured by the Spiral Aftereffect and Other Visual-perceptual Techniques," PERCEPTUAL AND MOTOR SKILLS, 1967, 25:841-854.

31. Apperson, S. V. "The Effectiveness of Orthoptic Training as a Means of Remedial Instruction of Reading," JOURNAL OF EXPERIMENTAL EDUCATION, 1940, 9:160-166.

32. Peters, H. B. "The Influence of Orthoptic Training in Reading Ability. Part II. The Problem, Study, and Conclusions," AMERICAN JOURNAL OF OPTOMETRY, 1942, 19:152-176.

33. Lyons, C. V., and Lyons, E. E. "The Power of Visual Training. Part III. A Loom for Productive Thinking," JOURNAL OF THE AMERICAN OPTOMETRIC ASSOCIATION, 1957, 38:651-655.

34. Worcester, D. A. "The Influence of Orthoptic Training on the Reading Ability of College Freshmen," JOURNAL OF EXPERIMENTAL EDUCATION, 1941, 9:167-174.

35. Olson, H. C., Mitchell, C. C., and Westberg, W. C. "The Relationship Between Visual Training and Reading and Academic Improvement," AMERICAN JOURNAL OF OPTOMETRY AND ARCHIVES OF AMERICAN ACADEMY OF OPTOMETRY, 1953, 30:3-13.

36. Khan, A. U. "Effect of Training for Visual Motor Difficulties in Severely Disturbed Children," PERCEPTUAL AND MOTOR SKILLS, 1968, 26:744.

37. Getman, G. N. HOW TO DEVELOP YOUR CHILD'S INTELLIGENCE. LuVerne, Minn.: Research Press, 1962.

38. Kephart, N. C. THE SLOW LEARNER IN THE CLASSROOM. Columbus: Charles E. Merrill, 1960.

39. Gesell, op. cit., page 133.

40. Myklebust, H. R., and Boshes, B. "Psychoneurological Learning Disorders in Children," ARCHIVES OF PEDIATRICS, 1960, 77:247-256.

41. McKee, G. W., et al. THE PHYSIOLOGY OF READINESS. Minneapolis: Programs to Accelerate School Success, 1964.

42. Halgren, M. R. "Opus in See Sharp," EDUCATION, 1961, 81:369-371.

43. Rutherford, W. L. "Perceptual-Motor Training and Readiness," a paper read at the annual meeting of the International Reading Association, Detroit, 1965.

44. Cohen, R. L. "Remedial Training of First Grade Children with Visual Perceptual Retardation," EDUCATIONAL HORIZONS, 1966-1967, 45:60-63.

45. Frostig, M. THE FROSTIG PROGRAM FOR THE DEVELOPMENT OF VISUAL PERCEPTION. Chicago: Follett, 1964.

46. Frostig, M. "Visual Perception in the Brain-Injured Child," AMERICAN JOURNAL OF ORTHOPSYCHIATRY, 1963, 33:665-671.

47. Money, J. "Dyslexia: A Postconference Review," in READING DISABILITY: PROGRESS AND RESEARCH NEEDS IN DYSLEXIA, edited by J. Money, Baltimore: Johns Hopkins Press, 1962. Page 29.

48. Hardesty et al., op. cit.

49. Rabinovitch, R. "Neuropsychiatric Factors," a paper read at the annual meeting of the International Reading Association, Detroit, 1965.

50. Money, op. cit., page 28.

51. Delacato, op. cit.

52. Delacato, C. H. NEUROLOGICAL ORGANIZATION AND READING. Springfield, Ill.: Charles C Thomas, 1966.

53. Glass, G. V., and Robbins, M. P. "A Critique of Experiments in the Role of Neurological Organization in Reading Performance." Denver: Laboratory of Educational Research, University of Colorado, 1967. (Mimeographed.)

54. Kershner, J. R. "Doman-Delacato's Theory of Neurological Organization Applied with Retarded Children," EXCEPTIONAL CHILDREN, 1968, 34:441-450.

55. Robbins, M. P. "A Study of the Validity of Delacato's Theory of Neurological Organization," EXCEPTIONAL CHILDREN, 1966, 32:517-523.

56. Flax, N. "Visual Function in Dyslexia," a paper presented at the annual meeting of the American Academy of Optometry, Chicago, 1967.

57. Ibid.

58. Schiffman, G. "Dyslexia as an Educational Phenomenon: Its Recognition and Treatment," in READING DISABILITY: PROGRESS AND RESEARCH NEEDS IN DYSLEXIA, edited by J. Money. Baltimore: Johns Hopkins Press, 1962.

59. Reinecke, R. "Eye Difficulties and Reading Problems: Report of the Charlestown Project," a paper presented at the Fifth International Conference for Children with Learning Disabilities, Boston, 1968.

60. Lancaster, W. B., et al. "Standards for Referral of School Children for an Eye Examination," AMERICAN JOURNAL OF OPHTHALMOLOGY, 1954, 37: 710-718.

61. Blum, H. L., Peters, H. B., and Bettman, J. W. VISION SCREENING FOR ELEMENTARY SCHOOLS. THE ORINDA STUDY. Berkeley: University of California Press, 1959.

62. Woolf, D. "The Visual Disability Syndrome," OPTOMETRIC WEEKLY, Jan. 21, 1965.

63. McQuarrie, C. W. "A 1964 Report on the Winter Haven Program Story." OPTOMETRIC WORLD, December, 1964.

64. Van Witsen, Betty. PERCEPTUAL TRAINING ACTIVITIES HANDBOOK. New York: Teachers College Press, 1967.

65. Hinds, Lillian. "The Euclid Visual Screening Program," a paper presented at the 21st Annual School Vision Forum and Reading Conference, Cleveland, 1968.

66. Arbital, I. "The Grossmont Vision Program," EXCEPTIONAL CHILDREN, 1968, 34:759-760.

STUDY QUESTIONS

1. According to Krippner, how many children in typical elementary school read one or more years below grade level?

2. Krippner presents two differing positions—the ophthalmological and the optometric—regarding the probable value of visual training. What factors seem to underlie the difference?

3. What three suggestions does Krippner offer to professionals concerned with reading disability?

4. This article is candid regarding areas of professional disagreement and/or uncertainty. What advantages or disadvantages do you see in such open discussion?

SECTION 3
TOWARD TEACHING

10: SPECIFIC READING DISABILITY:
AN APPROACH TO DIAGNOSIS AND TREATMENT

Archie A. Silver
Rosa A. Hagin

Silver and Hagin describe the syndrome of specific reading disability
and present a general approach to remediation. The reader might
wish to follow this article by reading the second paper by these
authors (Chapter 13), which details their analysis of the reading process and presents very specific intervention strategies. The long-term
followup and the evaluation of remedial procedures conducted by
Silver and Hagin are rare in the field and are highly commendable.

B. D. B.

eprinted with permission of the authors and publisher from THE JOURNAL OF
ECIAL EDUCATION, 1967, 1, 109-118.

This paper will attempt to describe the syndrome of *specific reading disability,* outline its natural history, and consider remedial measures. The material is based on the authors' work with children at New York University—Bellevue Medical Center, and with patients seen in private practice in psychiatry and psychology over the past 15 years. Studies of these children have been presented in a series of reports that give control data and statistical evaluation (Silver & Hagin, 1960, 1964, 1966; Silver, 1961).

DEFINITION

The authors define the term *specific reading disability* as indicating those children who, without evidence of structural damage to the central nervous system and without gross defects in the peripheral sensory apparatus, are retarded in reading with respect to both their mental age and their educational opportunities. These children have been described elsewhere as having *primary reading disability* (Rabinovitch, 1959), *specific* or *developmental dyslexia* (Critchley, 1964), *congenital word-blindness* (Bannatyne, 1966), *reading disability* (Money, 1962), or *strephosymbolia* (Orton, 1937). We prefer the term *specific reading disability* because it implies a defect intrinsic, i.e., specific, to language and does not imply assumptions in respect to etiology.

It is clear that not every child who is retarded in reading is suffering from specific reading disability as so defined. Reading retardation may spring from a variety of causes (Eisenberg, 1966). The child who has not had the opportunity to learn; the child whose reading grade, though below that of his class, is commensurate with his mental age; the child with classic evidence of neurological impairment; the child with sensory defects which impair the reception of stimuli—these children do not fit the diagnosis of specific reading disability. The diagnosis implies adequate intellectual and sensory abilities and conventional educational exposure, appropriate motivation to learn and, in spite of these attributes, retardation in reading.

These studies were made possible in part by funds granted by the Field Foundation and by the Carnegie Corporation of New York. The statements made and the views express are solely the responsibility of the authors.

GENERAL EVALUATION

The diagnosis specific reading disability requires evaluation in four areas: a) reading level, b) intellectual level, c) educational opportunity, and d) neurological status. Measurement in each of these may be subject to question as to reliability and validity. We must question, for example, the value of group tests of reading ability and intellectual level for atypical learners. We must also be certain that any test of intellectual functioning is not also a test of reading ability Furthermore, it has been claimed that all intelligence tests discriminate against the disadvantaged child and are therefore invalid as measures of his intellectual ability.

Recognizing these limitations, our experience has established the following individually administered battery of tests as useful in providing a baseline of data in each of the four areas. These, as well as other tests to be discussed later, are outlined below. (We should note that in our work we have attempted to use tests that have long clinical acceptance and are relatively easy to administer and score. We are constantly modifying and, hopefully, improving our techniques in order to understand better other areas of defect in these children.)

Tests for Reading Level

1. A test in oral reading, with emphasis upon the child's use of word-attack skills and the accuracy of his perceptual organization of the letter code (Wide Range Achievement Test [WRAT] : oral reading section).

2. A test for understanding of factual content, interpretation of language, ability to abstract from paragraphs, and use of vocabulary in context. (Metropolitan Reading Test, appropriate level.)

3. A test for spelling (WRAT spelling).

4. Written expression, through a sample composition.

OUTLINE OF TESTS USED

Neurological: Classical Examination Plus

1. Right-Left Discrimination
2. Handedness, eyedness, footedness
3. Extension Test

Perceptual Integrative

1. Visuo-motor
   a. Bender Visual-Motor Gestalt Test
   b. Visual Figure-Background: Marble-Board Test (Strauss and Werner)
   c. Reversible Figures
   d. Embedded Figures (Gottschaldt)

2. Auditory
   a. Auditory Discrimination
   b. Auditory Figure-Background
   c. Auditory Blending (Roswell-Chall)
   d. Matching Initial Consonants
   e. Matching Final Consonants

3. Tactile
   a. Face-Hand Test (M. Bender)
   b. Stereognosis
   c. Tactile Figure-Ground (Strauss & Werner)

4. Body Image
   a. Goodenough Drawing
   b. Finger Gnosis

5. Sequencing
   a. Objects
   b. Digits
   c. Words
   d. Sentences
   e. Days of the Week
   f. Months of the Year
   g. Clock Test (H. Head)

6. Educational
   a. Wide Range Achievement Test: Reading and Spelling Sections (Jastak)
   b. Appropriate level of Metropolitan Reading Test
   c. Writing Sampie

7. Articulation Inventory

PERCEPTUAL PROFILE

IDENTIFYING DATA

Name _____ WISC VIQ _____   Oral Reading _____

Age _____   PIQ _____   Reading Comprehension _____

                         FSIQ _____

Birthdate _____ Expectancy _____ Spelling _____

PROFILE OF TEST RESULTS

| Modality | Visual | Auditory | Tactile | Laterality | Body Image |

Modality	Visual			Auditory			Tactile	Laterality		Body Image	
	M	E	B	A	A F	S	T	E	L	F	D
	B	F	G	D	B	P	F B	L X	R	S	R

+

Base Line

−

+

Base Line

−

Key to Tests in Profile

MB = Marble Board

EF = Gottschaldt Embedded Figures

BG = Bender Visual-Motor Gestalt

AD = Auditory Discrimination

AFB = Auditory Figure-Background

SP = Articulatory Defect in Speech

TFB = Tactile Figure-Background

ELX = Abnormal Response on
        Extension Test

LR = Left Right Discrimination

FS = Finger Schema

DR = Figure Drawing

TEACHING PLAN

I. Laterality:
   Shift writing hand from right to left

II. Visual:
   A. Forms:
   B. Spatial Orientation:
      square puzzles
      pythagoras puzzle

III. Auditory:
   A. Sound Discrimination
   B. Word Discrimination
   C. Rhyming
   D. Auditory Sequences

IV. Tactile:
   Discrimination—Textures
   Discrimination—Size
   Discrimination—Forms:
   Tactile Dot Forms

V. Kinesthetic:
   Directionality Board
   Tracing: Movements/Simple
      Forms
   Rhythmic Writing

Intellectual Evaluation. Intellectual function is measured by the Wechsler Intelligence Scale for Children (WISC). Some writers suggest that the child with reading problems is penalized on the WISC verbal scale and that, therefore, the test's performance scale is a more valid measure of intelligence; others, however, report a lowered performance score. In our opinion, the full score plus study of all subtest scores offers the most effective measure of functioning intelligence. Furthermore, the use of *all* the WISC subtests offers an economical opportunity for collecting qualitative data to answer such questions as:

How does the child's potential ability differ from his actual functioning?

How effectively can he deal with the English language?—especially important in the case of children from non-English-speaking homes.

What are the characteristics of his speech production? Are there articulatory errors? mispronunciations? errors in the sequencing of words or syllables? auditory discrimination errors? omissions?

What are the child's language patterns? Are there neologisms or circumlocutions? What is the breadth of his vocabulary? What is the quality of his definitions—concrete, functional, and abstract?

How well does he understand quantitative concepts in dealing with time, size, distance, and number?

How does he deal with directional problems? Does he build Picture Arrangements from right to left? Does he reverse the symbols in Coding? Does he have difficulty orienting the split side of blocks?

How well does he focus attention with verbal directions? With non-verbal materials? How does he handle distractions?

How well can he abstract the points of problems?

Does he utilize a segmented approach to visual configurations or does he deal with perceptual gestalten?

Is he aware of his own errors in problem solving? Is he able to correct them within time limits?

Educational Opportunity. While a child's grade in school is a practical device for evaluating his educational opportunity and is in most cases a reliable one, the quantity and consistency of the child's exposure to education should be individually assessed. The quality of such exposure is more difficult to determine. We have found it useful to examine the child's school notebooks and papers for clues from the child's work and the teacher's corrections and comments.

Neurological Status. Our evaluation in this area attempts to determine not only classic neurological status in terms of cranial nerves, deep and superficial reflexes, muscle tone, power, synergy, and sensory evaluation of touch, pain, temperature, and joint position sense, but also the more subtle defects of patterned motor activity and those signs included under the syndrome of "minimal brain damage" to be discussed later.

PERCEPTUAL DEFECTS

When children who have been identified as having specific reading disability are then evaluated with detailed perceptual and cognitive measures (see opposite page), a syndrome will emerge, a syndrome in which a basic component appears to be disorientation in space and time. This disorientation reflects itself in specific temporal and spatial distortions in the visual, auditory, tactile, and kinesthetic modalities and in the orientation of the body-image in space. Although the children at Bellevue Medical Center come from disadvantaged backgrounds and the private patients from the upper-middle income level, the perceptual and neurological findings for the two groups are not dissimilar.

The Visual Modality. The Bender Visual-Motor Gestalt Test will reveal immaturities through persistence of verticalization and rotation and through difficulties in the construction of angles and in mid-line crossing, at inappropriate age levels. There will be difficulties in visual figure-background relations as measured by the Marble-Board, with angulation problems and tendencies to omit, displace, or rotate parts of the figure. Measurement of the rate of apparent change in ambiguous figures such as the Rubin Vase-Face Illusion will show an abnormally rapid rate of apparent change or no change at all. There are difficulties with such figure-background tests as the Gottschaldt. It is as though visual stimuli are shifted and rotated on the background of space. One can conjecture the difficulty such problems create for a child in the correct perception of letters, words, and phrases against the background of the printed page.

The Auditory Area. In this area the temporal sequencing of sounds is a major defect. Children with specific reading disability can apprehend the meaning of words they hear, but their grasp of sounds in temporal sequence is often distorted. This sequencing problem is a major one and will be seen in difficulties in perceiving similarities and differences in auditory configurations, in blending a sequence of sounds into a word pattern, and in isolating and matching initial and final sounds of words. Not only may the sequencing of individual sounds be defective, but also the sequencing of words in a sentence or of sentences in logical order. Thus, there may be difficulty in retaining or presenting ideas logically. For those children who survive the earlier grades and finally learn to read, sequencing defects may manifest themselves in the later grades as comprehension and organizational problems.

Children with specific reading disability also demonstrate figure-background problems in the auditory modality. If a background pattern is introduced into a verbal task, the children's motor response to the pattern will indicate their inability to free themselves from the intruding background stimuli. They generally have no difficulty in matching spoken words with pictures.

Tactile and Kinesthetic Perception. In this area, which is evaluated in part through response to Strauss and Werner's Tactile Figure-Ground Test, no statistically significant defect has been found. The defect does appear, however, in an occasional child.

Body-Image Concepts. In children with specific reading disability, most significant abnormality has been found in body-image concepts, particularly in the orientation of the body in space and in the orientation to a mirror image. In most of the children there is confusion in right-left orientation, not only in identifying right- or left-hand sides and in crossing the mid-line, but also in identifying right-left in their mirror image. In the Goodenough Draw-a-Person Test, body-image distortion is frequently seen in a peculiar downward displacement of the arms and the slanting of the figure in position on the page. Finger gnosis—the ability to identify one's fingers when they are hidden from sight and stimulated bilaterally—is frequently impaired.

In the above four areas of investigation alone, nine out of ten children with specific reading disability will demonstrate some defect. The most frequent are defects in right-left orientation and in visual perception, where the incidence is at about 90%, and where the areas may be considered as problems in spatial perception. At least 50% of the children will have problems in auditory perception, and we suspect that as we devise new methods of exploring this area, the incidence will be even higher. The outstanding auditory defect appears to be in the temporal sequencing of sounds, words, and ideas. Tactile perception, at least as measured by Strauss and Werner's Figure-Ground Test and by the absence of extinction phenomena, is relatively normal, with defects seen in perhaps 10% of the children. Finger gnosis is not clearly established in approximately four in ten. (It must be remembered that the data upon which these conclusions are based have been obtained for children aged 7 to 13.)

The significance of these perceptual defects is twofold:

    1. Specific reading disability is but one symptom of a defect that may involve all avenues of perception.

    2. With a perceptual evaluation such as outlined above, defects are found in more than one perceptual avenue. The defects may be charted in an individual "perceptual profile" of assets and deficits (see Figure 2), and from this profile, as will be seen below, appropriate remedial techniques may be determined.

As the perceptual profiles of children with specific reading disability are charted, patterns of defects emerge, and these may be grouped by areas of maximum defect. For example, there are those children with predominantly visual perceptual defects who, clinically, will display reading disability as their most prominent problem. Those with predominant problems in temporal sequencing of sounds will also have a reading disability, but often this may be compounded with a receptive-type aphasia, varying from mild to severe. The more severe may resemble the congenital word-deafness described by M. Creak (1936) and may obscure the associated reading disability or even make the child appear to be mentally retarded (Silver, Hagin, & Pfeiffer, 1965). Careful evaluation of the child's use of language may reveal additional problems in emissive speech and in the ability to find the appropriate word, although adequate ideation is present.

Where tactile and kinesthetic perceptual defects are found, the child will demonstrate poor handwriting, while the finding finger agnosia may accompany an arithmetic disability. Such combinations of reading disability with aphasia, apraxia, and agnosia lend support to the concept of specific reading disability as being but part of a complex of language defects, and the question arises as to an underlying causative condition.

CEREBRAL DOMINANCE FOR LANGUAGE

Theoretically, all the defects discussed above are related to spatial and temporal orientation. We have attempted to determine whether there is a common denominator for them—an underlying problem that will tie them together. Our tentative suggestion is that they may be related to the problem of cerebral dominance.

The issue of cerebral dominance has been a confused and controversial one. Part of the difficulty stems from the confusion of peripheral dominance with central or cerebral dominance. The emphasis has been upon observing which hand is used for skilled activity, which eye for sighting, and which foot for kicking, and determining the lack of agreement in eye, hand, and foot preferences. Mixed dominance has been said by some writers to be associated with reading disability (Orton, 1937); others have disagreed. There is real question, however, whether these peripheral preferences are really indicative of cerebral dominance. Harris' (1957) tests of peripheral dominance attempt to bridge the gap between peripheral dominance and *central* organization by testing a wide variety of peripheral preferences. His conclusion is that a dominant peripheral pattern is lacking in children with reading disability.

How can central dominance be effectively studied? Experimentally, injection of sodium amytal into each carotid artery (Penfield and Roberts, 1959), will suggest the dominant cerebral hemisphere for language. Direct stimulation of the brain in surgery has been utilized. Less drastic measures include the following:

1. Assessment of the *phi phenomenon* (i.e., the extent to which apparent movement is seen in two half-fields of vision), in which McFie (1952) found little or no apparent movement in children with reading disability and therefore concluded that the "neurophysiological organization corresponding to dominance was not normally established."

2. The dichotic presentation of auditory stimuli (Kimura, 1963), which again suggests that in children with reading disability clearcut dominance is not established.

Our own work has utilized the finding of Paul Schilder (Hoff & Schilder, 1927) that when the eyes are closed and the arms extended at shoulder level parallel to each other and to the floor, one arm will be higher than the other. In children with established dominance, the higher arm corresponds to that used for writing. In children with severe specific reading disability, this arm may be opposite to that used for writing, or neither arm will be elevated.

There is no doubt, in our opinion, of the validity of such findings. In a study of 100 third- and fourth-graders in a suburban school, we were able to identify 34 of 41 children who were reading below their mental age and grade placement. Conversely, of 41 children with abnormality on the extension test, 34 were retarded readers, an additional five had low scores on reading-readiness tests, one had a marked praxic difficulty, and one had a family history of reading disability.

The question is the meaning of these findings. We suggest that the elevated extremity is one which has the greater muscle tone and, hence, is an expression of cerebral dominance. If this is true, then we must conclude that in children with specific reading disability a clearcut dominant cerebral pattern for language has not been established.

This does not mean that the cause of specific reading disability is indeed a lack of cerebral dominance, but it does suggest that a lack of cerebral dominance is an important part of the syndrome. This concept is important not only for our understanding of the development of language but also, as will be seen below, for the management of language disabilities in general.

CHILDREN WITH MINIMAL BRAIN DAMAGE

There are a number of children who fit the above definition and description, but who in addition have minimal or so-called "soft" neurological signs (Bender, 1958). These signs are predominantly motor and include abnormalities in muscle tone, pronounced synkinetic activity, choreoform movements in the outstretched hands, awkwardness in fine motor performance, unequal or eccentric pupils, poor ocular convergence, sustained nystagmus on lateral or upward gaze, occasional hyperkineses, but, rarely, findings in the more classic neurological examination. These children generally have perceptual defects which are greater quantitatively and qualitatively than those associated with specific reading disability. We classify them as having specific reading disability with "organic" signs. Whether such children represent the most severe developmental defects or whether they have structural brain damage superimposed upon the developmental defect is not known (Zangwill, 1960). Yet, in severity and prognosis, they have the more difficult time. In prevalence, too, they are important. In our studies, at least three or four children out of each ten with reading disability have the minimal neurological signs described above. Because of the more guarded prognosis in treating these children, the importance of the neurological examination in locating them is not to be underestimated.

There is one other group that must be considered. This consists of the rare children who fit the diagnosis specific reading disability but who do not demonstrate perceptual defects on our tests. It may be that they have matured and learned to compensate for their defects, or that we have not yet learned how to find them, or that these children may represent a different etiological group. Perhaps their reading disability is due to emotional causes. In our experience, these children are rare—one in ten or twenty of the children that we see.

FOLLOW-UP STUDIES

If we follow these children from childhood into young adulthood (i.e., from about age 10 to about age 20) and retest them with the battery of tests they took as children, we find that although some maturation does occur in that there is quantitative improvement, basic perceptual problems tend to remain, and tell-tale evidence of the old reading disability persists.

In the visual motor area, for example, significant improvement is seen in decreased verticalization, but angulation problems still remain, while on the Marble-Board, surprisingly little maturation is seen. Auditory perception, difficult to evaluate, is still impaired, and tactile figure-ground problems can be found. Right-left discrimination is markedly improved, but the extension tests are still abnormal. These findings have been detailed in follow-up studies from our clinic (Silver & Hagin, 1964, 1966).

The differences between organically impaired and developmentally inadequate children become more pronounced as they grow older. Greater maturation is seen in those with developmental problems, particularly in right-left discrimination, in reproduction or orientation of visual symbols, and in finger schema. Both groups have persistent problems in the establishment of clearcut cerebral dominance.

More important is the finding that when oral reading quotients and IQ's are compared for the two groups, significant differences are not found, but reading comprehension is poorer in the organic group. Further, in comparing adequate and inadequate readers among these adults, we find that it is the adequate reader who shows greatest perceptual maturation, while the inadequate reader retains severe perceptual defects.

These follow-up studies made clear to us that, in spite of maturation in some perceptual areas, specific reading disability is a long-term problem, the signs of which can be detected in later life despite adequate vocational and social functioning. We cannot wait for children to "outgrow" their reading problems.

AN APPROACH TO REMEDIATION

Our follow-up findings also suggested the need for modifications in training methods. Our initial concept had been that compensation was a basic principle, i.e., that after assessing perceptual assets and deficits, we should train in the areas of greater perceptual strength, via the most intact modalities. Results of the follow-up studies, however, suggest that this technique does not appear to enhance perception or to effect lasting improvement in reading. Our efforts, therefore, in almost a complete reversal of our earlier approach, are now directed to the stimulation of the defective perceptual areas.

Our purpose now is actually to enhance cerebral maturation, to being neurological functioning to the point where a child is physiologically capable of learning to read. We are currently involved in an evaluation of this approach, working to devise methods for the stimulation of deficit perceptual areas and to subject these methods to controlled evaluation.

This method involves:

1. Total clinical assessment of neurological, psychiatric, psychological, and educational functioning to provide data for a profile of assets and deficits.

2. Teaching focused on the deficit areas as revealed by the perceptual profile.

3. Work within one modality, insofar as possible, before attempting intermodal tasks and before relating language to perception.

4. Individual teaching methods, which take a child through recognition, copying, and recall stages of perception.

5. Immediate feedback and prompts within the same modality as the technique then being used.

6. Opportunity for overlearning.

7. Awareness that the lack of clearcut cerebral dominance for language is a basic one with reading disabilities and consequent placing of emphasis upon consistent unilateral hand preferences, left-to-right progression, and correct orientation of figures in space and sounds in time.

8. Replicability through carefully defined techniques and record keeping on their use.

9. Provision for testing results through a cross-over experimental design in which each child serves as his own control.

We are now beginning the third year of a four-year study of perceptual stimulation (Silver, Hagin, & Hersh, 1965). In another year we hope to have some answers to the questions we have raised concerning the effect of these methods upon perceptual deficits, upon reading and spelling achievement, and upon the establishment of clearcut cerebral dominance. We also hope to know more about the response of various modalities to training and about the maintenance of gains after training has been terminated.

Extended Bibliography

annatyne, B. A suggested classification of the causes of dyslexia. WORD LIND BULLETIN, 1966, 1, 5-13.

ender, L. Report. BULLETIN OF THE ORTON SOCIETY, 1951, 1, 3.

ender, L. Problems in conceptualization and communication in children ith developmental alexia. In P. Hoch & J. Zubin (Eds.), PSYCHOPATHOLOGY F COMMUNICATION. New York: Grune & Stratton, 1958.

Benton, A. RIGHT-LEFT DISCRIMINATION AND FINGER LOCALIZATION. New York: Hoeber-Harper, 1959.

Birch, H., & Belmont, L. Auditory-visual integration in normal and retarded readers. AMERICAN JOURNAL OF ORTHOPSYCHIATRY, 1965, 34, 852-861.

Brain, R. SPEECH DISORDERS. Washington, D.C.: Buttenworth, 1961.

Creak, M. Reading difficulties in children. ARCHIVES OF DISEASES OF CHILDREN, 1936, 11, 143-156.

Critchley, M. DEVELOPMENTAL DYSLEXIA. London: Heinemann Medical, 1964.

Eisenberg, L. Reading retardation: psychiatric and sociological aspects. JOURNAL OF PEDIATRICS, 1966, 37, 352-365.

Frostig, M. Teaching reading to children with perceptual disturbances. In R. Flower, H. Gobman, & L. Lawson (Eds.), READING DISORDERS. Philadelphia: F. A. Davis Co., 1965.

Hagin, R. A. Some practical applications of diagnostic studies of children with specific reading disability. BULLETIN OF THE ORTON SOCIETY, 1961, 11, 13-18.

Hallgren, B. Specific dyslexia (congenital word-blindness). ACTA PSYCHIATRICA & NEUROLOGICA, 1950, Suppl. 65, 1-287.

Harris, A. J. Lateral dominance, directional confusion, and reading disability JOURNAL OF PSYCHOLOGY, 1957, 44, 283-294.

Head, N. APHASIA AND KINDRED DISORDERS OF SPEECH, Vol. II. Cambridge: Cambridge University Press, 1927.

Hecaen, H., & De Ajurriaguerra, J. LEFTHANDEDNESS: MANUAL SUPERIORITY AND CEREBRAL DOMINANCE. New York: Grune & Stratton, 1964.

Hermann, K. READING DISABILITY. Springfield, Ill.: Charles C Thomas, 1959.

Hoff, H., & Schilder, P. DIE LAGE REFLEXE DES MENSCHEN. Berlin: Springer, 1927.

Kimura, D. Speech lateralization in young children as determined by an auditory test. JOURNAL OF COMPARATIVE AND PHYSIOLOGICAL PSYCHOLOGY, 1963, 5, 899-902.

McFie, J. Cerebral dominance in cases of reading disability. JOURNAL OF NEUROSURGERY AND PSYCHIATRY, 1952, 15, 194-199.

Money, J. READING DISABILITY: PROGRESS AND RESEARCH NEEDS IN DYSLEXIA. Baltimore: Johns Hopkins Press, 1962.

Orton, S. T. READING, WRITING, AND SPEECH PROBLEMS OF CHILDREN. New York: Norton, 1937.

Penfield, W., & Roberts, L. SPEECH AND BRAIN MECHANISMS. Princeton, N. J.: Princeton University Press, 1959.

Rabinovitch, R. Reading and learning difficulties. In S. Arieti (Ed.), AMERICAN HANDBOOK OF PSYCHIATRY. Vol. II. New York: Basic Books, 1959.

Rawson, M. R. A bibliography on the nature, recognition, and treatment of language difficulties. ORTON SOCIETY, 1966.

Silver, A. A. Diagnostic considerations in children with reading disability. BULLETIN OF THE ORTON SOCIETY, 1961, 11, 5-12.

Silver, A. A., & Hagin, R. A. Specific reading disability: delineation of the syndrome and its relationship to cerebral dominance. COMPREHENSIVE PSYCHIATRY, 1960, 1, 126-133.

Silver A. A., & Hagin, R. A. Specific reading disability: follow-up studies. AMERICAN JOURNAL OF ORTHOPSYCHIATRY, 1964, 34, 95-102.

Silver, A. A., & Hagin, R. A. Developmental language disability simulating mental retardation. JOURNAL OF AMERICAN ACADEMY OF CHILD PSYCHIATRY, 1965, 4, 485-493.

Silver, A. A., & Hagin, R. A. Maturation of perceptual function in children with specific reading disability. THE READING TEACHER, 1966, January, 253-259.

Silver, A. A., Hagin, R. A., & Hersh, M. F. Specific reading disability: teaching through stimulation of deficit perceptual areas. Paper read at annual meeting, American Orthopsychiatric Ass'n., 1965.

Silver, A. A., Hagin, R. A., & Pfeiffer, E. The therapeutic nursery as an aid in the diagnosis of delayed language development. Paper read at annual meeting. American Orthopsychiatric Ass'n., 1966. (AMERICAN JOURNAL OF ORTHOPSYCHIATRY, in press.)

Zangwill, O. A. CEREBRAL DOMINANCE AND ITS RELATION TO PSYCHOLOGICAL FUNCTION. Springfield, Ill.: C. C. Thomas, 1960.

STUDY QUESTIONS

1. Silver and Hagin find disorientation in space and time to be a basic component of specific reading disability. How does this disorientation manifest itself in reading?

2. Describe the methods by which Silver and Hagin propose to enhance cerebral maturation. How would they know whether the methods were successful in achieving that goal?

3. Why did the authors shift from teaching to the intact modalities to teaching to areas of perceptual deficit?

4. What is their profile and how is it used?

11; TEACHING READING TO CHILDREN WITH PERCEPTUAL DISTURBANCES

Marianne Frostig

Frostig discusses, in classroom terms, the teaching of reading to children who have perceptual disturbances. The diagnosis of visual and auditory perceptual problems is clearly presented. The Developmental Test of Visual Perception is described, and specific teaching suggestions offered.
B. D. B.

Reprinted with permission of the author and publisher from READING DISORDERS, R. Flower, Helen Gofman, Lucie Lawson (Eds.), Philadelphia: F. A. Davis Co., 1965, pp. 113-127.

Of all aspects of human behavior, a person's modes of perception are the least evident. His language, his movements, even his intelligence and his emotional and social adjustment can be gauged at least roughly by observation. But perceptual ability is much less obvious, and can usually only be assessed by careful examination. The perceptual disturbances which characterize many children are therefore often overlooked.

The case of Stan provides an example. This 13½-year-old boy was referred to us as a poor learner who had shown inadequate school adjustment since he went to nursery school at 2½ years of age. The California Achievement Test, given when he was in grade A6, showed grade level scores of 5.2 for reading vocabulary, 4.4 for reading comprehension, 3.7 for language, 4.8 for arithmetic reasoning, 3.8 for arithmetic fundamentals, and 6.2 for spelling.

On an individual test of intelligence (WISC), he received a lower performance IQ (87) than verbal (126), but both scores were within normal range (full scale, 109). The Wepman Test of Auditory Discrimination revealed no auditory perceptual difficulties. There was nothing to indicate the cause of Stan's learning difficulties until his abilities in visual perception were tested.[1] His scores on the Marianne Frostig Developmental Test of Visual Perception showed him to be approximately five years retarded in the areas of eye-motor coordination, perception of position in space, and perception of spatial relationships.

MARIANNE FROSTIG DEVELOPMENTAL TEST OF VISUAL PERCEPTION

This test was an outcome of many years of observation of children such as Stan, whose learning difficulties could be attributed, at least in part, to disturbances in visual perception. The test comprises five subtests. The first of these, *eye-hand coordination,* explores a restricted area of motor skills. The child has to draw lines between guide lines without touching them, and to draw without guide lines from one point to another. Scores in this test predict the child's ability to do printing, writing, and such activities as pasting,

---

[1]Our research indicates that visual perception consists of relatively distinct processes, each of which may be disturbed independently of the others.

copying designs, and so on, but they have less implication for reading or arithmetic. Subtests II, III, IV, and V of the Developmental Test of Visual Perception are more specifically prognostic of reading ability than subtest I. They evaluate perception of *figure-ground relationships,* of *perceptual constancy,* of *position in space,* and of *spatial relationships* respectively. In the subtest for *figure-ground perception* the child is required to discriminate between intersecting figures and to find hidden figures. A child with disturbances in figure-ground discrimination tends to have difficulty in learning to read or spell because of his inability to perceive parts in their proper relation to wholes. This results in a difficulty in analyzing and synthesizing words and passages. A child with this disability will also be handicapped by a difficulty in finding and keeping his place on a page; and his understanding of what he is reading may be impaired by the fluctuating attention which frequently accompanies difficulty in figure-ground perception.

Perceptual constancy refers to the ability to recognize what is perceived as belonging to a certain class regardless of the image on the retina. For example, a clock seen from the side, from the back, and from the front looks entirely different from each angle, but can still be recognized in each instance as a clock. The exercises in the subtest for this ability (III) require the child to recognize a given shape, whatever its position, size, coloring, or background. Children who have this difficulty may learn to read a word in a particular style of print or context, but fail to recognize the word when it is presented in a different print or context. These are the children who learn to read their first pre-primer with gratifying facility, but seem to have forgotten everything when a new series is broached.

Perception of *position in space* refers to the ability to see an object in relation to one's own body; to see it as being in front, behind, or to the side, for instance. Children who have difficulty in this area are often unable to recognize the reversal or rotation of letters, so that a "b" may appear to them as a "p" or "d." In this test, the ability to perceive position in space is evaluated by requiring the child to recognize reversals and rotations in rows of similar figures.

Perception of *spatial relationships* refers to the ability to recognize the positions of objects or of reference points in relation to each other. Because this ability develops much later than perception of position in space, subtest V is given only to children of five years or older. (The other subtests can be used with children from 3½ years of age.) In this subtest the child is required to copy patterns by joining the appropriate dots in a given group of dots. Children with disabilities in this area are likely to perceive the letters in a word or words in a sentence as jumbled or interposed, and so be unable to learn to read. They will also probably have difficulty in writing, as they will not be able to perceive the parts of the letters in their proper relationship to each other.

The Developmental Test of Visual Perception thus allows an exploration of the child's developmental level in five areas of visual perception which clinical observation has shown to be closely related to learning ability. The child's strengths and weaknesses in each area can be estimated, a perceptual age level (based on norms obtained on over 2,100 unselected nursery school and public school children) can be assigned for each of the subtests, and a perceptual quotient (PQ) for the entire test may be calculated in a manner similar to that used in calculating the intelligence quotient (IQ). On the basis of this information, teaching programs can be planned which take into account the subject's visual perceptual assets and liabilities.

VISUAL PERCEPTION AND READING ABILITY

That a child's ability to learn to read is affected by his visual perceptual development has been demonstrated by an experiment initiated in May 1962 at the University Elementary School, University of California, Los Angeles.[2] A group of 26 children between the ages of 4½ and 6½ were exposed to reading material but not forced to use it; all those interested were given training in word attack skills, phonics, configuration, and context. But first the Frostig Test was administered, and eight of the children were found to have visual

[2]This experiment was under the direction of Mrs. Edith Appleton, kindergarten supervisor of University Elementary School.

perceptual quotients of 90 or below. It was predicted that these eight children would not attempt to learn to read because of their difficulties. This prediction proved to be highly accurate. In November 1962, the children were rated for reading achievement. None of the children with a visual perceptual quotient below 90 had begun to read; of the two children with a perceptual quotient of 90, one had learned to read very well, while the other had not. Only one of the children with a PQ above 90 showed reading difficulties. Research in other beginning reading situations, in which auditory reinforcement of visual methods was used by the teacher and in which all of the children were required to read, has shown a correlation of about .50 between the visual perceptual test and reading scores.[3]

DISABILITIES IN AUDITORY PERCEPTION

Children may also have difficulties in reading and spelling because of disturbances in *auditory* perception. The Wepman Test of Auditory Discrimination has been used successfully to explore this area by testing the child's ability to recognize the similarity or difference of similar paired words. In the pairs, "lack-luck," "man-man," for example, the child should recognize that the first two words are different, the latter two words the same. Wepman has shown convincingly that children with inadequate auditory discrimination show lower reading scores than those with high scores in auditory discrimination. The findings from these researches into the processes of visual and auditory perception lead to the conclusion that the teaching of reading should not be uniform for all children. The majority of children learn better when employing the visual sense modality (visile children) but many others are auditory learners (audile children) and learn better with a method of phonetic-phonemic-visual integration. (6, 7)

Used together, the Frostig and Wepman Tests can provide sufficient information to suggest what kind of perceptual training will best prepare a child for learning to read, and also what method of teaching him to read will prove most effective.

[3]This research was done at Hermosa Beach by the Frostig School, in Solano County by Mrs. Berkov, and in Glendora by Mrs. Waxman.

THE TEACHING OF BEGINNING READING

Effectiveness of Perceptual Training

Before discussing methods of teaching children with perceptual difficulties to read, it would be as well to consider the fundamental question, "Is perceptual ability a genetically determined ability which cannot be modified by training?" Our research with both the Hermosa Beach school system and our clinical cases suggests otherwise. In the Hermosa Beach experiment,[4] all of the children in both the morning and afternoon kindergarten classes of one school were ranked according to their score on the Frostig Test. They were marked off in pairs, and one child from each pair was selected for training by flipping a coin. Initial Frostig Test scores for the twenty training children ranged from 62 to 124, with eight children scoring below 90; the range for the twenty-two control children was 50 to 128, with six children scoring below 90 and two receiving a score of 90.

An experienced teacher from the clinical school met the two training groups of ten children each from March 28 to May 18, 1962, for a total of eighteen sessions of 85 minutes each (a period which included milk time, recess, etc.). She provided visual perceptual training by means of games and perceptual activities involving the manipulation of three-dimensional objects, exercises for body-image and concept, and workbook exercises.

The children in the control group remained with their regular teacher at the time of the training sessions. They followed the prescribed school curriculum, which included some perceptual exercises in all sense modalities.

Upon retesting, both groups gained on the average on the Frostig Test, but the training group gained significantly more. Using the median gain of 15 points as the cut-off, a two-by-two table produced a chi-square value of 9.9, significant at the .005 level. All children in the training group received a retest score of 90 or above (one girl received 90); four children in the control group fell below 90.

[4]The pilot training study at Hermosa Beach was conducted in cooperation with Dr. Dale Glick, Superintendent, Mr. Henry Levy, District Psychologist, and Mr. Lyle Smith, Principal of South School.

Responsiveness to perceptual training has been reported by many other writers. Vernon, for instance, after discussing the difficulty of a child learning to read a diagram, describes how a group of children aged ten to fourteen years were able to learn quite quickly how to match a cross-section of a doll with a drawing when they were given practice. "After a period of instruction as short as ten minutes even the youngest (children) improved their scores considerably." (5)

Methods of Teaching Reading Which Utilize Principles of Visual Perceptual Development

The present author has prepared workbooks to train each of the five areas of visual perception already mentioned. As these workbooks have been published (8), it would be inappropriate to say more about them here than that they consist of carefully graded pencil and paper exercises similar to those employed in the Developmental Test of Visual Perception. However, disabilities in visual perception require more than pencil and paper exercises alone, and the remainder of this paper will be devoted to suggestions for additional training, and for teaching reading by methods which take perceptual processes and disabilities into account.

Eye-Motor Coordination

Children with difficulties in eye-motor coordination often show a pattern of disturbed body movements, and are characterized by an inability to run, throw, climb, skip, or hop skillfully. These symptoms are presumed to be the result of poor progress in the early phase of sensory-motor development, which reaches its climax before the child is two years of age. As Kephart (2) and Radler and Kephart (3) have stressed, and as my clinical observations confirm, this developmental lag may well lead to emotional, social, and perceptual difficulties, which may in turn lead to poor school adjustment and so affect reading ability.

Physical exercises to develop the motor skills of hands, arms, legs, feet, and trunk are therefore to be strongly recommended for children with poor body-image and/or difficulties in learning to read or write. Such exercises are commonly included in the curricula of European elementary schools.

222

The skillful and quick coordination of eye movements and body movements (visual-motor skills) do not always have an influence on reading ability that can be termed decisive, but they need to be adequately developed to insure school adjustment. For exercises in eye-motor coordination the reader is referred to the books by Radler and Kephart, and Kephart, as well as to the perceptual training workbooks.

Figure-Ground Perception

To help children with difficulties in *figure-ground perception,* the teacher should write new words on a blackboard in big letters, while the children watch the movement of the chalk. This helps them to analyze and synthesize the shape of the letters and words correctly and to perceive the details as well as the whole word.

For one very bright youngster who had severe disturbances in figure-ground perception following encephalitis, this method was not sufficiently helpful. Words which intersected each other as shown in Figure 1 were therefore written out for him, at first while he watched, later, before he was permitted to look at them. He learned to solve these "word puzzles," and his reading improved rapidly. Another better known method is the use of color cues in writing; it is easier to analyze a word when the letters are written in different colors. Letters that are pronounced together should be written or printed in the same color, and silent letters, such as the "e" at the end of words, should be presented with stippled lines. As has already been indicated, it is difficult for children with defective figure-ground perception to scan. They should be given much practice in finding particular words or items in a dictionary, glossary, narrative, or table of contents.

Constancy

Children with difficulties in constancy are often made anxious by their inability to depend on their sense data. They may have difficulty in recognizing shapes in general, or they may be able to recognize shapes in one color, size, texture, or context, but fail to recognize the same shapes when presented with different attributes or in different contexts.

FIGURE 1

There should therefore be training in the recognition of shapes of three dimensional objects, presented both actually and pictorially. They should work with form boards, match depicted shapes, and do exercises involving sorting according to shape and size. The teacher must also be sure to present all the words that the child learns in a variety of styles, sizes, and colors. The use of chalk, crayon, a primary typewriter, and words cut from old pre-primers, all presented in both lower case letters and capitals, will provide variety. When the child has learned to identify words presented in various forms, it is usually possible for him to switch from one printed book to another without "forgetting" what he has learned.

Position in Space

Difficulty in the recognition of position in space is a considerable handicap in beginning reading. Many children show a maturational lag in this ability and exercises therefore should be done with whole classes as soon as possible after school entrance—either in kindergarten or first grade. The children should be made aware of directionality whenever possible during the ordinary daily activities, but specific exercises should also be introduced.

One method which has been found most worthwhile is to teach the children the arm movements which are appropriate to directions given by the teacher. When the teacher says "out," for instance, the children should stretch out their arms; when the teacher says "in," the arms are bent in toward the middle of the body; when the teacher says "down," they are stretched downwards, and upwards when the teacher says "up." Then the child stands at the blackboard with a piece of chalk in his hand, turning his face toward the board and doing the same exercises as before. He notices that the movements of his arm and hand cause him to make lines to the right, to the left, up, and down. This enables the teacher to help him, when he learns to write letters or numbers, by telling him the directions his movements should take. To teach the letter "a," for instance, the teacher should mark the starting point with a little cross near the edge of a box (Figure 2). The child is told that he must not transgress the lines of the box. As he draws his letter, the teacher says *"in and around* and *down,"* if he is right handed, or *"out,* and *around* and *down,"* if he is left handed. Children who reverse the letters in a word or digits in a number (e.g., saw-was, 19—91) will overcome the tendency if they learn to stress the first letter or digit as they read or write.

FIGURE 2

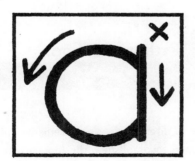

Spatial Relationships

Children with disabilities in the perception of spatial relationships are handi-capped in learning to spell as well as in learning to read. In reading they garble words and have difficulty in visual analysis and synthesis, especially of longer words. Spelling may seem a nearly impossible task. Before reading can be attempted with success, such children should learn to analyze and synthesize a variety of patterns, to work with mazes, copy structures, and reproduce patterns from memory. They improve if the words they are learn-ing are analyzed and the letters written in different colors, as discussed pre-viously. The use of letters of different sizes is often of help also. (4)

Eye Movement

The following techniques have been found helpful for children who have the faulty eye movements which sometimes accompany perceptual disturbances. Cut in a piece of cardboard a "window" just large enough to accommodate a portion of one line of text. Place it where the child is to read, and push it along the line as he reads. This will help him to focus his attention and to progress correctly with his eye movements. Another effective aid is a strip of cardboard with a black mark in the middle which is moved along below the lines in a smooth trailing motion, indicating the words to be read. A trailed pencil can also be used, or a marker as in Figure 3.

FIGURE 3

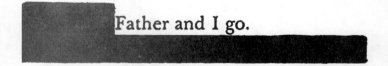

Father and I go.

Some children are able to direct their eye movements quite smoothly along a line, but have difficulty in accomplishing the fast backward movements to the beginning of the line below. These children can be helped if lines are drawn across the page below the rows of print, and slanted lines are drawn from the end of each horizontal line to the beginning of the next. The children are taught to follow the lines quickly with their eyes.

Exercises for eye movements need not be restricted to the reading period alone. At any time, the teacher can require the children to follow the track of objects which she moves from left to right, from their point of view. They should first be required to point at the objects, then follow them with the whole head and finally with the eyes alone.

Training in Auditory Perception

The child with disturbances in visual perception has great difficulty in learning to read if taught by the "sight" method alone. But when phonics are stressed, the child with a deficiency in auditory perception is unable to learn. Teaching should therefore proceed by favoring those methods which emphasize the child's preferred sense modality, but neither method should be used exclusively. Auditory and visual stimuli have to be associated to assure success in reading; and a multi-sensory approach affords children who have difficulties in a sense modality the maximum opportunity to learn to read.

Auditory training should include training in the discrimination of sounds, comparing the intensity of sounds, and perceiving rhythms.

In the first case, the child should be asked to identify and discriminate between sounds made by rubbing, shaking, or hitting a variety of objects or percussion instruments. For instance, the teacher might tap a stick on the table, on a metal plate, or on a glass; or rub blocks together both with and without sandpaper.

In order to help the child compare the intensity of sounds, the teacher can fill matchboxes with varying amounts of paper clips, buttons, or thumb tacks, shake the boxes and require the child to guess which box contains the largest or the least number of tacks. Or small bells may be put on rods and rung, and the child required to estimate the number of bells that he hears. A variety of noise-making materials can be used for similar exercises.[5]

Rhythms should first be presented in a very simple form—two short beats followed by a long beat, for instance—and then made more complicated. Percussion instruments can be used, but exercises involving part or all of the body are preferable, as in clapping, skipping, or hopping. Three running steps and a pause can be repeated, for example, or a skip and three steps, or four running steps and two slow steps, and so on; the more varied the exercises the better.

After initial training in auditory perception along these lines, the focus of auditory training should shift more and more to the sounds and letters of speech.

Practice should be given in differentiating between letters, and it is helpful to provide each child with a chart on which the letters of the alphabet are written. Each letter is marked when the child has learned its name and sound. These letters can then be combined into simple words for the child to read. Attention should at first be directed especially to the beginning and ending sounds in words, and later to the vowels. Words of two or three letters, such as *on, off, add, or, ox, in, it, if, is, tap, mat,* should be used at first, and longer words introduced later. The learning of one syllable words is an aid not only to children with disturbances in auditory perception, but also to those who substitute or transpose letters as they read, because they have difficulty in perceiving figure-ground and/or spatial relationships.[6]

Kinesthetic Reading Methods

The importance of a multisensory approach to reading has already been stressed. In addition to auditory and visual stimuli, kinesthetic and tactile

[5]It has not been found helpful to teach a child to differentiate between musical notes.

[6]It should be mentioned that we have not found it helpful to teach the rules of phonics. We agree with those who state that the exceptions to these results are too many and too confusing. Their emphasis tends to make learning to read an unhappy labor.

stimuli may be used. This is usually done by having the children trace or write the words or letters they are to learn. Children who learn best through kinesthetic stimuli are usually able to write well quite early, so that this does not normally prove a laborious process, but the teacher should note whether a child has poor eye-hand coordination, a tremor, or some other handicap which might make the process arduous. The child handicapped in this way may pay so much attention to the techniques of letter formation that he neglects to pay attention to the meaning of what he writes.

Kinesthetic perception may be strengthened by having the child write words on the blackboard or at his desk with his eyes closed. The teacher guides his hand and says the word while he repeats the kinesthetic pattern, until it is learned and he can reproduce it by himself. This "blind-writing" game is helpful both for the children who have difficulties in remembering what they have learned and for children whose visual perceptual disturbances are so severe that incorrectly perceived visual stimuli interfere with their performance.

Visualization

Training in visualization helps a child to understand what he reads by picturing the subject matter in his mind. For example, when a child reads a passage including the word "hat," he should be asked to imagine how a hat looks. Perhaps later the new word appears in a phrase, "Mary has a blue hat." The teacher may then ask, "Can you see Mary's blue hat?" If the child reads, "Jane walks to school. She walks slowly," the teacher might ask, "Can you imagine how Jane walks? Where did she go? Yes—to school! Imagine how the building looks—maybe like your school"—and so on. The child will also be helped to visualize if the story is discussed, with any unfamiliar word being repeated and defined and picturesque examples given of its use.

Motivation

Motivation plays a role in all learning, but never more than with children with perceptual disturbances, who have usually become discouraged by their continued inexplicable failure to learn. Once a child who is receiving training has started to learn, the experience of success usually provides its own motivation, but up to that point the most basic factor is the child's relationship to his teacher. He should be able to feel that he can trust his teacher to help him; and the relationship should be of such a quality that he should want to please his teacher.

There are other important motivations. It may be of advantage at first to make use of the child's normal egocentric attitude. A young child's interests center about himself, so the text which will interest him most is one which is written about himself. The teacher should compose stories about the child or the class, using the same vocabulary as that employed in the usual beginning readers, and collecting the work for each day into book form. Because much repetition is essential for children with perceptual handicaps, the new words for each day should be listed on the back of the page, and included in the next day's "chapter." The child should read a word correctly on at least three successive days before it is omitted and even then it should be reviewed after an interval. All of the techniques previously discussed should be used in making the book.

It should be emphasized in conclusion, that in teaching children with reading difficulties, variety is important from the point of view of both motivation and providing effective remedial training. Clinical experience has shown that auditory perceptual methods, visual perceptual methods, kinesthetic methods, and methods to help eye movements should be employed together, whenever possible.

SUMMARY

Diagnosis of perceptual disturbances and a test developed for this purpose have been discussed. The importance of a multisensory approach for children who have difficulties with perception in any sense modality has been documented with research findings.

Perceptual training methods (found effective both clinically and in a public school research program) have been described, together with techniques for teaching beginning reading that take perceptual disturbances into account. The importance of motivation has been stressed, and some techniques for enhancing motivation have been described.

Bibliography

1. Frostig, M., Lefever, D., and Whittlessey, J.: DEVELOPMENTAL TEST OF VISUAL PERCEPTION. Consulting Psychologists Press, Palo Alto, 1964.

2. Kephart, N.: THE SLOW LEARNER IN THE CLASSROOM. Charles E. Merrill Books, Columbus, 1960.

3. Radler, D., and Kephart, N.: SUCCESS THROUGH PLAY. Harper, New York, 1962.

4. Strauss, A., and Lehtinen, L.: PSYCHOPATHOLOGY AND EDUCATION OF THE BRAIN INJURED CHILD. Grune and Stratton, New York, 1947.

5. Vernon, M.: THE PSYCHOLOGY OF PERCEPTION. Penguin Books, Baltimore, 1962.

6. Wepman, J.: Auditory Discrimination, Speech, and Reading. ELEM. SCHOOL J., 60: 325-333, 1960.

7. Wepman, J.: Dyslexia: Its Relationship to Language Acquisition and Concept Formation. Money, J. (ed.). READING DISABILITY: PROGRESS AND RESEARCH NEEDS IN DYSLEXIA. The Johns Hopkins Press, Baltimore, 1962.

8. Frostig, M., and Horne, D.: THE FROSTIG PROGRAM FOR THE DEVELOPMENT OF VISUAL PERCEPTION. Follett Publishing Co., Chicago, 1964.

STUDY QUESTIONS

1. What is Frostig's position regarding teaching to the child's strengths or to his weaknesses?

2. If you were interested in raising children's scores in the Developmental Test of Visual Perception, what kind of activities would you teach the children? Be specific. If you were interested in increasing reading test scores, what activities would you suggest? Would the reading activities you suggest for children who have visual perceptual problems be different from ones suggested for those who do not?

3. What is Frostig's position regarding the role of physical (as contrasted to pencil-and-paper) activities?

12: THE EFFICACY OF AN AUDITORY AND A VISUAL METHOD OF FIRST-GRADE READING INSTRUCTION WITH AUDITORY AND VISUAL LEARNERS

Barbara D. Bateman

Bateman's study attempts to answer the question of whether initial reading instruction should be geared to the child's strong or weak learning modalities. Some authorities recommend teaching to the strengths, and others urge teaching to the weaknesses. The answer suggested by this study is that neither strategy can be recommended. The author contends that the teaching strategies should derive from the task to be learned, not from the child who is to learn it.

B. D. B.

Reprinted with permission from COLLEGE OF EDUCATION CURRICULUM BULLETIN, 1967, 23:278, Eugene, Oregon: University of Oregon, pp. 6-14.

Most educators probably agree with the proposition that reading instruction ideally should be geared to individual children's learning style. However, most attempts to do this kind of matching of method and child have actually centered on flexibility in planning for varying *rates* of learning and for interests rather than for *styles* of learning. Within regular classrooms, the basic method of teaching—i.e., of presenting the process of reading, has not been individualized. In contrast, some remedial teachers do, however, use radically different methods—e.g., kinesthetic, visual, phonics—with different children.

In a recent study of reading disabilities in children, de Hirsch, Jansky, and Langford (1966) compared relative strength in visual and auditory perceptual areas. All of the children rated as superior visual-perceptual subjects (N=3) in kindergarten achieved high scores on reading tests at the end of second grade, but of the superior auditory-perceptual children (N=7) only those who had received intensive phonic training were able to read satisfactorily. The authors concluded, therefore, that teaching methods should to a large extent be determined by modality strength and weakness. Conversely, Harris (1965) failed to find any significant association between the specific teaching method used and the presumed aptitude for that method. In addition to visual and auditory methods and aptitudes, he also explored kinesthetic patterns.

The basic purpose of this study was to explore the efficacy of an auditory approach to first-grade reading compared to a visual approach, both when children were homogeneously grouped by preferred learning modality (auditory or visual) and when they were not so grouped.

Subjects and Procedures

This study was initiated by the Highland Park, Illinois, school system[1] as part of its program to evaluate and continually improve first-grade reading instruction.

Portions of this material were presented at the International Reading Association Convention, Seattle, Washington, May, 1967, and are reproduced with permission of the International Reading Association.

[1]The excellent cooperation and assistance of the entire Highland Park school system including the members of the school board, the administration, the kindergarten and

In the spring of the year, eight kindergarten classes were given the Detroit Group Intelligence Scale and the Metropolitan Reading Readiness Test. In addition, the Illinois Test of Psycholinguistic Abilities (ITPA) was administered to the children in four of the classes.

On the basis of these test results the children were assigned to their first-grade classes. The four classes which were not administered the ITPA were designated as non-placement classes. Two of these non-placement classes received auditory method reading instruction and the other two received visual method instruction. These non-placement children were assigned to their first-grade classrooms in the usual manner utilized by the school system—an informal "sorting process" in which an effort is made to have all classes heterogeneous and similar to each other on CA and IQ and to control boy/girl ratio within each class. The classes were not known to differ from each other in any respect other than method of reading instruction employed by the teacher. There were no significant differences among the four classes on IQ, MA, or total reading readiness.

Each child in the other four classes—the placement classes—was labelled an "auditory" or a "visual" subject on the basis of his performance on the two ITPA subtests of memory which measure automatic-sequential language abilities and have been found to correlate with reading. The total group of placement children (N=87) was stronger in auditory memory (auditory-vocal sequential, subtest #8), where the mean language age was 80.75 months, than in visual memory (visual-motor sequential, subtest #9), where the mean language age was 71.30 months. The "typical" child in this group thus scored 9 months higher on auditory memory than on visual memory. The difference was used as the base line in the determination of whether a child was labelled "auditory" or "visual." If his auditory memory score exceeded

first-grade teachers, the guidance department, and especially Mr. Allen Trevor, Principal of Sherwood School, and Miss Sue Hunt, Director of Guidance Services, is gratefully acknowledged. Thanks are also due to the staff of the University of Illinois' Institute for Research on Exceptional Children who provided guidance, time, and personnel for all individual testing. Special thanks go to Sr. Joanne Marie, O.S.F., Ph.D., Cardinal Stritch College, for her assistance in the preparation of this paper, and to Miss Janis Wetherell, University of Illinois, for the statistical analyses.

his visual memory score by more than 9 months, he was designated an auditory subject and if it exceeded the visual by less than 9 months he was a visual subject. There were some borderline cases which were labelled on the basis of the total profile (comprised of four additional auditory tests and three additional visual tests).

Many of the children in the auditory group showed only a very slight preference for the auditory modality, and the same was naturally true in the visual group. But all the strong preference children were clearly in their appropriate group. The inclusion of "borderline" subjects has the effect of minimizing obtained differences.

Table 1 shows the constitution of all eight classes.

TABLE 1. EIGHT CLASSES

Tests given in Kdgtn.	Placement Classes	Subjects	Method	N	$\overline{IQ}$
Group IQ	1 ($A_S A_M$)	Aud.	Aud.	24	126.0
Reading Readiness	2 ($V_S A_M$)	Vis.	Aud.	24	124.7
	3 ($A_S V_M$)	Aud.	Vis.	20	124.8
ITPA	4 ($V_S V_M$)	Vis.	Vis.	<u>19</u>	126.2
				87	
	Non-Placement Classes				
Group IQ	5 (A-V$_S$, A_{M1})	Aud. & Vis.	Aud.	25	124.3
Reading Readiness	6 (A-V$_S$, A_{M2})	Aud. & Vis.	Aud.	23	127.0
	7 (A-V$_S$, V_{M1})	Aud. & Vis.	Vis.	25	121.6
	8 (A-V$_S$, V_{M2})	Aud. & Vis.	Vis.	<u>22</u>	125.6
				95	

Profile 1 shows the mean ITPA scores of the two Placement Classes of auditory subjects (N=44) and the two Placement Classes of visual subjects (N=43). The greatest differences occur in auditory memory and visual memory since these subtests were the bases on which the children were divided. However, the auditory subjects' mean score was slightly higher on all five auditory subtests and the visual subjects' score was higher on the four visual subtests.

PROFILE 1. ITPA PERFORMANCE OF AUDITORY (N=44) & VISUAL (N=43) SUBJECTS

	REPRESENTATIONAL LEVEL						AUTOMATIC-SEQUENTIAL		
	Decoding		Association		Encoding		Automatic	Sequential	
	1	2	3	4	5	6	7	8	9
CA	Auditory	Visual	Auditory Vocal	Visual Motor	Vocal	Motor	Auditory Vocal	Auditory Vocal	Visual Motor
9-0									
8-6									
8-0									
7-6									
7-0									
6-6									
6-0									
5-6									
5-0									
4-6									
4-0									
3-6									
3-0									
2-6									

—— Aud. 87.8 81.5 88.2 76.5 84.6 80.4 83.4 90.9 66.9 Months

- - - Vis. 87.0 82.4 84.7 81.1 82.7 82.8 82.7 70.6 75.7 Months

237

The auditory method classes utilized the Lippincott beginning program and the visual method classes used the Scott, Foresman series. None of the teachers of the placement groups was told whether his class was composed of auditory or of visual subjects (the two auditory-method teachers guessed correctly which group they had within the first few weeks of school, but this was not confirmed for them). All eight first-grade teachers in the study attended in-service orientation sessions in which the use of only those supplementary reading materials and techniques consistent with the basic approach used in that classroom (auditory or visual) was emphasized and discussed.

Only one instance of "contamination" was discovered in which a teacher of a non-placement visual method class employed some supplementary auditory materials.

At the end of first grade the Gates Primary Word Recognition and Paragraph Reading tests were administered to all eight classes. Each pupil's scores on these two tests were averaged to obtain his reading grade. A spelling test (author-constructed) consisting of 12 words and 6 nonsense words was also administered to all subjects.

Results—Non-Placement Classes

The results obtained are presented in three sections: 1) a comparison of the auditory and visual methods in the non-placement classes; 2) a comparison of the auditory and visual methods with auditory and visual subjects; 3) a comparison of good and poor readers from the placement classes. Summary data for the non-placement classes are presented in Table 2.

The 2 point IQ difference between the combined auditory method classes (N=48) and visual method classes (N=47) was not significant. The auditory method was significantly superior (t=2.17, p<.05) to the visual method. The mean reading achievement of the children in the auditory classes was 3 1/3 months higher than in the visual classes.

The same clear superiority of the auditory method over the visual is seen in the spelling scores as presented in Table 3.

TABLE 2. NON-PLACEMENT CLASSES (N=95) READING AND SPELLING ACHIEVEMENT

	N	Class Subjects - Method		IQ	Average Rdg. Grade X̄	SD	Spelling X̄ No. Right
	25	A-V,	A_{M1}	124.3	3.34	1.14	7.04
	23	A-V,	A_{M2}	127.0	3.27	.57	6.57
Total	48	Auditory	Method	125.6	3.31	.91	6.81
	25	A-V,	V_{M1}	121.6	2.95	.51	2.88
	22	A-V,	V_{M2}	125.6	3.00	.53	2.65
Total	47	Visual	Method	123.5	2.98	.52	2.77

TABLE 3. NON-PLACEMENT CLASSES SPELLING ACHIEVEMENT

Spelling Score	Auditory Method Classes	Visual Method Classes
0-5 words right	14 (29%)	39 (83%)
6+ words right	34 (71%)	8 (17%)
N	48	47

The above data reveal that when children were heterogeneously grouped without regard to preferred learning modality, the auditory method of instruction produced results significantly superior to those of the visual method in both reading and spelling.

Results—Placement Classes

Analysis of variance (two-way fixed effects model) of reading achievement revealed that for the four placement classes the auditory method was significantly superior to the visual method (F = 16.38, 1 df, p < .01) and that the auditory subjects were significantly superior to the visual subjects (F = 9.28, 1 df, p < .01). Method accounted for 14 per cent of the variance and subjects for 7 per cent. There was no interaction between subject and method (F = 1.62, NS). Table 4 summarizes reading and spelling achievement of the four placement classes.

TABLE 4. PLACEMENT CLASSES READING AND SPELLING ACHIEVEMENT

N	Placement Classes Subjects - Method		IQ	Average Rdg. Grade X	SD	Spelling X No. Right
24	A	A	126.0	3.62	.37	11.29
24	V	A	124.7	3.43	.38	7.92
20	A	V	124.8	3.34	.59	7.85
19	V	V	126.2	2.90	.51	1.79

The superiority of the A_SA_M group and the poorer performance of the V_SV_M group in reading are apparent.

Analysis of variance of spelling scores revealed the auditory subjects were superior to the visual subjects (F = 49.4, 1 df, p < .01) and the auditory method was superior to the visual method (F = 42.7, 1 df, p < .01). Method accounted for 24 per cent of the variance and subjects for 28 per cent. Again, there was no interaction between subject and method (F = 2.0, 1 df, NS).

Good Readers versus Poor Readers

The children in the placement classes who scored at the 3.9 grade level or above were designated "good" readers and those who scored below 2.9 grade level were "poor" readers. These highly arbitrary cutoffs were dictated by the necessity of choosing points which would yield groups of a size suitable for study.

Of the sixteen good readers, 14 had received the auditory method and only 2 the visual method. Of the 18 poor readers, 16 were visual subjects, 12 of whom had received the visual method.

The clear superiority of the auditory method over the visual and the less marked superiority of the auditory subjects (as found in the analysis of variance) are both apparent in Table 5.

TABLE 5. CLASS PLACEMENT OF GOOD AND POOR READERS

	N	A_SA_M	A_SV_M	V_SA_M	V_SV_M	A_S	V_S	A_M	V_M
Good	16	10	2	4	0	12	4	14	2
Poor	18	1	4	1	12	5	13	2	16

The mean IQ of the good readers was 129.6 compared to 120.2 for the poor readers. Table 6 shows the IQ breakdown by preferred modality.

TABLE 6. IQ OF GOOD AND POOR READERS

	N	A_S	V_S	T
Good	16	127.8	135.0	129.6
Poor	18	111.4	123.6	120.2

The visual subjects who were good readers were substantially above the average IQ for the total group, while the auditory subjects who were poor readers were appreciably below the group mean in intelligence. These data again confirm the earlier observation that children who prefer the visual modality are handicapped, relative to those who prefer the auditory modality, in reading. An interesting possibility is suggested—did the few visual subjects who became "good" readers by the end of first-grade also become more auditorily oriented?

When the ITPA profiles of the 16 good readers and 18 poor readers were plotted (see Profile 2) it was immediately apparent that the psycholinguistic patterns were different in shape as well as in level. The level difference was to be expected since the IQs and MAs of the good readers were higher than those of the poor readers. The good readers were predominantly auditory subjects (12 of 16) so their highly auditory profile is not unexpected. However, the poor readers were predominantly visual subjects (13 of 18) but their profile is not predominantly visual. Profile 1, presented earlier, shows that the mean difference between the total group of auditory subjects and the total group of visual subjects on auditory-vocal automatic is less than one month. Yet on Profile 2 it is 15 months. Also, Profile 1 shows only a 2-month superiority of the auditory subjects in vocal encoding, while the good readers (Profile 2) are 15 months higher than the poor readers. This suggests that, given good auditory memory, other auditory-vocal skills (incidental verbal learning and vocal expression) may play a more important role in reading than previous ITPA studies have indicated.

The poor readers' ITPA profile differs from their "parent" visual group in that they show a peak in motor encoding and are below the total visual group in visual memory. The low visual memory might be related to the presence of the 5 auditory subjects in the poor reader group. But this assumption poses a difficulty in accounting for the strong showing of the poor readers in motor encoding which is a visual-motor test. The high motor encoding score of the poor reader does suggest that some very active (hyperactive?), "acting-out" children may have difficulty adjusting to the auditory-vocal world of reading.

The unexpected finding that the A_SA_M group produced 10 good readers and only 1 poor reader, while the V_SV_M group had 12 poor and no good readers, has precluded the kind of inter-group comparisons of good and poor readers that would have been most meaningful, in regard to psycholinguistic abilities.

There was no overlap whatever between the distribution of spelling scores of the good readers ($\overline{X}$ = 12.3 words correct) and the poor readers ($\overline{X}$ = 2.2 words correct).

PROFILE 2. ITPA PERFORMANCE OF GOOD (N=16) AND POOR (N=18) READERS

CA	REPRESENTATIONAL LEVEL						AUTOMATIC-SEQUENTIAL		
	Decoding		Association		Encoding		Automatic	Sequential	
	1	2	3	4	5	6	7	8	9
	Auditory	Visual	Auditory Vocal	Visual Motor	Vocal	Motor	Auditory Vocal	Auditory Vocal	Visual Motor

ood $\overline{IQ}$ 129.6
oor $\overline{IQ}$ 120.2

— Good	16	91.6	82.8	89.2	82.6	93.1	79.8	92.5	91.9	76.8	Months
- - Poor	18	84.7	81.7	82.6	79.9	78.2	83.8	77.3	75.1	73.6	Months

Summary and Discussion

The major findings of this study may be very simply stated: the auditory method of reading instruction was superior to the visual method for both reading and spelling; the auditory-modality-preferred subjects were superior in both reading and spelling to the visual-modality-preferred subjects; and there was no interaction between subjects' preferred modality and the method of instruction used.

Within the fields of remedial and corrective reading one of the recurring issues centers on whether instruction should be geared to the child's pattern of cognitive strengths or to his weaknesses. It was hoped that this study might provide evidence on this point as two groups ($A_S A_M$ and $V_S V_M$) were taught to their strengths and two groups ($A_S V_M$ and $V_S A_M$) to their weaknesses. However, one of the strength groups was significantly superior ($A_S A_M$) to all other groups and the other ($V_S V_M$) was significantly inferior. The weakness groups ($A_S V_M$ and $V_S A_M$) were intermediate in results produced and were highly similar to the non-placement classes. One way to talk about these results is to say that it is not enough to ask, "Should we teach to the child's strengths or his weaknesses," but that we must specify about which child we are asking. The data from this study suggest the answer would then be to teach to his strengths if he is an auditory learner or to his weakness if he is a visual learner. However, a much simpler way of stating all this is to say that the auditory method is superior, regardless the child's own pattern of learning.

It is, of course, possible that this may be true for a homogeneous, above-average intelligence group such as this, and still not be true for the extreme cases found in a reading disability population.

The close correspondence found between reading and spelling achievement was striking and possibly supportive of the observation that both reading and spelling are basically processes of making sound-symbol associations.

The findings of this study support those of Harris (1965) who found no interaction between subject and method and those of Bliesmer and Yarborough (1965) who compared the effectiveness of 10 beginning first-grade programs of reading, including Lippincott and Scott, Foresman and found the Lippincott program was significantly superior to the Scott, Foresman on every measure of reading employed (Stanford Achievement Tests subtests of Word Reading, Paragraph Meaning, Vocabulary, Spelling, and Word Study Skills). The 484 children included in this study were from middle and lower socio-economic levels, in contrast to the higher level of the present investigation. Bliesmer and Yarborough use the description "synthetic approach, in which sound-symbol relationships (letter sounds) are taught before words are taught" to designate what the present study called "auditory method" and they use "analytic approach of going from sight words to sounds" to describe what this study called "visual method." In the Bliesmer-Yarborough study the four "auditory methods" (including Lippincott) were all significantly superior to the three "visual methods" (including Scott, Foresman).

The evidence appears to be mounting that reading is basically a sound-symbol association process and should perhaps be taught to all children as such. The assumption has often been made by many (including the writer) that some kind of matching procedure in which instruction is differentially geared to individual children, replete with their individual differences, must be better than an arbitrary application of one method to all children. However, it is just possible that our lack of knowledge of adequate or best methods of teaching given set of behaviors such as reading has made this assumption too easy.

Limitations of the Present Study and Suggestions for Further Research

One of the major limitations of this study is that the sample was drawn entirely from a high socio-economic level. The general ability and achievement level was unusually high (e.g., only one child in the entire sample had a group IQ of below 100) and it is somewhat ironic to describe a first-grader who reads at a 9 grade level as a "poor" reader! However, it should not be overlooked that the major findings of this study in regard to the superiority of the auditory method have also been obtained on low and middle socio-economic level children (Bliesmer and Yarborough, 1965).

The second major limitation appeared only when the results were available—namely, the auditory method produced only two poor readers while the visual method produced only two good readers, thus making many planned analyses impossible.

This study yielded many data which remain unanalyzed, and also suggests further data gathering. Examples of possible analyses include: a) correlational studies including both predictive and content validity studies employing the subtests of the ITPA, the Detroit Group Intelligence Scale, and the Metropolitan Reading Readiness Tests; b) redefinition of good and poor readers to allow comparisons of those two groups within each modality preference; c) ITPA retest of good and poor readers to check for any changes in preferred modality, as a function of method of instruction employed.

References

Bliesmer, E. P. and Yarborough, Betty H. "A Comparison of Ten Different Beginning Reading Programs in First Grade." PHI DELTA KAPPAN 46 (June, 1965), 10:500-504.

De Hirsch, Katrina; Jansky, Jeanette J.; and Langford, W. S. PREDICTING READING FAILURE: A PRELIMINARY STUDY. New York: Harper & Row, 19 144 pp.

Harris, A. J. "Individualizing First-Grade Reading According to Specific Lear Aptitudes." Office of Research and Evaluation, Division of Teacher Educatio City University of New York, (April, 1965). Mimeographed, 12 pp.

STUDY QUESTIONS

1. What does this study suggest about teaching to the strengths versus teaching to the weaknesses?

2. Why was one program described as "auditory" and the other as "visual?"

3. Explain in your own words what the author means by the suggestion that "lack of knowledge of adequate teaching procedures has made too easy the assumption of efficacy in matching child and technique."

13: STRATEGIES OF INTERVENTION IN THE SPECTRUM OF DEFECTS IN SPECIFIC READING DISABILITY

Archie A. Silver
Rosa A. Hagin

Silver and Hagin relate certain teaching strategies both to the nature of the reading process and to the patterns of perceptual strengths and weaknesses revealed by the child with reading problems. The background of the authors' position regarding the desirability of teaching to the weaknesses is both interesting and important. The stimulation of deficit perceptual areas appears very promising and will be of substantial interest to clinicians and teachers.

    B. D. B.

Reprinted with permission of the authors and publisher from BULLETIN OF THE ORTON SOCIETY, 1967, 17, 39-46.

Because defects can occur with the encoding, decoding, and associative aspects of language, the manifestations of specific reading disability can vary widely among children. This implies that the treatment approaches utilized with these children will also vary, and that " ready made" programs will succeed only to the extent that they coincide with a child's unique pattern of assets and deficits.

This paper will:
1) describe a theoretical progression of skills involved in reading.
2) relate some strategies of intervention with learning disabilities to this progression.
3) present some data concerning one type of intervention, perceptual stimulation, which is the subject of an investigation now under way at New York University, School of Medicine.

The child with specific reading disability is one who, despite adequate intelligence, intact senses, conventional instruction, and normal motivation, has difficulty in learning to read. To help understand what went wrong, it is helpful to break down the reading process in terms of the behavior responses required. This has been done in the following chart which is a theoretical job analysis of the process of learning to read:

Perceptual Skills	Word Recognition	Getting Meanings	Study Skills
Visual Perception	"Sight" Words	Words	Location
Auditory Perception	Context Cues	Factual	Selection
L-R Orientation	Phonic Cues	Comprehension	Organization
Figure-Background-Perception	Structural Cues	Interpretation	Retention

Among the skills in visual perception are: 1) the discrimination of likenesses and differences in complicated asymmetric forms, 2) the recognition of these forms in correct orientation in two-dimensional space, 3) the organization or "chunking" into letter groups. Reading also requires auditory skills: the discrimination and matching of sounds, the blending of isolated sounds so that a recognizable word results, and the accurate sequencing of sounds in time.

Children in our project surprise their teachers with the auditory difficulties they present. For example, one bright ten-year-old told his teacher that he preferred "tambourines to oranges because they are easier to peel." Another demonstrated a variation on sequencing by observing that "Although Columbus is given credit for discovering America, this is not necesselery so."

To read English, the child must also accept the arbitrary convention of left to right progression. Though at age five or six he may not have a name for the sides, he must learn which is "the side that things begin on" and "the direction in which the lines go." The child must also learn to deal with figure and background because reading involves words in context. He must learn to attend to words or parts of words along a line, to inhibit attention to embedding stimuli, and to make an accurate return sweep to the succeeding line as he comes to the end of a line.

Word recognition may involve the use of several methods of decoding. Words may be recognized on "sight" which is probably a response to such signal cues as letter combinations, downstrokes, and tall letters. Another method of word recognition is the use of context cues, the guessing of what makes sense in terms of the ideas in the content and the grammatical conventions of the language. Further along in the reading process, the child begins to use phonic cues, either by drawing his own conclusions about the letter code or by applying rules which have been taught. Of course, in English these principles are usually qualified by a number of exceptions, so that the child must use these skills with what Gibson has termed "a set for diversity." (2) Finally, as his reading skills develop, the child learns to use such word structure cues as compounds, prefixes, suffixes.

Basic in the getting of meanings is a rich oral vocabulary. This goes beyond the vague definitions which may be adequate for the concrete operations of daily life. Reading requires the child to select from a range of multiple definitions the exact meaning implicit in the context.

The study skills area is one in which reading becomes a tool for acquiring information. It is in this area that problems of sequencing again become apparent for the specific language disability; here not so much as a perceptual, but as a conceptual activity. The locating aspect of the study skills requires the child to retrieve an element within a sequence, a skill which one might take for granted unless one has observed the difficulties reading disability children frequently have with it. We find bright children in our work who begin paging at the front of the dictionary to find a word beginning with T, and others who are not quite sure whether Thursday comes before or after Friday until they have repeated the whole sequence. Selection, because it involves both sequencing and figure and background relationships, may also offer hazards for reading disability children. Most interesting of all to us are the organizational problems which these children have. We find children who have learned to "read" in the conventional sense of decoding and comprehending, but who have great difficulty applying what they read because they cannot organize ideas into logical sequences. This problem may be manifested by the college student who writes his term papers with a "scissors and paste" technique, lifting passages from books and inserting them into the structure provided by a brief textbook treatment of his topic. In the same way, younger children may find it difficult to translate reading content into behavior responses, as for example with a recipe, even though they may have "understood" the material well enough to earn a perfect score with multiple questions based on the content.

Although one can talk about these behaviors one at a time and organize them in a chart, they are not learned in this logical fashion. They are interrelated to the extent that one could draw many arrows to show how one kind of behavior facilitates another. To illustrate this interrelatedness, we might cite the example of a boy who read the sentence:

> "In the pocketbook was one cent."

in the following fashion:

> "In the pocketbook was one pen—no, in the pocketbook was one Kent—what's a kent?—s—oh—In the pocketbook was one cent!"

On the first trial he depended upon language cues and judicious use of picture cues as well. Then he realized that *penny* was too long a word to be written c-e-n-t and so he shifted to phonics. The generalization of the soft *c* followed by *e* or *i* eluded him, but he realized that *Kent* was incorrect because it was meaningless. He switched to a context cue provided by the word pocketbook and, with a combination of phonics and context, unlocked the word.

Teaching often consists of isolating and giving practice with fragments of these behaviors of the job analysis. Not only must one isolate and teach mastery of these skills, but one must also encourage a set for diversity so that the child can draw upon those skills which are appropriate for a task, rather than plodding along with a set of behaviors which, although they may have been mastered thoroughly, are inappropriate. An illustration of this kind of response is seen with a youngster who first came to us for evaluation at age five. He had numerous perceptual problems except in the auditory modality and a meagre and inexact oral vocabulary. Despite recommendations that the formal teaching of reading be delayed, instruction with the Initial Teaching Alphabet (which depends upon phonic regularity) was begun upon his entry into grade one. This boy learned to decode very well with this medium, for when he came back for reevaluation at age 7, he was able to score at the 7th grade level on an oral reading test. However, his comprehension of even very easy and interesting material was so limited that he was unable to score on standardized tests of reading comprehension or to explain what he had just read aloud without error. It seemed to us that he had missed out on very basic foundations for reading and that this decoding ability was a splinter skill with little practical utility. Such an approach for this child emphasized only one aspect of one area of the job analysis and neglected more basic areas of deficiency in perception and meanings.

The point in the job analysis at which one chooses to intervene depends upon one's beliefs about the etiology of reading disability in general, and the specific diagnostic picture of the child one is to teach. One may believe that reading disability is a kind of maladaptive behavior and thus one must find motivation (usually through a book that the child really wants to read) so that all problems will disappear. This approach begins by asking the child what he is interested in and then locating that one book, brightly colored, new and shiny—about spacemen, cowboys, or pro football. The tutor prepares challenging discussion questions beforehand, and the lesson starts with optimism. If the child is a specific language disability (and the chances are about 9 in 10 in our population that he *is,* if he is seriously retarded in reading and has normal intelligence), perceptual and associative problems will soon appear. Because no provision has been made for these aspects of the reading process, the youngster will plod through his bright and interesting book, calling *was saw,* puzzling over *b* and *d,* forgetting the phonemes for the graphemes v and h, missing lines in the return sweeps. The tutor will work harder and harder trying to give contextual cues. Finally he will give up and merely "tell" the boy the words he doesn't know. He may decide to read aloud "to give the pupil practice with oral language" or he may discard the book for one of the commercial games "to build rapport." As can be imagined, the prognosis is guarded if one intervenes in this fashion with a specific language disability.

Another type of intervention is the "homework helper" whose assistance with school assignments is directed to the study skills and meaning areas of our job analysis. Although this approach may be appropriate with children who have been inadequately taught for whatever environmental reasons, this kind of intervention does not touch the basic problems of specific reading disability. Thus, although the child may get some emotional support from these sessions, he will not learn to read in the sense that this job analysis represents reading.

The corrective reading programs in many schools address themselves to the comprehension aspects of reading and deal with word recognition only as it relates to the practice material and with perception not at all. Practice material is presented to the children in the form of workbooks, drill pads, or kits. The pupils read the material to themselves and demonstrate their "comprehension" through the selection of multiple choice answers. The effectiveness of this type of intervention depends not only upon the quality of the materials used and the learner's ability to work for himself, but also upon the criteria for the selection of students, for this program, too, does not deal with the basic defects of specific reading disability.

Special remedial programs have, for some time, intervened at the word recognition area of the job analysis. Because these programs are often clinically oriented, there is provision for some diagnostic study and some awareness of perceptual defects in the children. Two approaches are seen: one is the attempt to bombard the child with all kinds of sensory stimuli (the VAKT and the Fernald tracing techniques are examples currently in use); another is to identify the child's intact perceptual channels and to choose a teaching approach which exploits these high points (e.g., to teach phonics to children with good auditory discrimination or to teach a sight approach to children who have been called "good visualizers"). Our early work followed this "intact channels" approach. However, follow-up study of children taught during 1949-1951 led us to reexamine our assumptions about the retraining of children with specific reading disabilities.

In 1961-1962 it was possible to reexamine patients ten to twelve years after completion of our work with them. These follow-up studies are reported in detail elsewhere. (9)

Our neurological and perceptual assessment of these patients showed the tenacity of perceptual deficits which could be detected despite adequate educational, vocational, and social functioning. Although there was improvement in reading in these patients, it was not as great as might be expected from the levels of intellectual functioning they demonstrated. Furthermore, it was the adequate readers who showed the greatest improvement in perception, while it was the inadequate readers in whom perceptual problems persisted.

These studies suggested the need for departure from established training procedure. We chose to intervene directly (11) with perception in order to learn:
1) the effect of stimulation of deficit areas upon perception;
2) the effect of perceptual stimulation on reading and spelling achievement;
3) the effect of perceptual stimulation on cerebral dominance for language.

254

We are nearing completion of a study in which we have devised and tested methods of perceptual stimulation. (11) This study utilizes a crossover design in which each subject serves as his own control with contrasting treatments of perceptual stimulation given in fifty individual sessions twice weekly (as the experimental condition) and fifty contact sessions utilizing individual teaching from a basal reading series (as the control condition). Training is planned to focus upon the deficit perceptual areas which our clinical evaluation has revealed. Work is directed toward improving perception through training 1) with a recognition-discrimination stage; 2) with a copying stage; 3) with a recall stage. Techniques are directed toward one perceptual modality at a time, insofar as possible, before the child attempts intermodal tasks, or attempts to relate language and perception.

We have completed three years of this four-year study of intervention in the perceptual areas of the job analysis. Although final conclusions must await completion of the study in 1968, our impressions from case material as well as preliminary views of the data suggest that perceptual stimulation is important in the retraining of children with specific reading disabilities. However, we are also persuaded that retraining involves more than teaching children to draw better Benders or not to say that they eat "tambourines," "necesselery." The nature of the defects and the changes that have occurred with training have led us to consider the possibility of an underlying organizing principle, manifested in perception and related to the development of language, which might be basic in acquiring these symbolic behaviors. Evidence suggests that this principle is the neurological organization corresponding to cerebral dominance for language.

Although there are many unanswered questions about this brain mechanism, a substantial neurological literature (6, 12) has described the language defects which accompany its disturbance. As yet we do not know how cerebral dominance is established in children, or how to determine it for sure without the use of surgical procedures. A number of tests are being used to infer the dominant side for language. Kimura (4) has used the Broadbent technique of dichotic auditory presentation of digits; McFie (5) has used the phi-phenomenon; Barton, Goodglass and Shai (1) have used tachistoscopic presentation of stimuli

to the visual fields. In our own work we have utilized the Extension Test
which is based upon the observation of Paul Schilder (3, 7) that when the
eyes are closed and the arms extended at shoulder level parallel to each other
and to the floor, one arm will be higher than the other. In normal readers
the elevated arm usually corresponds to the hand used for writing; in children
with severe reading disability the extended arm may be opposite from that
used for writing or neither arm may be elevated. Results with this measure
have been described in detail elsewhere. (10) We suggest that the elevated
extremity is the one which has the greater muscle tone and hence is an expression of cerebral dominance for language. The abnormal responses suggest
to us that a clearcut cerebral pattern for language has not been established.
Because 91% of the children in our experimental population initially demonstrated abnormal responses on the Extension Test, we have been interested in
results on retesting. Retest data show that in a significant number of cases
improvement on the extension test occurred following the perceptual training
phase of the experiment at a level exceeding chance when evaluated by
McNemar's Test for the Significance of Changes: (8)

Subjects Showing Improvement on the Extension Test

	%	x^2	p
During Perceptual Stimulation Phase	66	11.7	.001
During Control Phase	18		n.s.

This improvement occurred at a level exceeding chance both in subjects for
whom the perceptual stimulation phase came first (p = .001) and in subjects
whose perceptual stimulation phase followed the control phase (p = .03).

When results of the Extension Test were related to oral reading scores, we
found that subjects who had shown improvement on the Extension Test
tended to demonstrate significant gains in reading (greater than .5 of a grade)
more consistently than those who did not show such changes:

Subjects Showing Significant Gains in Reading

	%	x^2	p
Subjects showing improvement on Extension Test	79	17.05	.001
Subjects showing no improvement on Extension Test	56	3.27	n.s.

It is important to emphasize the tentative nature of these findings and to avoid unwarranted generalizations. We do, however, permit ourselves some cautious optimism concerning both the practical and theoretical validity of intervention by stimulation of deficits in the perceptual areas with children with specific reading disability.

To Summarize:

A job analysis of the behaviors involved in learning to read is proposed. Four interrelated areas (perceptual skills, word recognition, getting meanings, and study skills) comprise this job analysis. Teaching is seen as intervention at some point in the job analysis in order to give practice with various aspects of these behaviors. Current strategies of intervention have been considered in relation to the spectrum of defects in specific reading disability. Preliminary data concerning changes associated with one experiment in intervention, stimulation of deficit perceptual areas, have been presented. These data suggest that there may be an underlying principle, the neurological organization corresponding to cerebral dominance for language, which is basic to the acquisition of the symbolic behavior required in learning to read.

References

1. Barton, M. H., Goodglass, H., and Shai, A. 1965. Differential recognition of tachistoscopically presented English and Hebrew words in right and left visual fields. PERCEPT. MOT. SKILLS . 21:431-437.

2. Gibson, E. J. 1965. Learning to read. BULLETIN OF THE ORTON SOCIETY. 15:32-48. Reprinted from SCIENCE, V148:No. 3673 (21 May, 1965).

3. Hoff, H. and Schilder, P. 1927. DIE LAGE REFLEXE DES MENSCHEN. Springer, Berlin, Germany.

4. Kimura, D. 1961. Cerebral dominance and the perception of verbal stimuli. CANAD. J. PSYCHOL. 15:166-171.

5. McFie, J. 1952. Cerebral Dominance in cases of reading disability. JOUR. NEUROL. NEUROSURG. AND PSYCHIATRY. 15:194-199.

6. Mountcastle, V. B. 1962. INTERHEMISPHERIC RELATIONS AND CEREBRAL DOMINANCE. Johns Hopkins Press. Baltimore, Maryland.

7. Schilder, P. 1935. IMAGE AND APPEARANCE OF THE HUMAN BODY. Paul, Trench and Tubner, London, England.

8. Siegel, S. 1956. NONPARAMETRIC STATISTICS FOR THE BEHAVIORAL SCIENCES. McGraw-Hill. New York, N. Y.

9. Silver, A. A. and Hagin, R. 1964. Specific reading disability—follow-up studies, AM. JOUR. ORTHO. 35:95-102.

10. Silver, A. A. and Hagin, R. 1967. Specific reading disability: an approach to diagnosis and treatment. JOUR. OF SPECIAL EDUCATION. Winter, 1967.

11. Silver, A. A., Hagin, R., and Hersh, M. 1965. Specific reading disability: teaching through stimulation of deficit perceptual areas. AM. JOUR. ORTHO. 38 (July, 1967).

12. Zangwill, O. L. 1960. CEREBRAL DOMINANCE AND ITS RELATION TO PSYCHOLOGICAL FUNCTIONING. Oliver and Boyd, London, England.

STUDY QUESTIONS

1. Why is the prognosis guarded when "motivation remediation," "homework helpers," or "comprehension emphasis" programs are used with children who have specific reading disability?

2. Why did Silver and Hagin reject their early approach to retraining children with specific reading disabilities?

3. Distinguish between multi-sensory and intact-modality approaches.

4. Compare the tentative conclusions reached by Silver and Hagin with those of Kass regarding the nature of the "underlying organizing principle" of language behaviors.

5. What is the Extension Test? What is it used for?

14: READING EXPECTANCY FROM DISABLED LEARNERS

John McLeod

McLeod discusses a question and problem of real concern to those
who must make decisions about which children are to be provided
with remedial reading help and when such service should be terminated. Often, IQ is used in determining the expected reading level
for a given child. This widespread practice may not be as valid as
we would like.

B. D. B.

───────
eprinted with permission of the author and publisher from JOURNAL OF LEARNING
ᴵSABILITIES, 1968, 1, 97-105.

A question that has to be faced every day in the classroom and educational clinic, but one that is perhaps not always faced up to, is that which seeks to establish the criterion against which reading disability can be defined. And in practice, perhaps the corollary to that question, namely, "When is a child no longer a disabled reader?" is even more important.

A respect for the law of parsimony is a characteristic of science, but educational psychology's penchant for simple answers to questions of complex human behaviour, particularly in the area of learning disability, has tended towards paucity rather than parsimony of explanation.

The most common technique for estimating the seriousness of reading retardation is succinctly expressed by Wilson (1967).

> A comparison of the best estimates of reading potential with the best estimates of reading achievement will result in an arithmetical difference. Finding that potential exceeds achievement, concern is legitimate that the child is not working up to his capacity. (p. 36)

To measure a child's reading achievement presents no particular problem. To measure *potential*—what might have been, or what the future will unfold—is a different matter however. The general interpretation of research findings by psychologists has been, correctly summarised by Hermann (1959), that reading disability is not a specific condition, but rather a nonspecific reaction to a series of environmental factors. Thus, if only a panacea or philosopher's stone could be unearthed to define the individual's latent or innate capacity, then this could be compared with his actual achievement and any discrepancy would be rectified by environmental modification through remedial instruction.

The panacea made its appearance in the first decade of the present century in the form of Binet's scale, the impact of which has been such that with over two-thirds of the century gone, the educator can still be "encouraged to view scores from intelligence scales as indicators of potentials for reading." (Wilson 1967, p. 39)

A child's measured mental age is intepreted as his reading potential, and so the subtraction of Reading Age from Mental Age produces a tangible quantified estimate of his reading retardation.

It is rather remarkable that the simple subtraction of Reading Age from Mental Age is still fashionable as an index of retardation, while the equally simple and equally respectable accomplishment quotient (Reading Age)/(Mental Age) is not. If a child's Reading Age equals his Mental Age, then his Accomplishment Quotient is equal to unity. Burt (1937, p. 36) contended that:

The teacher may gauge his own efficiency, as well as the child's . . .
by his success in keeping the (accomplishment quotient) of all his
pupils close to 100 per cent.

Thorndike and Gates (1929, p. 227) declared that the purpose of the Accomplishment Quotient:

Is to make it possible to reveal not only absolute achievement along
any line, but also attainment in proportion to capacity of the indi-
vidual for productivity in that line.

The theoretical validity of the Accomplishment Quotient may be now rejected (Vernon, 1958) but, in the area of reading disability at any rate, it is still very much in evidence in practice. Bond and Tinker (1967) assert that:

No child should ordinarily be considered disabled in reading unless there
is a discrepancy between his learning capacity or general verbal intelli-
gence and his reading performance. (p. 168)

Consider a ten-year-old child whose measured mental age is seven years and whose reading achievement is also at the seven-year level. According to popular practice, and with the backing of Bond and Tinker, this child is not a disabled reader because he is "working up to capacity." If his measured mental age had been at the ten-year level, then he would be regarded as a disabled reader, but what if his measured mental age had been seven years and his reading achievement was at the ten-year level?

It is a tribute to the power of the dogma of psychological orthodoxy that psychologists and teachers have continued to accept that a child's achievement cannot exceed his measured mental age (i.e., that his Achievement Quotient cannot be higher than his Intelligence Quotient) in spite of the evidence to the contrary which has been sitting under their very noses every day of the week. Thus, in what is generally a very wise and valuable book, Adams (1964, pp. 464-469) advises that diagnostic work is indicated for students whose test scores suggest underachievement, but for students whose test scores suggest overachievement, she recommends a retest in case the IQ has been underestimated.

Underlying common practice then, at least at the stage of initial diagnosis, there appear to be two implicit assumptions:

1) An intelligence test is a valid measure of a child's reading achievement. And if the intelligence test does not indicate what the child's reading level actually *is*, then it indicates what it *ought* to be.

2) A child's reading achievement level should not exceed his measured intelligence level.

Let us examine some of the theoretical implications and empirical evidence related to these two assumptions.

DOES AN INTELLIGENCE TEST MEASURE WHAT READING ACHIEVEMENT OUGHT TO BE?

The technique of factor analysis enables the intercorrelations between a battery of tests to be accounted for in terms of a relatively small number of, hopefully more basic factors. At the same time, factor analysis permits a test to be described in terms of these more basic factors. If there is perfect correlation between two tests, then their factor patterns will be identical; as correlation decreases from unity, so the contrast in the factor structure underlying the tests becomes more pronounced.

In administering an intelligence test to establish a child's reading potential, a test which correlates highly with reading (and, therefore, one which would have high predictive validity) must inevitably have a considerable loading with a verbal factor. This disqualifies it from consideration and there has to be recourse to an intelligence test which is free from this verbal contamination. As Wilson (1967, p. 35) observes:

Unless group intelligence tests have non-language features, they are not particularly useful in estimating the reading potential of children with reading problems.

Unfortunately—and inevitably—the correlation between the non-verbal intelligence test and reading is significantly lower than unity. Remedial teaching of the disabled reader, which aims at raising his reading achievement level to that of his measured intelligence, thus seems to be expected to increase the modest observed correlation between reading test and intelligence test until it approximates to unity, which presumably means that remedial teaching will alter the factor structure of the tests.

But, of course, the correlation between intelligence and reading is not perfect. In the course of an experimental inquiry into reading disability at the Grade Two level, I made a factor analysis of some 33 variables and extracted five significant factors (McLeod, 1967, 1968). A selection of obtained factor loadings is presented in Table 1, loadings of 0.4 or less being suppressed.

TABLE 1.

Test	Rotated Factors[*]				
	I	II	III	IV	V
WISC Full Scale IQ	.52	.52	.57	—	—
WISC Verbal IQ	.59	.67	—	—	—
WISC Performance IQ	—	—	.86	—	—
Reading Achievement	.65	—	—	.46	—

[*]Factors interpreted as: I Integrative-Sequential; II Encoding; III Visual-Motor; IV Auditory Language Input Capacity; V Planning.

It will be observed that reading achievement, but not measured intelligence, has a substantial loading on Factor IV (interpreted as an Auditory Language Input Capacity factor), which suggests the significance for reading ability of a factor which is not measured by intelligence tests. A child who is deficient in skills related to Factor I might be expected to have poorly developed reading skills coupled with low verbal IQ, whereas a child deficient in Factor IV could have adequate measured intelligence, yet impaired reading ability. For this latter type of child, measured intelligence is unlikely to be a valid index of reading achievement expectancy.

CAN READING ACHIEVEMENT LEVEL EXCEED MEASURED INTELLIGENCE?

The scattergram in Figure 1 illustrates the distribution of a Grade Four class, crossclassified according to Mental Age and Reading Age as assesed by the Australian Council for Educational Research's Junior Non-Verbal Intelligence Test and the GAP Reading Comprehension Test (McLeod, 1956) respectively.

There is a positive correlation between the two tests, so that most of the children's scores lie fairly close to the diagonal extending from the upper right-hand corner to the lower left-hand corner. If Mental Age is interpreted as a level of educational expectancy, and if the convention is adopted of regarding a child as "working up to expectancy" if his Reading Age and Mental Age are within 12 months of each other, then the 24 of the 40 children in this class whose scores are located between the two "staircases" are working up to expectancy.

The children whose test performances place them outside this diagonal band, in the direction of the lower right-hand area, each have Reading Ages at least a year behind their Mental Ages, and it has been common practice to label such children as underachievers. But the children whose test performances place them outside the "staircase" of Figure 1 in the direction of the upper left-hand corner, have Reading Ages more than 12 months in advance of their Mental Ages. Therefore, to be consistent, these children ought to be termed "overachievers." It can be seen that, for this particular class at any rate, the number of overachievers is the same as the number of underachievers, and it is inevitable that for test scores which have been standardised for a given population, the distribution of test score differences must be centred around zero, i.e., some differences will be positive and some negative.

FIGURE 1. SCATTERGRAM OF READING AGES PLOTTED AGAINST MENTAL AGES

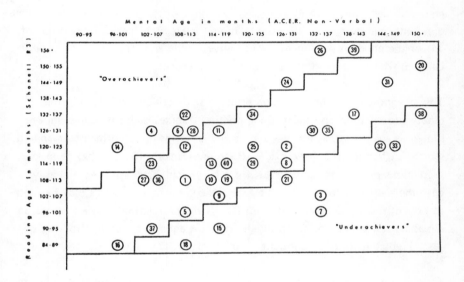

As Reynolds (1963) has observed, the use of Mental Age to establish an expectancy level seems to depend mainly on the evidence which shows that measured intelligence predicts achievement to some degree within most programmes. There has been a tendency to use the modest degree of academic prediction afforded by intelligence tests as a basis for specifying expectancy or capacity. Actually, every child is achieving just exactly as well as he should be expected, argues Reynolds, if only enough were known about prediction. A partial illustration of Reynolds' contention is afforded by the study from which the entries of Table 1 were derived. A correlation of 0.63 between WISC IQ and Reading

Age was increased to a multiple correlation of 0.85 when reading achievement was predicted from children's weighted factor scores. (McLeod, 1967a)

REGRESSION EFFECT IN PREDICTION

A further shortcoming of the IQ, as a basis for the assessment of reading expectancy, is that it over-estimates the number of "underachievers" at higher levels of intelligence. In Figure 1, for example, the incidence of "underachievers" progressively decreases from 60 per cent (i.e., three out of five) in the case of children with mental ages of 12 years or more, down to 14 per cent (two out of 14) of the children with mental ages between nine and ten, and none at all in children whose mental age is lower than nine years.

This phenomenon is the regression effect first described by Galton in the nineteenth century, and must occur whether standardised test results are presented as age norms, as in Figure 1, as Grade norms or as normalised standard scores. Attempts have been made, (Bond and Tinker, 1967, p. 92) to make predictions of reading achievement from IQ which correspond more closely with the facts of experience. The facts of experience themselves may be used to predict reading achievement from IQ. If the correlation between scores on a reading test and those on an intelligence test equals "r," then it follows that

Predicted Reading Quotient = 100 (1-r) + r.IQ

Thus, if the correlation between reading and intelligence is (say) 0.65, then the predicted Reading Quotient of a child with IQ 125 would be 116. If, further, the reliability of the test is known, then the standard error of an individual score is

$$15 \sqrt{1\text{-Reliability}}$$

Thus, if the standard deviation of Reading Quotient distribution is 15, and if the particular reading test has a reliability of (say) 0.91, then the standard error of estimate of an individual Reading Quotient is

$$SD \sqrt{1-0.91,}$$

i.e., 4.5

To be confident at the five per cent level of probability that a child's actual Reading Quotient is significantly lower than that predicted, it must fall short of prediction by at least 1.64 times its standard error, i.e., by 7.38 points in the present hypothetical example. Thus, given a correlation of 0.65 between an intelligence test and a reading test whose reliability is 0.91, a child with measured IQ of 125 should have a Reading Quotient of less than 109 before it could be confidently assumed that his level of reading achievement was significantly lower than that which would be predicted from his IQ.

But the derivation of modified formulae serves only to offset spurious statistical effects. In order to estimate the reading achievement level which can reasonably be expected from an individual child, it is necessary to consider the individual in rather more detail.

THE CASE OF JIMMY H.

Jimmy was a complete non-reader in Grade Three when he was first referred for treatment, at eight and one-half years of age. He was sixth in a warm affectionate family of nine, and while financial circumstances were straitened, the home could not be described as culturally deprived.

Jimmy's birth was easy, and he passed the developmental milestones of sitting up and walking well within the normal times. He did not speak, however, until the age of two, and his speech, which was not really intelligible until about the age of three, was still immature when he began school. During infancy he had two bad falls, requiring stitches, and he had always been overactive. Originally left-handed, he now held his pen in his right hand, and had difficulty in distinguishing right from left. At the age of two he had been hospitalized.

Jimmy's Full Scale IQ on the WISC was 112, his Verbal IQ being 110 and Performance IQ 113. He failed to score on the Neale (1958) Analysis of Reading Ability and his Reading Age on the Schonell (1958) Word Recognition Test was 5.1 years.

According to the Illinois Test of Psycholinguistic Abilities, Jimmy had an overall Language Age of eight years four months, which was only four months below his chronological age. The profile of his performance on the various subtests (Figure 2) shows that Encoding, both Vocal and Motor, was above average, but that Visual-Motor Association was very retarded, as was, to almost as great an extent, Visual Decoding and Visual-Motor Sequencing. His weaknesses were almost exclusively in the visual modality; in all skills involving auditory stimuli, he was either average or above average.

FIGURE 2. THE PSYCHOLINGUISTIC PROFILE OF JIMMY

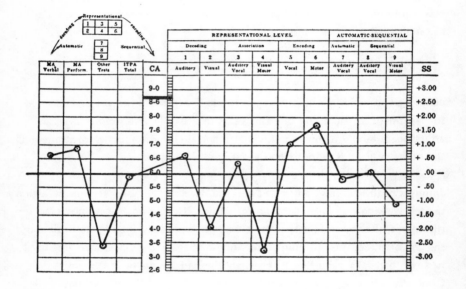

Treatment

Jimmy had several symptoms which are generally associated with developmental dyslexia. To diagnose him as "dyslexic" fixed the label. The pattern of his test behaviour indicated remedial action.

Using the ITPA profile as a diagnostic blueprint, a remedial programme which involved specific training in the deficient areas was designed and, where possible, use was made of Jimmy's superior abilities—his above average auditory and encoding abilities—in order to develop the areas of deficiency.

No formal reading instruction was given for the first two terms (20 lessons). Instead, a remedial language programme was undertaken in an effort to improve: a) Visual Decoding, b) Visual Association, c) Visual Sequencing and d) left/right discrimination (Atkinson, 1967).

After 20 weekly lessons, his Reading Age had reached six years five months according to Schonell's test, and seven years two months according to the Neale test.

It was at this point that some formal reading instruction was introduced, making use of his auditory skills. Jimmy quickly established a knowledge of the phonic value of letters and soon he was analysing and blending three letter words quite easily, at first, however, with little carry-over into meaningful reading. Before long he was using his still rather restricted phonic knowledge as an aid to word recognition when reading.

He was an industrious boy who was keen to learn to read, and he showed steady improvement in his reading until he was working just above a seven-year level, when some deterioration was observed, not only in his reading, but in his all round performance. He was late for his lessons and arrived without some of his books; he did not seem able to remember many of the skills which he had previously mastered. There was some evidence that his out-of-school activities were proving rather too onerous at this period. Consolidation and revision of both language skills and formal reading instruction in various contexts were used at this point and, after some weeks, Jimmy was ready to go on, moving with the same steady improvement that had occurred earlier.

Results

When this boy was discharged after five terms (1.7 years) of treatment, he was reading at about an average eight-year level. Schonell's Word Recognition Test gave a Reading Age of seven years 10 months and Neale Analysis of Reading, seven years 11 months for reading accuracy and nine years one month for comprehension.

Was the treatment successful? According to the view that a child should "read up to potential"—potential being measured by an IQ test—then treatment had been far from successful. He was about 10 years two months when discharged, and had an IQ of 112, so that his Mental Age was about 11½ years and his reading was three and one-half years retarded relative to his Mental Age. Even if the Bond and Clymer formula[1]

$$\text{Expected Reading Age} = (\text{Years in school} \times \text{IQ}) \times 5.0$$

is invoked, Jimmy was still two and a half years behind expectancy.

But when he had been first referred for treatment, after more than three years in school, his Reading Age had been below the norms of any reading test. His measurable progress prior to remediation had been zero. During one and two-third years' treatment, he had made about three years of measurable progress, and while these bald figures cannot express adequately the overall change in his educational morale, they *do* indicate that his progress had been lifted from zero to about 180 per cent, in terms of months of progress per month of attendance.

Jimmy's case was closed, at least temporarily, because it was the general consensus of opinion at the clinical case conference that he was levelling off and had reached a stage where he might be losing more than he was gaining by taking time off from school.

WHEN IS A CHILD NO LONGER A DISABLED READER?

Earlier in this article, it was stated that Mental Age is commonly regarded as

[1]Formula modified to yield Reading Ages instead of Grade Placements.

an index of reading expectancy at the time of *initial* diagnosis. Reading clinic case files bear silent testimony to the fact that mental age level is not always retained as the reading target to be achieved; at any rate, many cases are closed where reading achievement has fallen short of this target. The clinician whose education and training have taken place within an ideological climate that has caused him to take for granted that intelligence tests provide an index which is a target for, and limitation of, reading ability, will probably harbour a feeling of guilt that such cases have been closed prematurely. His justification of such closures is likely to be of a logistical nature; in the very nature of things, there is a comparatively rapid turnover of children who are brought "up to capacity" while the number of those who are resistant to remediation inevitably accumulates. But the incidence of "specific skill deficiency," "dyslexia," "minimal cerebral dysfunction"—indeed, all the cases "for whom our predictive devices, poor as they are, don't work" (Reynolds, 1963)—are not so rare that they can be regarded as exceptions.

To answer the question, "When is a child no longer a disabled reader?" represents a clinical problem requiring a clinical judgment, not a problem that can be solved by a mechanical formula. The question itself needs to be rephrased into operational terms. Instead of asking, "Is Jimmy a disabled reader?" the operational question is, "Is Jimmy's reading ability now sufficiently developed to enable him to cope adequately with the regular classroom learning of content subjects, without specialist remediation reading?"

TARGET OF READING EXPECTANCY

Long-term forecasting of a disabled reader's response to remediation is, like long-range weather forecasting, a hazardous procedure. It is trite to assert that in the field of learning disabilities diagnosis must be continuous, but in practice, it means that expectancies must be *short-term* expectancies. In order to specify immediate objectives, it is necessary to locate and identify the stage of development of skills that are relevant to the learning deficiency.

The analysis of these skills has to be a *behavioural* analysis. What the child can do has to be described in terms of actual specific operations which he cannot.

Any remediational method attempts, in essence, to locate the fault, i.e., where the break or breakdown occurs, go back to that point—and maybe a little beyond it—to a stage where growth was healthy, patch it up, grafting remedial experiences on to the healthy development, and move on from there.

Appropriate remediation can be indicated if relevant skills which are basic to, rather than merely correlated with, reading ability are known. Current research (Bateman, 1965, McLeod, 1967) suggests that such relevant basic skills are likely to be in terms of the ITPA model, at the Automatic-Sequential level of organization and in the Auditory-Vocal Modality, e.g., phonemic discrimination, sound blending, immediate auditory memory span, etc.

The possibility of valid long-term prediction of reading potential depends upon: a) the extent to which these skills can be trained; and b) the extent of any transfer effect to reading from the training of such skills. It might be that some disabled readers will, with well-planned remediation based on sound research, be able to achieve a reading level comparable with, or superior to, their measured intelligence level. On the other hand, it may be that for some, a ceiling of 4th or 5th Grade level in reading is the most that can reasonably be anticipated.

All this might appear a more indecisive and, therefore, less satisfactory answer to the question of reading expectancy of disabled readers than is furnished by the straightforward use of an easily obtained numerical index such as the IQ. Charles Osgood, architect of a theoretical framework within which much of current psycholinguistic research is being carried out, once made the impenitent apology that one claim which he had never made for his theory was that it was simple. Why should the answer to questions involving some of the most complex activities of the complex human organism *be* simple?

References

Adams, Georgia S., MEASUREMENT AND EVALUATION, N.Y. Holt, Rinehart and Winston, 1964.

Atkinson, Joan K., READING IMPROVEMENT THROUGH PSYCHOLINGUISTIC REMEDIATION. Slow Learning Child, Nov. 1967, 14, 2, 103-115.

Bateman, Barbara D., THE ILLINOIS TEST OF PSYCHOLINGUISTIC ABILITIES IN CURRENT RESEARCH, Urbana, Institute for Res. on Except. Children, 1965.

Bond, G. and Tinker, M. A., READING DIFFICULTIES: THEIR DIAGNOSIS AND CORRECTION, N.Y. Appleton-Century-Crofts, 1967.

Burt, C., THE BACKWARD CHILD, London, Univ. of London Press, 1937.

Hermann, K., READING DISABILITY: A MEDICAL STUDY OF WORD-BLINDNESS AND RELATED HANDICAPS. Copenhagen, Munkgsaard, 1959.

McLeod, J., THE GAP READING COMPREHENSION TEST, Melbourne, Heinemann, 1965.

McLeod, J., Dyslexia in Young Children: a Factorial Study, with Special Reference to the Illinois Test of Psycholinguistic Abilities, IREC PAPERS IN EDUCATION, Vol. 2, No. 1, Univ. of Illinois, Inst. for Res. on Exceptional Children, 1967.

McLeod, J., Perceptual Bases of Reading, In READING INSTRUCTION: AN INTERNATIONAL FORUM. First World Congress on Reading, Paris 1966, Newark, Internat. Reading Assoc., 1967a.

McLeod, J., PERCEPTION OF SPOKEN LANGUAGE BY CHILDREN WITH READING DISABILITIES, Zeitschrift für Phonetic, Sprachwissenschaft und Kommunikationsforschung (in press) 1968.

Neale, Marie D., NEALE ANALYSIS OF READING ABILITY, London, Macmillan, 1958.

Reynolds, M. C., A Strategy for Research, EXCEPTIONAL CHILDREN, 1963, 29, 5, 213-219.

Schonell, F. J. & Schonell, F. Eleanor, DIAGNOSTIC AND ATTAINMENT TESTIN Edinburgh: Oliver & Boyd, 1950.

Thorndike, E. L. and Gates, A. I., ELEMENTARY PRINCIPLES OF EDUCATION, N. Y., Macmillan, 1929.

Vernon, P. E., The Relation of Intelligence to Educational Backwardness, EDUC. REVIEW, 1958, 9, 7-15.

Wilson, R. M., DIAGNOSIS AND REMEDIAL READING FOR CLASSROOM AND CLINIC, Columbus, Ohio, Merrill, 1967.

STUDY QUESTIONS

1. How does McLeod answer the question: Does an intelligence test measure reading expectancy?

2. How does he answer the question: Can reading achievement exceed measured intelligence?

3. How does McLeod suggest that reading expectancy be determined?

4. Give an example of what McLeod means by a "behavioral analysis."

SECTION 4
TEACHING

15: LEARNING TO READ

Eleanor J. Gibson

Gibson analyzes the reading process per se. She presents evidence regarding the nature of three phases of learning to read: 1) visual differentiation of written symbols; 2) converting letters to sounds; and 3) utilizing higher-order units of structure. The reader is urged to evaluate the extent to which various commercial reading programs take into account the considerations outlined in Gibson's outstanding analysis.

      B. D. B.

Reprinted with permission of the author and publisher from SCIENCE, 1965, 148, 1066-1072. Copyright © 1965 by the American Association for the Advancement of Science.

Educators and the public have exhibited a keen interest in the teaching of reading ever since free public education became a fact. (1) Either because of or despite their interest, this most important subject has been remarkably susceptible to the influence of fads and fashions and curiously unaffected by disciplined experimental and theoretical psychology. The psychologists have traditionally pursued the study of verbal learning by means of experiments with nonsense syllables and the like—that is, materials carefully divested of useful information. And the educators, who found little in this work that seemed relevant to the classroom, have stayed with the classroom; when they performed experiments, the method was apt to be a gross comparison of classes privileged and unprivileged with respect to the latest fad. The result has been two cultures: the pure scientists in the laboratory, and the practical teachers ignorant of the progress that has been made in the theory of human learning and in methods of studying it.

That this split was unfortunate is clear enough. True, most children do learn to read. But some learn to read badly, so that school systems must provide remedial clinics; and a small proportion (but still a large number of future citizens) remain functional illiterates. The fashions which have led to classroom experiments, such as the "whole word" method, emphasis on context and pictures for "meaning," the "flash" method, "speed reading," revised alphabets, the "return" to "phonics", and so on, have done little to change the situation.

Yet a systematic approach to the understanding of reading skill is possible. The psychologist has only to treat reading as a learning problem, to apply ingenuity in theory construction and experimental design to this fundamental activity on which the rest of man's education depends. A beginning has recently been made in this direction, and it can be expected that a number of theoretical and experimental studies of reading will be forthcoming. (2)

This article is adapted from a paper read at a conference on Perceptual and Linguistic Aspects of Reading, sponsored by the Committee on Learning and the Educational Process of the Social Science Research Council and held at the Center for Advanced Study in the Behavioral Sciences, Palo Alto, California, 31 October 1963.

Analysis of the Reading Process

A prerequisite to good research on reading is a psychological analysis of the reading process. What is it that a skilled reader has learned? Knowing this (or having a pretty good idea of it), one may consider how the skill is learned, and next how it could best be taught. Hypotheses designed to answer all three of these questions can then be tested by experiment.

There are several ways of characterizing the behavior we call reading. It is receiving communication; it is making discriminative responses to graphic symbols; it is decoding graphic symbols to speech; and it is getting meaning from the printed page. A child in the early stages of acquiring reading skill may not be doing all these things, however. Some aspects of reading must be mastered before others and have an essential function in a sequence of development of the final skill. The average child, when he begins learning to read, has already mastered to a marvelous extent the art of communication. He can speak and understand his own language in a fairly complex way, employing units of language organized in a hierarchy and with a grammatical structure. Since a writing system must correspond to the spoken one, and since speech is prior to writing, the framework and unit structure of speech will determine more or less the structure of the writing system, though the rules of correspondence vary for different languages and writing systems. Some alphabetic writing systems have nearly perfect single-letter-to-sound correspondences, but some, like English, have far more complex correspondence between spelling patterns and speech patterns. Whatever the nature of the correspondences, it is vital to a proper analysis of the reading task that they be understood. And it is vital to remember, as well, that the first stage in the child's mastery of reading is learning to communicate by means of spoken language.

Once a child begins his progression from spoken language to written language, there are, I think, three phases of learning to be considered. They present three different kinds of learning tasks, and they are roughly sequential, though there must be considerable overlapping. These three phases are: learning to differentiate graphic symbols; learning to decode letters to sounds ("map" the letters into sounds); and using progressively higher-order units of structure. I shall consider these three stages in order and in some detail and describe experiments exploring each stage.

Differentiation of Written Symbols

Making any discriminative response to printed characters is considered by some a kind of reading. A very young child, or even a monkey, can be taught to point to a patch of yellow color, rather than a patch of blue, when the printed characters YELLOW are presented. Various people, in recent popular publications, have seriously suggested teaching infants to respond discriminatively in this way to letter patterns, implying that this is teaching them to "read." Such responses are not reading, however; reading entails decoding to speech. Letters are, essentially, an instruction to produce a given speech sound.

Nevertheless, differentiation of written characters from one another is a logically preliminary stage to decoding them to speech. The learning problem is one of discriminating and recognizing a set of line figures, all very similar in a number of ways (for example, all are tracings on paper) and each differing from all the others in one or more features (as straight versus curved). The differentiating features must remain invariant under certain transformations (size, brightness, and perspective transformations and less easily described ones produced by different type faces and handwriting). They must therefore be relational, so that these transformations will not destroy them.

It might be questioned whether learning is necessary for these figures to be discriminated from one another. This question has been investigated by Gibson, Gibson, Pick, and Osser. (3) In order to trace the development of letter differentiation as it is related to those features of letters which are critical for the task, we designed specified transformations for each of a group of standard, artificial letter-like forms comparable to printed Roman capitals. Variants were constructed from each standard figure to yield the following 12 transformations for each one: three degrees of transformation from line to curve; five transformations of rotation or reversal; two perspective transformations; and two topological transformations (see Figure 1 for examples). All of these except the perspective transformations we considered critical for discriminating letters. For example, contrast V and U; C and U; O and C.

FIGURE 1. EXAMPLES OF LETTER-LIKE FIGURES ILLUSTRATING DIFFERENT TYPES OF TRANSFORMATIONS

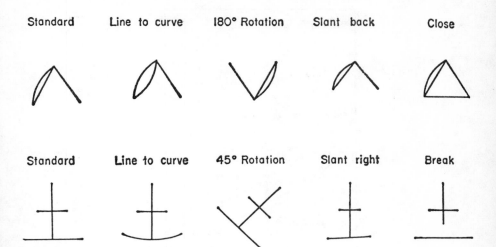

The discrimination task required the subject to match a standard figure against all of its transformations and some copies of it and to select only identical copies. An error score (the number of times an item that was not an identical copy was selected) was obtained for each child, and the errors were classified according to the type of transformation. The subjects were children aged 4 through 8 years. As would be expected, the visual discrimination of these letter-like forms improved from age 4 to age 8, but the slopes of the error curves were different, depending on the transformation to be discriminated (Figure 2). In other words, some transformations are harder to discriminate than others, and improvement occurs at different rates for different transformations. Even the youngest subjects made relatively few errors involving changes of break or close, and among the 8-year-olds these errors dropped to zero. Errors for perspective transformations were very numerous among 4-year-olds and still numerous among 8-year-olds. Errors for rotations and reversals started high but dropped to nearly zero by 8 years. Errors for changes from line to curve were relatively numerous (depending on the number of changes) among the youngest children and showed a rapid drop among the older—almost to zero for the 8-year-olds.

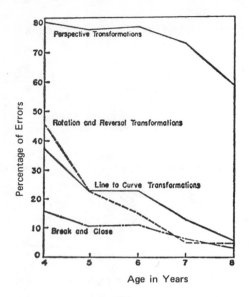

Age in Years

The experiment was replicated with the same transformations of real letters on the 5-year-old group. The correlation between confusions of the same transformations for real letters and for the letter-like forms was very high (r = + .87), so the effect of a given transformation has generality (is not specific to a given form).

What happens, in the years from 4 to 8, to produce or hamper improvement in discrimination? Our results suggest that the children have learned the features or dimensions of difference which are critical for differentiating letters. Some differences are critical, such as break versus close, line versus curve, and rotations and reversals; but some, such as the perspective transformations, are not, and must in fact be tolerated. The child of 4 does not start "cold" upon this task, because some of his previous experience with distinctive features of objects and pictures will transfer to letter differentiation. But the set of letters has a unique feature pattern for each of its members, so learning of the distinctive features goes on during the period we investigated.

TABLE 1. NUMBER OF ERRORS MADE IN TRANSFER STAGE BY GROUPS WITH THREE TYPES OF TRAINING

Group	Type of training		Errors
	Standards	Transfor-mations	
E1	Same	Different	69
E2	Different	Same	39
C	Different	Different	101

If this interpretation is correct, it would be useful to know just what the distinctive features of letters are. What dimensions of difference must a child learn to detect in order to perceive each letter as unique? Gibson, Osser, Schiff, and Smith (4) investigated this question. Our method was to draw up a chart of the features of a given set of letters (5), test to see which of these letters were most frequently confused by prereading children, and compare the errors in the resulting "confusion matrix" with those predicted by the feature chart.

A set of distinctive features for letters must be relational in the sense that each feature presents a contrast which is invariant under certain transformations, and it must yield a unique pattern for each letter. The set must also be reasonably economical. Two feature lists which satisfy these requirements for a specified type face were tried out against the results of a confusion matrix obtained with the same type (simplified Roman capitals available on a sign-typewriter).

Each of the features in the list in Figure 3 is or is not a characteristic of each of the 26 letters. Regarding each letter one asks, for example, "Is there a curved segment?" and gets a yes or no answer. A filled-in feature chart gives a unique pattern for each letter. However, the number of potential features for letter-shapes is very large, and would vary from one alphabet and type font to another. Whether or not we have the right set can be tested with a confusion matrix. Children should confuse with greatest frequency the letters having the smallest number of feature differences, if the features have been chosen correctly.

FIGURE 3. EXAMPLES OF A "FEATURE CHART." WHETHER THE FEATURES CHOSEN ARE ACTUALLY EFFECTIVE FOR DISCRIMINATING LETTERS MUST BE DETERMINED BY EXPERIMENT

Features	A	B	C	E	K	L	N	U	X	Z
Straight segment										
Horizontal	+			+		+				+
Vertical		+		+	+	+	+			
Oblique /	+			+					+	+
Oblique \	+			+			+		+	
Curve										
Closed		+								
Open vertically								+		
Open horizontally			+							
Intersection	+	+		+	+				+	
Redundancy										
Cyclic Change		+		+						
Symmetry	+	+	+	+	+			+	+	
Discontinuity										
Vertical	+				+				+	
Horizontal				+		+	+			+

We obtained our confusion matrix from 4-year-old children, who made matching judgments of letters, programmed so that every letter had an equal opportunity to be mistaken for any other, without bias from order effects. The "percent feature difference" for any two letters was determined by dividing the total number of features possessed by either letter, but not both, by the total number possessed by both, whether shared or not. Correlations were then calculated between percent feature difference and number of confusions, one for each letter. The feature list of Figure 3 yielded 12 out of 26 positive significant correlations. Prediction from this feature list is fairly good, in view of the fact that features were not weighted. A multidimensional analysis of the matrix corroborated the choice of the curve-straight and obliqueness variables, suggesting that these features may have priority in the discrimination process and perhaps developmentally. Refinement of the feature list will take these facts into account, and other methods of validation will be tried.

Detecting Distinctive Features

If we are correct in thinking that the child comes to discriminate graphemes by detecting their distinctive features, what is the learning process like? That it is perceptual learning and need not be verbalized is probable (though teachers do often call attention to contrasts between letter shapes). An experiment by Anne D. Pick (6) was designed to compare two hypotheses about how this type of discrimination develops. One might be called a "schema" or "prototype" hypothesis, and is based on the supposition that the child builds up a kind of model or memory image of each letter by repeated experience of visual presentations of the letter; perceptual theories which propose that discrimination occurs by matching sensory experience to a previously stored concept or categorical model are of this kind. In the other hypothesis it is assumed that the child learns by discovering how the forms differ, and then easily transfers this knowledge to new letter-like figures.

Pick employed a transfer design in which subjects were presented in step 1 with initially confusable stimuli (letter-like forms) and trained to discriminate between them. For step 2 (the transfer stage) the subjects were divided into three groups. One experimental group was given sets of stimuli to discriminate which varied in new dimensions from the *same standards* discriminated in stage 1. A second experimental group was given sets of stimuli which deviated from *new standards,* but in the same dimensions of difference discriminated in stage 1.

A control group was given both new standards and new dimensions of difference to discriminate in stage 2. Better performance by the first experimental group would suggest that discrimination learning proceeded by construction of a model or memory image of the standards against which the variants could be matched. Conversely, better performance by the second experimental group would suggest that dimensions of difference had been detected.

The subjects were kindergarten children. The stimuli were letter-like forms of the type described earlier. There were six standard forms and six transformations of each of them. The transformations consisted of two changes of line to curve, a right-left reversal, a 45-degree rotation, a perspective transformation, and a size transformation. Table 1 gives the errors of discrimination for all three groups in stage 2. Both experimental groups performed significantly better than the control group, but the group that had familiar transformations of new standards performed significantly better than the group given new transformations of old standards.

We infer from these results that, while children probably do learn prototypes of letter shapes, the prototypes themselves are not the original basis for differentation. The most relevant kind of training for discrimination is practice which provides experience with the characteristic differences that distinguish the set of items. Features which are actually distinctive for letters could be emphasized by presenting letters in contrast pairs.

Decoding Letters to Sounds

When the graphemes are reasonably discriminable from one another, the decoding process becomes possible. This process, common sense and many psychologists would tell us, is simply a matter of associating a graphic stimulus with the appropriate spoken response—that is to say, it is the traditional stimulus-response paradigm, a kind of paired-associate learning.

Obvious as this description seems, problems arise when one takes a closer look. Here are just a few. The graphic code is related to the speech code by rules of correspondence. If these rules are known, decoding of new items is predictable.

Do we want to build up, one by one, automatically cued responses, or do we want to teach with transfer in mind? If we want to teach for transfer, how do we do it? Should the child be aware that this is a code game with rules? Or will induction of the rules be automatic? What units of both codes should we start with? Should we start with single letters, in the hope that knowledge of single-letter-to-sound relationships will yield the most transfer? Or should we start with whole words, in the hope that component relationships will be induced?

Carol Bishop (7) investigated the question of the significance of knowledge of component letter-sound relationships in reading new words. In her experiment, the child's process of learning to read was simulated by teaching adult subjects to read some Arabic words. The purpose was to determine the transfer value of training with individual letters as opposed to whole words, and to investigate the role of component letter-sound associations in transfer to learning new words.

A three-stage transfer design was employed. The letters were 12 Arabic characters, each with a one-to-one letter-sound correspondence. There were eight consonants and four vowels, which were combined to form two sets of eight Arabic words. The 12 letters appeared at least once in both sets of words. A native speaker of the language recorded on tape the 12 letter-sounds and the two sets of words. The graphic form of each letter or word was printed on a card.

The subjects were divided into three groups—the letter training group (L), the whole-word training group (W), and a control group (C). Stage 1 of the experiment was identical for all groups. The subjects learned to pronounce the set of words (transfer set) which would appear in stage 3 by listening to the recording and repeating the words. Stage 2 varied. Group L listened to and repeated the 12 letter-sounds and then learned to associate the individual graphic shapes with their correct sounds. Group W followed the same procedure, except that eight words were given them to learn, rather than letters. Learning time was equal for the two groups. Group C spent the same time-interval on an unrelated task. Stage 3 was the same for the three groups. All subjects learned to read the set of words they had heard in stage 1, responding to the presentation of a word on a card by pronouncing it. This was the transfer stage on which the three groups were compared.

At the close of stage 3, all subjects were tested on their ability to give the correct letter-sound following the presentation of each printed letter. They were asked afterward to explain how they tried to learn the transfer words.

Figure 4 shows that learning took place in fewest trials for the letter group and next fewest for the word group. That is, letter training had more transfer value than word training, but word training did produce some transfer. The subjects of group L also knew, on the average, a greater number of component letter-sound correspondences, but some subjects in group W had learned all 12. Most of the subjects in group L reported that they had tried to learn by using knowledge of component correspondences. But so did 12 of the 20 subjects in group W, and the scores of these 12 subjects on the transfer task were similar to those of the letter-trained group. The subjects who had learned by whole words and had not used individual correspondences performed no better on the task than the control subjects.

It is possible, then, to learn to read words without learning the component letter-sound correspondences. But transfer to new words depends on use of them, whatever the method of original training. Word training was as good as letter training if the subject had analyzed for himself the component relationships.

Learning Variable and Constant Component Correspondences

In Bishop's experiment, the component letter-sound relationships were regular and consistent. It has often been pointed out, especially by advocates of spelling reform and revised alphabets (8), that in English this is not the case. Bloomfield (9) suggested that the beginning reader should, therefore, be presented with material carefully programmed for teaching those orthographic-phonic regularities which exist in English, and should be introduced later and only gradually to the complexities of English spelling and to the fact that single-letter-to-sound relationships are often variable. But actually, there has been no hard evidence to suggest that transfer, later, to reading spelling-patterns with more variable component correspondence will be facilitated by beginning with only constant ones. Although variable ones may be harder to learn in the beginning, the original difficulty may be compensated for by facilitating later learning.

FIGURE 4. LEARNING CURVES ON TRANSFER TASK FOR GROUP
TRAINED ORIGINALLY WITH WHOLE WORDS (W), GROUP
TRAINED WITH SINGLE LETTERS (L), AND CONTROL
GROUP (C)

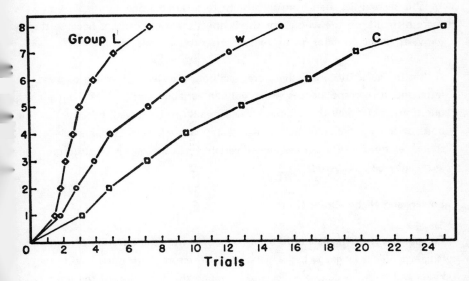

A series of experiments directed by Harry Levin (10) dealt with the effect of learning variable as opposed to constant letter-sound relationships, on transfer to learning new letter-sound relationships. In one experiment, the learning material was short lists of paired-associates, with a word written in artificial characters as stimulus and a triphoneme familiar English word as response. Subjects (third-grade children) in one group were given a list which contained constant graph-to-sound relationships (one-to-one component correspondence) followed by a list in which this correspondence was variable with respect to the medial vowel sound. Another group started with a similarly constructed variable list and followed it with a second one. The group that learned lists with a variable component in both stages was superior to the other group in the second stage. The results suggest that initiating the task with a variable list created an expectation of learning set for variability of correspondence which was transferred to the second list and facilitated learning it.

In a second experiment, the constant or variable graph-sound relation occurred on the first letter. Again, the group with original variable training performed better on the second, variable list. In a third experiment adult native speakers of English and Spanish were compared. The artificial graphs were paired with nonsense words. Again there was more transfer from a variable first list to a variable second list than from a constant to a variable one. Variable lists were more difficult, on the whole, for the Spanish speakers, perhaps because their native language contains highly regular letter-sound relationships.

A "set for diversity" may, therefore, facilitate transfer to learning of new letter-sound correspondences which contain variable relationships. But many questions about how the code is learned remain to be solved, because the true units of the graphic code are not necessarily single letters. While single-letter-sound relations in English are indeed variable, at other levels of structure regularity may be discovered.

Lower- and Higher-Order Units

For many years, linguists have been concerned with the question of units in language. That language has a hierarchical structure, with units of different kinds and levels, is generally accepted, though the definition of the units is not easily reached. One criterion of a unit is recodability—consistent mapping or translation to another code. If such a criterion be granted, graphic units. must parallel linguistic units. The units of the writing system should be defined, in other words, by mapping rules which link them to the speech code, at all levels of structure.

What then are the true graphic units? What levels of units are there? Exactly how are they mapped to linguistic units? In what "chunks" are they perceive

We must first try to answer these questions by a logical analysis of properties of the writing and speech systems and the correspondences between them. Then we can look at the behavior of skilled readers and see how units are processed during reading. If the logical analysis of the correspondence rules is correct, we should be able to predict what kinds of units are actually processed and to check our predictions experimentally.

Common sense suggests that the unit for reading is the single grapheme, and that the reader proceeds sequentially from left to right, letter by letter, across the page. But we can assert at once and unequivocally that this picture is false. For the English language, the single graphemes map consistently into speech only as morphemes—that is, the names of the letters of the alphabet. It is possible, of course, to name letters sequentially across a line of print ("spell out" a word), but that is not the goal of a skilled reader, nor is it what he does. Dodge (11) showed, nearly 60 years ago, that perception occurs in reading only during fixations, and not at all during the saccadic jumps from one fixation to the next. With a fast tachistoscopic exposure, a skilled reader can perceive four unconnected letters, a very long word, and four or more words if they form a sentence (12). Even first graders can read three-letter words exposed for only 40 milliseconds, too short a time for sequential eye movements to occur.

Broadbent (13) has pointed out that speech, although it consists of a temporal sequence of stimuli, is responded to at the end of a sequence. That is, it is normal for a whole sequence to be delivered before a response is made. For instance, the sentence "Would you give me your _____?" might end with any of a large number of words, such as "name" or "wallet" or "wife." The response depends on the total message. The fact that the component stimuli for speech and reading are spread over time does not mean that the phonemes or letters or words are processed one at a time, with each stimulus decoded to a separate response. The fact that O is pronounced differently in COAT and BOMB is not a hideous peculiarity of English which must consequently be reformed. The O is read only in context and is never responded to in isolation. It is part of a sequence which contains constraints of two kinds, one morphological and the other the spelling patterns which are characteristic of English.

If any doubt remains as to the unlikelihood of sequential processing letter by letter, there is recent evidence of Newman (14) and of Kolers (15) on sequential exposure of letters. When letters forming a familiar word are exposed sequentially in the same place, it is almost impossible to read the word. With an exposure of 100 milliseconds per letter, words of six letters are read with only 20 percent probability of accuracy; and with an exposure of 375 milliseconds per letter, the probability is still well under 100 percent. But that is more than 2 seconds to perceive a short, well-known word! We can conclude that, however graphemes are processed perceptually in reading, it is not a letter-by-letter sequence of acts.

If the single grapheme does not map consistently to a phoneme, and furthermore, if perception normally takes in bigger "chunks" of graphic stimuli in a single fixation, what are the smallest graphic units consistently coded into phonemic patterns? Must they be whole words? Are there different levels of units? Are they achieved at different stages of development?

Spelling Patterns

It is my belief that the smallest component units in written English are spelling patterns. (16) By a spelling pattern, I mean a cluster of graphemes in a given environment which has an invariant pronunciation according to the rules of English. These rules are the regularities which appear when, for instance, any vowel or consonant or cluster is shown to correspond with a given pronunciation in an initial, medial, or final position in the spelling of a word. This kind of regularity is not merely "frequency" (bigram frequency, trigram frequency, and so on), for it implies that frequency counts are relevant for establishing rules only if the right units and the right relationships are counted. The relevant graphic unit is a functional unit of one or more letters, in a given position within the word, which is in correspondence with a specified pronunciation. (17)

If potential regularities exist within words—the spelling patterns that occur in regular correspondence with speech patterns—one may hypothesize that these correspondences have been assimilated by the skilled reader of English (whether or not he can verbalize the rules) and have the effect of organizing units for perception. It follows that strings of letters which are generated by the rules will be perceived more easily than ones which are not, even when they are unfamiliar words or not words at all.

Several experiments testing this prediction were performed by Gibson, Pick, Osser, and Hammond. (18) The basic design was to compare the perceptibility (with a very short tachistoscopic exposure) of two sets of letter-strings, all nonsense or pseudo words, which differed in their spelling-to-sound correlation. One list, called the "pronounceable" list, contained words with a high spelling-to-sound correlation. Each of them had an initial consonant-spelling with a single, regular pronunication; a final consonant-spelling having a single regular pronunciation; and a vowel-spelling, placed between them, having a single regular pronunciation when it follows and is followed by the given initial and final consonant spellings, respectively—for example, GL/UR/CK. The words in the second list, called the "unpronounceable" list, had a low spelling-to-sound correlation. They were constructed from the words in the first list by reversing the initial and final consonant spellings. The medial vowel spelling was not changed. For example, GLURCK became CKURGL. There were 25 such pseudo words in each list, varying in length from four to eight letters. The pronunciability of the resulting lists was validated in two ways, first by ratings, and second by obtaining the number of variations when the pseudo words were actually pronounced.

The words were projected on a screen in random order, in five successive presentations with an exposure time beginning at 50 milliseconds and progressing up to 250 milliseconds. The subjects (college students) were instructed to write each word as it was projected. The mean percentage of pronounceable words correctly perceived was consistently and significantly greater at all exposure times.

The experiment was later repeated with the same material but a different judgment. After the pseudo word was exposed, it was followed by a multiple-choice list of four items, one of the correct one and the other three the most common errors produced in the previous experiment. The subject chose the word he thought he had seen from the choice list and recorded a number (its order in the list). Again the mean of pronounceable pseudo words correctly perceived significantly exceeded that of their unpronounceable counterparts. We conclude from these experiments that skilled readers more easily perceive as a unit pseudo words which follow the rules of English spelling-to-sound correspondence; that spelling patterns which have invariant relations to sound patterns function as a unit, thus facilitating the decoding process.

In another experiment, Gibson, Osser, and Pick (19) studied the development of perception of grapheme-phoneme correspondences. We wanted to know how early, in learning to read, children begin to respond to spelling-patterns as units. The experiment was designed to compare children at the end of the first grade and at the end of the third grade in ability to recognize familiar three-letter words, pronounceable trigrams, and unpronounceable trigrams. The three-letter words were taken from the first-grade reading list; each word chosen could be rearranged into a meaningless but pronounceable trigram and a meaningless and unpronounceable one (for example, RAN, NAR, RNA). Some longer pseudo words (four and five letters) taken from the previous experiments were included as well. The words and pseudo words were exposed tachistoscopically to individual children, who were required to spell them orally. The first-graders read (spelled out) most accurately the familiar three-letter words, but read the pronounceable trigrams significantly better than the unpronounceable ones. The longer pseudo words were seldom read accurately and were not differentiated by pronunciability. The third-grade girls read all three-letter combinations with high and about equal accuracy, but differentiated the longer pseudo words; that is, the pronounceable four- and five-letter pseudo words were more often perceived correctly than their unpronounceable counterparts.

These results suggest that a child in the first stages of reading skill typically reads in short units, but has already generalized certain regularities of spelling-to-sound correspondence, so that three-letter pseudo words which fit the rules are more easily read as units. As skill develops, span increases, and a similar difference can be observed for longer items. The longer items involve more complex conditional rules and longer clusters, so that the generalizations must increase in complexity. The fact that a child can begin very early to perceive regularities of correspondence between the printed and spoken patterns, and transfer them to the reading of unfamiliar items as units, suggests that the opportunities for discovering the correspondences between patterns might well be enhanced in programming reading materials.

I have referred several times to *levels* of units. The last experiment showed that the size and complexity of the spelling patterns which can be perceived as units increase with development of reading skill. That other levels of structure, both syntactic and semantic, contain units as large as and larger than the word, and that perception of skilled readers will be found, in suitable experiments, to be a function of these factors is almost axiomatic. As yet we have little direct evidence better than Cattell's original discovery (12) that when words are structured into a sentence, more letters can be accurately perceived "at a glance." Developmental studies of perceptual "chunking" in relation to structural complexity may be very instructive.

Where does meaning come in? Within the immediate span of visual perception, meaning is less effective in structuring written material than good spelling-to-sound correspondence, as Gibson, Bishop, Schiff, and Smith (20) have shown. Real words which are both meaningful and, as strings of letters, structured in accordance with English spelling patterns are more easily perceived than nonword pronounceable strings of letters; but the latter are more easily perceived than meaningful but unpronounceable letter-strings (for example, BIM is perceived accurately, with tachistoscopic exposure, faster than IBM). The role of meaning in the visual perception of words probably increases as longer strings of words (more than one) are dealt with. A sentence has two kinds of constraint, semantic and syntactic, which make it intelligible (easily heard) and memorable. (21) It is important that the child develop reading habits which utilize all the types of constraint present in the stimulus, since they constitute structure and are, therefore, unit-formers. The skills which the child should acquire in reading are habits of utilizing the constraints in letter-strings (the spelling and morphemic patterns) and in word-strings (the syntactic and semantic patterns). We could go on to consider still superordinate ones, perhaps, but the problem of the unit, of levels of units, and mapping rules from writing to speech has just begun to be explored with experimental techniques.

Further research on the definition and processing of units should lead to new insights about the nature of reading skill and its attainment.

Summary

Reading begins with the child's acquisition of spoken language. Later he learns to differentiate the graphic symbols from one another and to decode these to familiar speech sounds. As he learns the code, he must progressively utilize the structural constraints which are built into it in order to attain the skilled performance which is characterized by processing of higher-order units—the spelling and morphological patterns of the language.

Because of my firm conviction that good pedagogy is based on a deep understanding of the discipline to be taught and the nature of the learning process involved, I have tried to show that the psychology of reading can benefit from a program of theoretical analysis and experiment. An analysis of the reading task—its discriminatory and decoding aspects as well as the semantic and syntactical aspects—tells us *what* must be learned. An analysis of the learning process tells us *how*. The consideration of formal instruction comes only after these steps, and its precepts should follow from them.

References and Notes

1. See C. C. Fries, LINGUISTICS AND READING (Holt, Rinehart, and Winston, New York, 1963), for an excellent chapter on past practice and theory in the teaching of reading.

2. In 1959, Cornell University was awarded a grant for a Basic Research Project on Reading by the Cooperative Research Program of the Office of Education, U.S. Department of Health, Education, and Welfare. Most of the work reported in this article was supported by this grant. The Office of Education

has recently organized "Project Literacy," which will promote research on reading in a number of laboratories, as well as encourage mutual understanding between experimentalists and teachers of reading.

3. E. J. Gibson, J. J. Gibson, A. D. Pick, H. Osser, J. COMP. PSYCHOL. 55, 897 (1962).

4. E. J. Gibson, H. Osser, W. Schiff, J. Smith, in A BASIC RESEARCH PRO-GRAM ON READING, Final Report on Cooperative Research Project No. 639 to the Office of Education, Department of Health, Education, and Welfare.

5. The method was greatly influenced by the analysis of distinctive features of phonemes by Jakobsen and M. Halle, presented in FUNDAMENTALS OF LANGUAGE (Mouton, The Hague, 1956). A table of 12 features, each in binary opposition, yields a unique pattern for all phonemes, so that any one is distinguishable from any other by its pattern of attributes. A pair of phonemes may differ by any number of features, the minimal distinction being one feature opposition. The features must be invariant under certain transformations and essentially relational, so as to remain distinctive over a wide range of speakers, intonations, and so on.

6. A. D. Pick, J. EXP. PSYCHOL., in press.

7. C. H. Bishop, J. VERBAL LEARNING VERBAL BEHAV. 3, 215 (1964).

8. Current advocates of a revised alphabet who emphasize the low letter-sound correspondence in English are Sir James Pitman and John A. Downing. Pitman's revised alphabet, called the Initial Teaching Alphabet, consists of 43 characters, some traditional and some new. It is designed for instruction of the beginning reader, who later transfers to traditional English spelling. See I. J. Pitman, J. ROY. SOC. ARTS 109, 149 (1961); J. A. Downing, BRIT. J. EDUC. PSYCHOL. 32, 166 (1962); _____, "Experiments with Pitman's initial teaching alphabet in British schools," paper presented at the Eighth Annual Conference of International Reading Association, Miami, Fla., May 1963.

9. L. Bloomfield, ELEM. ENGL. REV. 19, 125, 183 (1942).

10. See research reports of H. Levin and J. Watson, and H. Levin, E. Baum, and S. Bostwick, in A BASIC RESEARCH PROGRAM ON READING (See 4).

11. R. Dodge, PSYCHOL. BULL. 2, 193 (1905).

12. J. McK. Cattell, PHIL. STUDIES 2, 635 (1885).

13. D. E. Broadbent, PERCEPTION AND COMMUNICATION (Pergamon, New York, 1958).

14. E. Newman, AM. J. PSYCHOL., in press.

15. P. A. Kolers and M. T. Katzman, paper presented before the Psychonomic Society, Aug. 1963, Bryn Mawr, Pa.

16. Spelling patterns in English have been discussed by C. C. Fries in LINGUIS-TIC AND READING (Holt, Rinehart, and Winston, New York, 1963), p. 169 ff. C. F. Hockett, in A BASIC RESEARCH PROGRAM ON READING (see 4), has made an analysis of English graphic monosyllables which presents regularities of spelling patterns in relation to pronunciation. This study was continued by R. Venezky (thesis, Cornell Univ., 1962), who wrote a computer program for obtaining the regularities of English spelling-to-sound correspondence. The data obtained by means of the computer permit one to look up any vowel or consonant cluster of up to five letters and find its pronunciation in initial, medial, and final positions in a word. Letter environments as well have now been included in the analysis. See also R. H. Weir, FORMULATION OF GRAPH-EME-PHONEME CORRESPONDENCE RULES TO AID IN THE TEACHING OF READ-ING, Report on Cooperative Research Project No. 5-039 to the Office of Education, Department of Health, Education, and Welfare.

17. For example, the cluster GH may lawfully be pronounced as an F at the end of a word, but never at the beginning. The vowel cluster EIGH, pronounced /Ā/ (/ej/), may occur in initial, medial, and final positions, and does so with

nearly equal distribution. These cases account for all but two occurrences of the cluster in English orthography. A good example of regularity influenced by environment is [C] in a medial position before I plus a vowel. It is always pronounced /S/ (social, ancient, judicious).

18. E. J. Gibson, A. D. Pick, H. Osser, M. Hammond, AM. J. PSYCHOL. 75, 554 (1962).

19. E. J. Gibson, H. Osser, A. D. Pick, J. VERBAL LEARNING VERBAL BEHAV. 2, 142 (1963).

20. E. J. Gibson, C. H. Bishop, W. Schiff, J. Smith, J. EXP. PSYCHOL., 67, 173 (1964).

21. G. A. Miller and S. Isard, J. VERBAL LEARNING VERBAL BEHAV. 2, 217 (1963); also L. E. Marks and G. A. Miller, ibid. 3, 1 (1964).

STUDY QUESTIONS

1. What are the three phases of learning which follow the child's learning to use spoken language? Give an example of each.

2. Is the rat reading when he learns to jump to a yellow card and not to a red card? Why or why not?

3. Gibson reports a study by Bishop on letter and word training. What are the implications of this study for first-grade teachers?

4. What are "spelling patterns?" What do they have to do with teaching reading?

5. Why is it necessary to analyze the reading task? What else must be analyzed before a scientific pedagogy of reading instruction can be developed?

6. If Gibson were to design a first-grade reading program, which commercial programs might it resemble? (see Chall's LEARNING TO READ)

16: TEACHING READING TO CHILDREN WITH LOW MENTAL AGES

Siegfried Engelmann

Engelmann places responsibility for the child's learning to read on the program which purports to teach him that skill. He outlines the analysis of reading that forms the basis for a new reading program (DISTAR, published by SRA), which has been successful in teaching reading to children who, by traditional predictions and procedures, would be highly likely to fail to learn to read. The editor has selected this article in the hope and belief that Englemann's philosophy, as presented here, heralds a new and constructive approach to the teaching of reading to all children.

B. D. B.

Reprinted with permission of the author and publisher from EDUCATION AND TRAINING OF THE MENTALLY RETARDED, 1967, 2, 193-201.

Little progress has been made in developing effective reading instruction for children with low mental ages, i.e., below six and one-half years. In fact, little progress has been made in developing effective approaches for school age children with average mental ages (MA's). Although the average child learns to read, he does not usually learn very quickly; some average children have extreme difficulties, although they are intelligent and seem to have the mental equipment necessary to read.

Why does this situation exist? The answer seems to be that the authors of reading programs have typically approached in an awkward way the problem of teaching children to read. They have worked with average children of about six and one-half years. These children are relatively sophisticated. They have a pretty good idea of what reading is and they know what they are supposed to do in a new learning situation. They know how to treat words as sounds and not merely as signals that convey content. They play word games; they rhyme and alliterate. They probably know letter names and have a fair idea of some letter sounds. These children are able to learn to read from a variety of approaches, so they are thus able to compensate for gaps in an instructional program. They often learn in spite of the program. If the program does not provide adequate instruction for a particular subskill such as rhyming or blending, the children usually learn anyhow.

When the author of a beginning reading approach works with such children, he cannot clearly see the relationship between the effectiveness of his program and the children's reading performance. He cannot clearly see which skills he has successfully taught, which skills were taught before the child began the program, and which were obliquely induced through instruction. In other words, the author cannot refer to the performance of the children after they have received instruction and specify how much of it he is responsible for and how much of it is accounted for by home and previous training. Typically, he presumes that he is responsible for a great deal more than he deserves credit for. But since most of the children learn to read, it is difficult to discredit his presumption. For example, he may introduce exercises that are supposed to teach comprehension. He can refer to most of the children in the class who have received the instruction and note that they do comprehend. He may then conclude that his exercises were a success. But it is quite possible that these children would have comprehended well without the instruction he provided; it may be that their performance is not clearly a function of the instruction they have received. The author may justify readiness exercises in a similar manner, noting that the children who received the instruction are ready to read. However, much of the readiness training may be quite irrelevant to the problems associated with learning to read. If one provides a broad enough scope of tasks, one will undoubtedly hit upon some tasks that actually do prepare the child. In the process, however, one may provide many tasks that accomplish little.

When the author works with children who may have mastered skills that are necessary to read, there are relatively few checks on his imagination. He may identify skills that are basically irrelevant to the act of translating those clusters of squiggles on the printed page into word sounds, and he may fail to identify subskills that are crucial to the translation process. It might be difficult for us to demonstrate possible weaknesses in his program for the simple reason that most of the children who receive instruction perform well. It can be pointed out that a certain number of children who receive the instruction do not perform well, but the author is not usually compelled to take responsibility for these children. These children can be viewed in two ways: as children who fail because they have not received adequate instruction, or as children who fail because they lack aptitude, readiness, or intelligence. By attributing their failure to a lack of aptitude rather than a lack of appropriate instruction, the author can write them off, maintaining that his program is designed for "average" children. There is a certain appeal to this argument. Children do vary in aptitude, as any teacher knows, and it seems reasonable that not all can learn from a given approach. The danger in this argument, however, is that it leaves the author unbridled. He is provided with a floating standard. If the children succeed, the program is responsible; if they fail, the children are responsible. The instruction is exonerated from all responsibility for failure. Obviously, this situation is not healthy and does not promote better instruction. Rather, it encourages post hoc justification of what happened, with no fixed standard against which to measure the effectiveness of various approaches.

There have been comparisons of different reading approaches, but such comparisons do not tell us precisely in what areas a given program is strong or weak, and they do not effectively discredit the approach that is relatively poor in comparison with others. The author of an approach that does not do well in comparative studies may contend that his program achieves objectives that are not measured or taken into consideration in the comparison, such as an appreciation of reading. The act of reading is so broad and involve that it may be difficult to demonstrate that he is mistaken.

Solving the Problem

To solve the problem of providing better reading instruction for children who may have trouble with traditional approaches (including preschool and mentally retarded children), we must identify the various trouble spots encountere by those children in learning to read. Obviously, we cannot do this by worki with children who are more sophisticated than those with reading trouble, because more sophisticated children often do not encounter the severe difficulti that the children with less reading aptitude encounter. Therefore, children that are more sophisticated don't provide the kind of feedback that is necessa to identify the primary problems in learning to read. An analysis of the readi code provides important information about what is involved in reading, but it doesn't tell which skills are relatively difficult to learn and which are easy. T only way one discovers what the central problems are is to work with childre who have low MA's. These children are ideal subjects for developing solid instructional approaches for these reasons: a) they learn slowly, which means that the method developer can observe the problems they encounter in some detail; and b) they probably have not learned or even partially learned the key subskills in reading outside of the instructional setting, which means that if they learn to handle a particular subskill, we can credit the instruction with their learning.

The method developer working with low MA children is less likely to use a floating standard, less likely to say that those children who fail lack aptitude. All of his subjects lack aptitude: therefore, he is in a better position to accep the idea that if the children fail, the instruction has failed, and if they learn,

306

the instruction has succeeded. This attitude is potentially productive because it allows the method developer to look at each segment of reading behavior and see whether or not he can teach it. It is difficult to evaluate an approach by looking at it as a whole. An approach is more productively viewed as a series of components, each of which can be separately evaluated and subsequently improved. This kind of evaluation assumes that we clearly understand what the components are. The best way to find out is to work with the children who will tell us through their performance. The slow learning child does this. When he comes to a gap in instruction, he doesn't merely pause before working through the gap. He stops and he may remain stopped for weeks. His performance tells the curriculum designer when a technique works and when it doesn't work. The performance of the more sophisticated child does not.

A New Reading Program

The reading program that we are currently using in the Bereiter-Englemann preschool certainly does not represent the ultimate in reading instruction, but it is a good start. The program was developed by working with preschool children. Some were culturally deprived (with entering Stanford-Binet IQ scores of about 91; others were middle class children (with entering IQ scores of about 113); all were four years old. After 48 hours of classroom instruction, the culturally disadvantaged children read on the 1.25 grade level (Wide Range Achievement scores) and the middle class children read on the 2.3 grade level. Another group of disadvantaged children who received instruction for two school years read on the 2.6 grade level at the end of their kindergarten year. Not one child read below the 1.6 grade level, although some of these children wouldn't have been expected to read by the second or third grade if they had received traditional instruction.

While our work has been primarily focused on culturally disadvantaged children, it has implications for teaching reading to mentally retarded children for the following reasons:

1. Over one-third of the disadvantaged children we work with have entering IQ scores in the 80's, which place them on the fringe of the mentally handicapped.

2. Typically, IQ scores of four- and five-year-old children who have IQ scores in the 80's will drop as the children get older, which means that these children are potentially mentally handicapped at age four.

3. The mental ages of these children are as low as many children in special classes. An eight-year-old child who has an IQ score of 75 has a mental age of six years. The initial mental age of the disadvantaged children we work with is less than four years. This means that many of the children we have taught to read have less knowledge of the world and fewer skills than children who do not learn to read in special classes.

4. The younger child is often more difficult to teach than the older child with the same mental age because the younger child is generally more difficult to motivate, has a shorter interest span, and knows less about the type of classroom behavior that is expected of him.

Thus the approach that we use should work with all children who have MA's of four and above, whether they are classified as mentally retarded, culturally deprived, or gifted children.

The Method. Our motto in trying to work out a successful reading approach was simply to "keep the baloney out of the program." We did not analyze the reading code as the linguist or the educator typically analyzes it. We tried to determine what kind of behavior is demanded of the children, asking ourselves, What must they be able to do? Next we tried to develop tasks to teach them the appropriate behavior. And finally, we tried to remain sensitive to the children's reaction to the presentations. If they stalled and failed to learn a skill such as blending, we tried to make the rule for blending more obvious so that the children could see more clearly what they were expected to do. If various approaches seemed to make little difference in the children's progress we used the approach that seemed most economical and manageable, but we did not close the book on the issue. We recognized that it may be possible to supplant the drill with an approach that is far superior.

The children were taught in small groups, averaging about five children each. They were grouped homogeneously, according to performance in the classroom. The method of instruction demanded a great many responses from the children, so that the teacher received maximum feedback and the children received maximum corrected practice. Each daily reading period lasted from 15 to 20 minutes. The goal of instruction was to pack as much learning into these periods as possible.

We were particularly interested in identifying the places at which the children encountered difficulties. The first stumbling block encountered by our low MA children was in learning that the letters in a word stand for sounds that are sequenced in time. When a person says the word "Batman," some of the parts occur before other parts, and the order of the parts (or sound elements) is fixed. The words "manbat" or "tabman" are not the same as "Batman," because in these words, the order of parts has been violated. The instruction must therefore teach the naive child a) that the spoken word is composed of parts, b) that the parts occur in a fixed order in time, and c) that the reading code represents the passage of time through a left to right progression of symbols.

To teach the child to focus on parts of words, the teacher introduces rhyming and alliteration tasks. In rhyming, the child must hold part of the word constant—the ending—and vary the other part. "Okay, I want to hear some words that rhyme with superman. . . . Here's one: boo—perman. Here's another: foo—perman. And another: moo—. . . ." To teach alliteration (in which the beginning part stays the same and the ending changes) the teacher says, "I want some words that start out the same way as SSSS-uper. Here's one: SSSS-ister. Another: SSSS-ee. Another: SSSS—. . . ."

If the child has not mastered rhyming and alliteration skills, he will probably have an extremely difficult time reading. Specifically, he'll have difficulty understanding how similar words are similar. Similar words are similar because part of one word is the same (makes the same sound) as a part of the others. If the child cannot hear the way in which "car" is the same as "far," he is not in a very good position to look for the sameness in the orthography of the two words.

To teach the children the rule for mapping the passing of time from left to right, the teacher begins by demonstrating how to sequence events from left to right. The teacher claps her hands together and follows this action by tapping herself on the head with one hand. "I'm doing it the right way," she says, and invites the children to do it with her, pausing between each trial. After the children have produced the pair of actions a number of times, the teacher says, "My turn. Watch me and tell me if I'm doing it the right way." She then produces the actions either in the correct or the reverse order. "Did I do it the right way?" Not all the children will be able to see the difference. Some will insist that the sequence head tap-hand clap is the right way.

After the teacher has made the children aware of the right way using a variety of examples, she symbolizes the actions and presents them on the chalkboard from left to right. For the hand clap she uses this symbol: "- - - -" (demonstrating how it is formed by holding her hands at the ends of the line and bringing them together in a clap); for the head tap, she introduces this symbol: "O." She draws an arrow on the board pointing from left to right. She claps her hands and makes the corresponding symbol at the tail of the arrow. "I'm drawing a picture of what I did." She then follows with the head tap, and makes the symbol for it near the head of the arrow. She asks the children to read what happened. "Start here and go with the arrow." After demonstrating how the code works, she presents a series of examples in which the children are asked to do what the symbols tell them to do. For example, she may present the following series and have the children read it and do what it says.

FIGURE 1. SAMPLE CODE SERIES

As the children become increasingly proficient in working with the code, she can introduce other symbols and introduce more difficult tasks, such as having a child symbolize a series of events that is produced either by the teacher or by another child.

the children learn the rules for translating events that occur in time onto
ace, they are also introduced to the conventional sound symbols used in
ding. Initially, the following sounds are presented: "ă," "ŏ," "e," "m,"
" "r," "s," and "n." There is no particular difficulty involved in teaching
se. Young disadvantaged and retarded children learn the symbol slowly,
t they succeed in time. The teacher should be careful not to overload the
ldren by presenting too many examples. She must also be careful not to
sent the same objects unless she wants to induce mislearning. She must
sent many different examples of each letter, as it appears on cards and on
chalkboard in different colors and different sizes. All letters are presented
sounds; "a" is identified as the short "a" sound ("and"); "f" is the un-
ced sound that occurs at the beginning of such words as "fan."

ese initial letters are selected not on the basis of frequency of occurrence
on the basis of linguistic considerations, but on the basis of specific dif-
ulties the low MA child has in learning to read. Stated differently, they
selected because they allow for the most precise demonstration of the
ationship between the unblended word and the blended word. Typically,
disadvantaged child and the retarded child have trouble learning to blend.
e can walk into virtually any third grade class for disadvantaged children
note many children making the same type of error. They can sound out
vord such as "cat," saying, "cu-ah-tu." But they cannot put the pieces
ether to form a word. When asked, "What word is that?" they either
ug or repeat, "cu-ah-tu." Their failure to see the similarity between "cu-
tu," and "cat" is not without cause. The relationship between "cu-ah-
' and "cat" is not particularly obvious. The parts of the unblended word
separated by pauses in time; the parts of the blended word are not. There
sounds in the unblended word that do not appear in the blended word.
e relationship between blended and unblended words can be made more
vious by the following method:

st, the teacher introduces only those words that begin with a continuous
nd, not a stop sound. Such words as "cat" are not introduced. Such
rds as "fan" and "ran" are introduced. Next, the teacher teaches the chil-
n to blend without pausing between letters. The child is taught the

311

convention that one sound is held until the next one is produced. When th child attempts to sound out the word "ran," he says, "rrraaannn." In this unblended word there are no pauses; there are no extra sounds. Its relation ship to "ran" is therefore quite obvious.

After the child has learned to process simple two and three letter words com posed of continuous sound letters, he is introduced to words that contain st sounds. The stop sounds are first introduced at the end of three sound wor "rat," "rag," and "rab."

The stop sounds are then moved to the beginning. To demonstrate how the work, the teacher begins a series of familiar endings, such as: "an," "an," and "an." She introduces familiar continuous sound beginnings: "fan," "ran," and "man." She then erases these beginnings and introduces stop sound beginnings: "can," "gan," and "tan." Before attacking a word she c attention to the vowel. "What does this say? Yes: ă. So this word is ca— By calling attention to the vowel, the teacher allows the child to produce th sounds of the first and second letter together—"că"—thereby eliminating son of the difficulties associated with stop sounds.

The conventions introduced to demonstrate blending make a significant dif- ference in the performance of the children.

The teacher next introduces a long vowel convention. A long line drawn over a vowel changes the sound to the letter names, "a," "e," "i," "o," and "u." The teacher proceeds quickly to exercises in which the children first sound out and identify a familiar word, such as "rat." The teacher then draws a line over the vowel, "rat," and the children sound out the new word "rate."

The children now have a large enough repertoire of sounds to begin reading small stories. Initially, the teacher avoids any of the vowel sounds that have not been introduced (such as the vowel sounds in the words "all," "foil," etc.) and she avoids such combinations as "th" and "ch."

312

She limits herself to those sounds the child has learned and she spells all words phonetically. For example, she spells the word "said" as "sed," and the word "have," "hav." The following is an example of the kind of story the teacher might introduce:

A cat līks mēt.
Hē ēts mēt and he runs.
Hē has fun.

These stories familiarize the children with the conventions involved in moving from one line of text to the next.

The teacher then introduces new sound combinations—"th," "ch," "oo," "ee," "oi," and "oy"—and expands the scope of her stories.

The final step, which is actually taken in gradual stages starting when the children begin reading stories, is to introduce irregularly spelled words. These are presented as "funny words," that is, words that are spelled a sound at a time, the way any other word is spelled, but that are pronounced as if they were spelled differently. Handling irregulars in this way is extremely important. The child must learn that the spelling of words is not arbitrary. The word "have" is always spelled the same way; however, it is pronounced as if it were spelled differently, without the final "e." "It looks like 'hav-ĕ,' but we don't say 'hav-ĕ,' we say, 'hav.' " Unless irregulars are handled this way, a certain number of children will abandon any kind of phonetic attack, trying to remember individual words and making wild guesses such as calling the word "have," "got."

Some irregular words are introduced early so that the child doesn't get the idea that the reading code is perfectly regular. The initial irregular words the teacher introduces are: "he," "she," "we," "me," "go," "so," and "no." These are presented by erasing the diacritical marks over the vowel. To prompt the children on how to sound out these words, the teacher simply indicates with her finger (drawing an imaginary line over the vowel) that the vowel should be treated as a long vowel.

After the children have become reasonably familiar with the initial set of irregulars, the teacher introduces other common words that are not as neat as the originals: "to," "want," "like," "was," "were," etc. These are carefully programed so that the child receives sufficient exposure on one or two of them every day until these are mastered. Then, the next pair is introduced while the previous pair is continued as a fairly regular schedule.

Implications

The major implication of our work seems to be that children with relatively low mental ages (initially less than four years) can learn to read if the instruction is adequately geared to give them instruction on all of the subskills demanded by the complex behavior we call reading. Furthermore, virtually all children with mental ages of four or over can learn to read. Their progress is relatively slow, but all can progress from one subskill to the next until they are reading. With the emphasis on subskills, the teacher is in a position to know precisely what skills a child has not learned. She therefore knows which skills to work on. When a child masters a given skill, the teacher can proceed to the next one.

If a child has a mental age of four to six years, the chances are overwhelming that he can learn to read, if the instructional program is adequate. Such programs are not commercially available, however, and the teacher of the mentally retarded child is therefore faced with a dilemma. Should she continue to use material that has been proven to be inadequate to teach mentally retarded children to read, or should she wait until programs are commercially available? She should not wait, because the children she is teaching cannot wait. They cannot place themselves in a state of suspended animation for several years, at which time adequate programs will probably be on the market. She must do the best she can. Specifically, this means:

> 1. She should recognize that the most difficult skills the child must learn are not gross comprehension or experiential skills, but skills in learning how to translate a written word into a series of sounds and putting these sounds together to form a spoken word.

2. She should be extremely skeptical of published materials that do not concentrate on these skills; she should not use a given method merely because it works on normal children; she should not introduce whole words.

3. She should be cautious about assuming that different children "learn in a different way" and must be treated differently. If the criterion of performance is the same for all children, the steps they must take to arrive at that criterion must be the same; therefore, the instruction should be basically the same, in that it should concentrate on the skills that the children must learn in order to achieve the desired criterion of performance (which is to be able to translate clusters of symbols into words).

4. She should work with i.t.a. if possible, recognizing that the program as published is inadequate, but also recognizing that it provides the children with clear demonstrations of the relationship between sounds and symbols, since one symbol stands for one and only one sound.

5. She should not try to teach all of the symbols, but merely enough of them to allow for word building; she should not initially program stop sound consonants ("b," "d," "c," "g," "h," "k," "p," and "t") but only those consonants which can be blended continuously ("f," "j," "l," "m," "n," "r," and "s").

6. She should introduce word blends early with the continuous sound convention.

7. She should simultaneously teach the children the verbal skills of saying words fast, saying words slowly, rhyming, and alliterating. Saying words fast is a blending task; the teacher says a word such as "ta—ble" and asks the children to "Say it fast—'table.' " Saying words slowly is an unblending task in which the teacher says words and asks children to say it slowly, a sound at a time. ("Listen: 'man.' Say it slowly—'mmmaaannn.' "). The focus of rhyming should be a task in which the children are assigned an ending, the teacher says various beginnings, and the children say the ending and identify the word. ("Here are some

words that rhyme with table: 'ta-ble,' 'ra-ble,' 'ma—,' 'ca—,' 'sta—.' ")
The focus of alliteration should be a task in which the children are assigned a beginning to which the teacher attaches various endings; the children must then identify the word. (Children say "sss." Teacher follows
with " 'and'—What word is that?" Children say, "ssss." Teacher follows
with " 'eee'—What word is that?")

8. She should introduce stop sounds only after the children have learned
to handle continuous sound blends.

9. She should introduce irregulars very cautiously (but relatively early);
she should treat these as "funny words," pointing out that they are
sounded out in the same way other words are, but aren't pronounced
that way.

Teaching reading to children with low mental ages is not easy because these
children must learn a great deal before they can hope to read. Their progress
is much slower than that of children with higher mental ages. But they can
and should be taught if the aim of education is to educate. There is nothing
unique about the problems encountered by mentally handicapped children.
The problems are the same as those encountered by any child with a relatively
low mental age. To read, all children must learn the set of skills. The child
with a higher mental age has already been taught many of these before he
steps into the classroom. By focusing on these skills and forgetting about
such empty labels as "dyslexia" and "perceptually handicapped," a teacher
can succeed with children who have mental ages of four or over. The secret
of success is simply to provide the children with adequate instruction.

STUDY QUESTIONS

1. School System 101 has been using the "Mervin and Mabel" reading program. At the end of first grade, standardized reading achievement tests show that 20% of the children are reading substantially above grade level, 50% are at or near grade level, and 30% are substantially below grade level. The administrators note that those figures are approximately the same as exist throughout the entire state, so they conclude that the "Mervin and Mabel" reading program is adequate. Give three specific objections Englemann would raise against that conclusion.

2. Why does Engelmann urge that a reading program be developed with children who have mental ages appreciably below 6 years?

3. Engelmann lists nine specific do's and don'ts for reading teachers: The first three are controversial. Present the traditional point of view regarding each of these three. How would Engelmann defend his position?

4. What are the specific behaviors which constitute reading, according to Engelmann? Does Engelmann recommend teaching these specific things differently to different children, depending on the child's strengths and weaknesses?

17: IMPROVED LEARNING CONDITIONS IN THE ESTABLISHMENT OF READING SKILLS WITH DISABLED READERS

Norris G. Haring
Mary Ann Hauck

Haring and Hauck present evidence suggesting that if the conditions under which learning to read is expected to occur are appropriately controlled and manipulated, children will learn effectively and efficiently. They thus forge another link in the chain of reason and data suggesting that a child's failure to learn to read is but a reflection of our failure to teach him. Responsibility is shifting from the child to the reading program.

B. D. B.

Reprinted with permission of the authors and publisher from EXCEPTIONAL CHILDREN, 1969, 35, 341-352.

Children with severe reading disabilities are currently receiving national attention and concern. These are children who apparently have failed to acquire the necessary responses to be successful in reading. Their reading performances typically exhibit low rates of total performance, high rates of error, and marked deficiency in visual to auditory and auditory to visual association, as well as other related deficiencies in discrimination. Research providing reliable information about this serious behavior problem is extremely urgent. Neither medicine nor education has conducted research, which can be replicated and utilized in the natural school setting, that provides answers to the identification, treatment, and prevention of the problems presented by these children.

Medically oriented professionals (Critchley, 1966; Hermann, 1959; Money, 1962) have referred to these children as dyslexic, a term often meant to suggest that the child has a reading disability associated with minimal neurological dysfunctioning. This label attached to children who read poorly may or may not be appropriate, and the present investigators in no way acknowledge the existence of such a medical entity. These children, nevertheless, remain a serious problem to educators.

There are widely varying reading deficits among children which might result from either biological or experiential factors. By the time reading behavior becomes important to children, however, it is far too late to be concerned about etiology. The concern to the educator is with procedures which will predictably establish reading responses with children having severe reading disabilities. The concern of the present investigation was the establishment of reading skills in four boys with severe reading disability using systematic instructional procedures.

Analysis of Reading Behavior

The process of using systematic procedures began with an analysis of reading behavior. This analysis included a) an assessment of the entering skills each student had acquired; b) specification of terminal reading skills each student should acquire; c) specification of successive approximations to these terminal reading skills that would be viewed as progress in skill development; and d) an assessment of the kinds of stimuli which could function as reinforcing events to the individual child.

TABLE 1. ENTERING AND TERMINAL LEVELS OF READING SKILLS
OF SUBJECTS

Student			Entering Levels		Terminal Levels	
	Grade	Programed Material	Basal Reader	Word recognition	Basal Reader	Programed Material
RD	5	Primer	Primer	2.8	4-1	4.2
M	4	Primer	Primer	2.5	3-1	3.9
R	4	Primer	3.1	3.1	4-2	4.5
P	3	Primer	Primer	2.5	2-2	3.5

As social reinforcers had well demonstrated their weakness in shaping skill development in these boys, other stimuli which were already strong reinforcers to these four students had to be used. An extensive repertoire of skills cannot be built without the use of variables that are motivating to the child (Ferster, 1961). Although candy (Hewett, 1964), trinkets (Staats, Staats, Schutz, & Wolf, 1962), a combination of both (Bijou & Sturges, 1959), and opportunity to engage in a desired activity (Homme, deBaca, Devine, Steinhorst, & Rickert, 1963) have all been demonstrated as strong reinforcers, the most powerful extrinsic reinforcer for accelerating responses has proved to be token reinforcement (Bijou & Baer, 1966; Ferster & Skinner, 1957; Ferster & DeMyer, 1961) because it is appropriate to changing conditions of deprivation. Token reinforcement procedures use reinforcing events which have become motivating by their temporal occurrence (pairing) with other more basic reinforcers. Points (Haring & Kunzelmann, 1966), chips (Bijou, 1958), stars and checkmarks (Birnbrauer, Wolf, Kidder, & Tague, 1965), exchangeable for time to engage in an activity of one's choice (Haring & Kunzelmann, 1966) or for a wide variety of store items (Staats et al., 1962; Staats & Butterfield, 1965), have functioned as powerful motivators in skill development (Zimmerman & Zimmerman, 1962).

320

The present investigation used token reinforcement in the form of points as counter numbers and later as marbles exchangeable for edibles, trinkets, and more expensive store items that were known to be highly reinforcing. Space and equipment were unavailable for investigating effects from tokens exchangeable for activity time. Information useful for establishing a store of reinforcers was obtained from the students and their parents during informal conversations that initiated the entering assessments.

Terminal reading goals were established as reading at grade level, as in basal readers and Sullivan Programmed Books. Successive approximations of the terminal goals were built into the commercially programed reading materials in minute and successive response requirements.

METHOD

Subjects

Four elementary school boys (grades 5, 4, 4, and 3) severely disabled in reading but average or above average in intelligence, were diagnostically evaluated by the experimenters as one to 5 years retarded in reading skills. Entering reading behaviors are categorized in Table 1 under entering grade level, word recognition level from the Gates-McKillop Diagnostic Reading Tests, instructional reading level determined by informal basal reading tests, and placement in Sullivan Programmed Reading Books determined by the Sullivan Placement Test. All four boys presented reading skills at the primer level in Sullivan Programmed materials. Only one boy, R, read above the primer level in a basal reader.

Materials and Apparatus

Reading materials were sequentially ordered in frames with answers adjacent to each presentation to allow for individual progress and effective sequencing of skills. A slider covered the answer until a written response was completed.

321

The highly structured reading environment contained a teacher station, four student stations, and a reinforcement area. A podium behind the four student served as the teacher station at which the teacher performed her observations and made verbal contact with each boy through a microphone to the headsets worn by each boy. She whispered instructions, provided directional prompting cues during oral reading, and manipulated switches to reinforce oral responses throughout the experiment. At the student stations, students completed all written and oral reading work, and manipulated a switch at the outside edge of their carrels to record correct and incorrect written responses.

The reinforcement area contained edibles, trinkets, and toys priced at various point values based on actual retail value. Items with retail value of 15 cents or more had point values based on 400 points per 15 cents. Five cent items were valued at 200 points, 10 cent items at 350 points, and one cent items at 50 points. Pellets of candy, gum, and peanuts were valued at 25 points. Reinforcers were packaged separately except for pellets of candy and gum which were bottled for dispensing one at a time.

Design and Procedures

Obtaining continuous evaluation and making ongoing decisions for the development of terminal behaviors required that the effects of reinforcement variables on written and oral reading responses be continuously measured through each change in variables. The five periods of the design included two baseline periods and three modification periods (See Table 2). The study continued for 91 days with a 65 minute session each day—the students' only formal reading period. Reading material remained constant throughout the five periods except that content became progressively more complex.

Response specification. Two types of responses from each student were measured: written responses and oral responses. A written response was defined by the response requirement of each programed frame: a) circling the correct word or picture, b) drawing a line to the correct word or picture, c) writing one letter or several letters, or d) writing a whole word. Each constituted one written response. One oral response was defined as each word read orally from a) lists of new words, b) word discrimination groupings, and c) sentences appropriate to each unit in the programed books.

TABLE 2. BASELINE AND MODIFICATION PERIODS OF EXPERIMENT

Independent Reinforcement Variables	Periods					
	A	B	C	D	E	F
	Without answers	With answers	Counters	Continuous reinforcement token reinforcement	Variable ratio token reinforcement	Variable ratio token reinforcement
Material	Programed Material		Programed Material			Basal reader
Period type	Baseline periods		Modification periods			

Baseline periods. The four boys served as their own controls in two ways. First, each brought with him an academic history exhibiting from one to four years of low rates of performance in reading. Secondly, during the first 2 weeks of the experiment, the students made reading responses to the programed material without receiving any reinforcement beyond what the programed format offered, i.e., immediate confirmation of answers and/or appropriate sequencing of textual material. These measures, especially the latter, were considered as representing the number of correct reading responses each student made under conditions prior to the experimental conditions—response data which served as a baseline from which to compare behavior change.

Adaptation. Prior to the first baseline period, 4 days of adaptation introduced procedures for: a) written responding to programed reading, b) oral responding to appropriate stimuli from cards and teacher directions through earphones; and c) switch use.

323

Period A. During the 4 days of Period A, answer columns were stapled together, visible answers were blacked out, and verbal correction of oral responses was not given. Under these conditions, which approximated classroom assignments for which answer feedback is often delayed, each response was followed by the next frame and movement of a switch by the student to record his response.

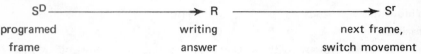

S^D R S^r

| programed | writing | next frame, |
| frame | answer | switch movement |

Period B. The 7 days of this period provided a typical programed format. After making each written response, the student obtained answer confirmation from the adjacent answer column. Verbal correction of oral responses was given by the teacher. The student recorded the accuracy of his answer by moving a switch at his carrel to the right if he was correct and to the left if incorrect.

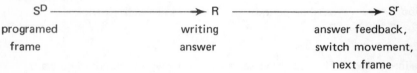

S^D R S^r

programed	writing	answer feedback,
frame	answer	switch movement,
		next frame

During this period the programed format was modified permanently to avoid misuse of the answers. This enabled measurement of responses emitted before answers were known. Answers were cut from the books, perforated at the top, and hung backwards on hooks in front of the student. The cut pages were stapled into books. The modified format required the student to write responses to a complete page of frames, remove the answer column from the hook, place it next to the corresponding frames, and correct his written responses.

Period C. Following the baseline period, a counter, which tallied the number of correct responses being made, was installed at each carrel and functioned as the only change in variables for the next 12 days.

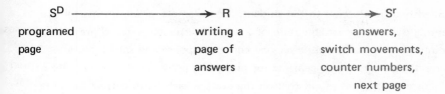

S^D ──────────────→ R ──────────────→ S^r
programed   writing a   answers,
page   page of   switch movements,
                               answers   counter numbers,
                                                                next page

This running account of the number of correct responses emitted proved to be important information for both the student and his neighbor.

Although the counter directly influenced behavior, the more important process for modification of the student's skills was the systematic application of reinforcement following two basic procedures: acquisition and maintenance reinforcement. During the initial modification procedures (Period D), when each student's correct reading responses occurred at a very low rate, it was necessary to reinforce each correct reading response. When each student had exhibited a high, stable rate of correct reading responses over a number of sessions, reinforcement was presented only intermittently (Period E), but no less systematically, to maintain the high output of correct responses each boy was exhibiting.

Period D: Acquisition reinforcement. Throughout the 21 days of Period D, counter numbers functioned as points (token reinforcement) with exchange value for edibles, trinkets, and more expensive items. Correct responses were reinforced continuously. Each correct written or oral response immediately earned one point, and each student set up his own chained reinforcement schedule of continuous reinforcement (CRF) components by his choice of the reinforcers for which he would work. During the first week, points had exchange value for store items varying from 25 points to 1,000 points. During the second week expensive items were introduced for purchase requiring point saving over many days or several weeks.

Period E: Maintenance reinforcement. Correct responses during the 47 days of Period E were reinforced intermittently. Arrangements for reinforcement changed progressively from presentation following a variable ratio (VR) of every two responses (VR 2) to VR 4, VR 5, VR 7, VR 10, VR 15, and VR

25, without instruction to the student. For example, arrangements for presenting points on a variable ratio of 2 correct responses entailed presenting points variably, sometimes after one correct response and sometimes after 2 correct responses. Arrangements for presenting points on a variable ratio of 10 correct responses meant that on the average each tenth correct response received a point, although in fact sometimes a marble would be earned after one response, or after 3 responses, or sometimes only after 20 correct responses.

The objective of intermittent reinforcement was to maintain, as the number of reinforcements per responses progressively decreased, the high stable rate of performance which developed during continuous reinforcement. Intermittent reinforcement of correct responses initially was very frequent, but progressively became less frequent as responding appeared to stablilize with each change in schedule. Except for the initial instructions indicating that sometimes, following a number of correct responses, the student would earn a marble worth 10 points, no instructions were given when reinforcement arrangements changed.

Marbles worth 10 points each took the place of counter points as token reinforcement to give the experimenters the flexibility necessary for intermittent reinforcement with crude, nonautomatic equipment. The series of numbers within a ratio schedule were determined randomly to enable randomly varied reinforcer presentation controlled from the teacher's podium. Following a predetermined number of correct responses registered on a student's counter at the teacher's podium, the teacher flipped a microswitch which activated a stimulus light at a student carrel indicating to the student he had made enough correct responses to have earned a marble. The boy responded to the stimulus light by manipulating an apparatus attached to his carrel which dispensed a marble.

Period F. This month of transition was designed as another step in the reinforcement of successive approximations to the terminal behavior—"normal reader functioning under natural contingencies." The independent variables which changed were the instructional materials. As Figure 1 indicates, a three-

326

mponent chained sequence of responding required a) reading a word list, b) ding a story from the basal reader, and c) making a choice between reading a basal book or a library book. Silent reading preparation preceding the portunity to read orally for points constituted the basic procedure in each mponent. The points earned and the reinforcement given for correct oral ding were credited to the student contingent on daily completion of all ee components. Word lists containing words not known during silent prepaion or oral responding were grouped to emphasize common word parts, dertions, and/or syllable division. Comprehension was measured by responses oral questions from the teacher after oral reading and by answers to written ltiple choice questions following story completion.

tially, the students were assigned to read only one basal reader page silently fore having the opportunity to read orally for points. But within one week, s requirement had changed to silently reading 3 pages before oral reading d, finally, they were required to read a complete story. Initially, when a dent orally read a randomly selected paragraph for points, he earned one int per word in each line of print read correctly. But within a week, read- the total paragraph correctly was required before any points were earned. is incorporated an essential feature of skill development: progressive in- ase in task difficulty as performance data exhibit readiness.

inforcement was provided only for correct oral responding, as follows: a) m the word list, 5 points per word within each group of similar words read rrectly, but no points for words in a group if errors occurred within it; b) m the basal reader, initially one point per word from a line of print read thout error and later from a paragraph read without error, but no points if y errors were made in either instance; c) during the "choice" component, points per word from a paragraph read without error if the basal reader was osen, and one point per word from a paragraph or page if a library book s chosen. All material to be read orally was randomly selected from pages eady read silently, except the words on the word list. Correct oral answers oral comprehension questions received 5 points. Correct written answers written comprehension questions received 10 points. Following Period F, e same reading procedures were continued but under the direction of the cher in the student's public school classroom.

FIGURE 1. CHAINED SEQUENCE OF RESPONDING REQUIRED IN PERIOD F

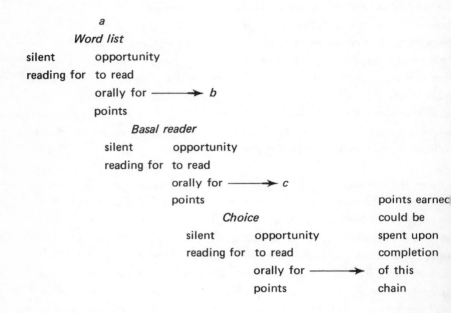

Teacher Instruction

The teacher paced the students together through side one of the Sullivan Primer the first 2 days of the adaptation period to establish the procedural chain for functioning in the experimental environment. From that time on each student progressed individually.

All other reading instruction from the teacher was given during oral reading in the Sullivan material for Periods A through E and in the basal readers and word lists during Period F. When a student mispronounced a word while reading orally, the teacher directed him to the word for another try by repeating the word immediately preceding the word mispronounced. With this cue, the student returned to the mispronounced word for a second try. If he failed on this try, the teacher provided directional cues highlighting the beginning, middle, or ending of the word. For example, the teacher would say, "Look at the beginning of the word again." If the student failed with this cue, he was told the sound of the part missed, and finally told the word, if necessary. The first cue was often sufficient; the latter two were rarely needed. Mispronounced words were programed for a word list the next day.

The teacher diagnostically recorded mispronunciations during oral reading. With microswitches she recorded the interval and content of her verbal interaction with a student as well as the number of correct oral responses a student was making. The latter data also registered on the student's counter.

Teacher Communications

Teacher communication was almost totally preplanned and prepared in script form. Scripts controlled teacher communication for: a) giving initial procedural directions, b) repeating directions upon request or upon teacher observation of improper responding to directions, c) requesting oral reading, d) stopping behavior harmful to others or to equipment, e) dispensing final reinforcers, and f) commencing or dismissing class.

Student Procedures

The two basic procedures for the students entailed writing answers in their programed books and orally reading from word cards at the teacher's requests. Oral reading was programed to correspond with progress in the books.

During reinforcement periods, points earned, spent, and saved were recorded in common bank savings books. At any time a student had earned enough points or marbles to make a purchase he had the option to make a purchase, although students usually waited until the session ended.

Response Recording

A 20 pen event recorder automatically recorded the occurrence of correct oral responses, and the occurrence and content of teacher communication as well as correct and incorrect written responses. A daily check of the student's switch use was obtained from a book count of the actual number of correct and incorrect written responses.

RESULTS

Results will be discussed under three categories: a) comparison of response data between baseline and modification periods, b) reading skill progress and c) reinforcer preference.

Average Response Data

Baseline performance. Response data for both baseline periods (Period A, with no answer confirmation given, and Period B, with immediate answer confirmation given) were similar for all four students. Whether or not the student was provided immediate confirmation of answers, the total number of correct responses made daily was low. Correct responding, which occurred at the rate of about four per minute when the child was reading, was irregularly interspersed with responding to stimuli other than reading materials. Almost half of each session was spent in behavior incompatible with making reading responses, resulting in an overall average of 2.8 correct responses per session. Over the last few days of the baseline period, a rapid decrease in the number of reading responses and a rapid increase in the amount of time spent not reading were evident. Figure 2 exhibits for each student the average number of correct responses made each session and the average number of 5 minute intervals spent not making reading responses.

Counters (Period C). After counters were installed, dramatic changes occurred in reading performance. Students made correct responses at the baseline rate of 4 per minute but typically made over 300 each session, resulting in an overall rate of 4.5 responses per session. Responding became stable throughout the session with very few five-minute intervals when the student was not making reading responses. Although response rate varied extremely over sessions for each student, compared to rate during continuous reinforcement (Period D), counters did function as conditioned reinforcers. Average response rates were significantly higher for three of the four boys compared to baseline rates. Misuse of the programed format by the fourth boy, M, before answers were clipped from the frames prevented accurate comparison of his overall baseline rate with rates between other periods. Comparison between his rate during Period A when he could not misuse the answers and his rate during any modification period, however, indicates a very significant difference.

Acquisition reinforcement (Period D). Systematic application of reinforcers following each correct response during the first week of this modification period resulted in: a) establishing stable reading rates throughout each session; b) accelerating response rates to 6.2 and 8.5 correct responses per minute; and c) producing daily rates as high as 400 to 550 correct responses. Table 3 exhibits the significantly higher average response rates which occurred for three of the four students under continuous reinforcement compared to baseline conditions.

TABLE 3. COMPARISON OF AVERAGE TOTAL RESPONSES PER PERIOD

Subjects	Average Total Responses				
	Baseline Periods		Modification Periods		
	A	B	C	D	E
RD	115	228	335*	334*	316*
M	121	335a	337*	267	240
R	219	94	295*	319*	209*
P	180	174	221*	297*	213*

*Chi square test revealed significantly higher ($p < .001$) average total responses
aMisuse of answers

Two boys, P and RD, averaged about 100 more correct responses every session, while R averaged almost 200 more correct responses. It may be of importance to note that M responded during Period D almost as fast as he misused the answers during the baseline conditions of Period B.

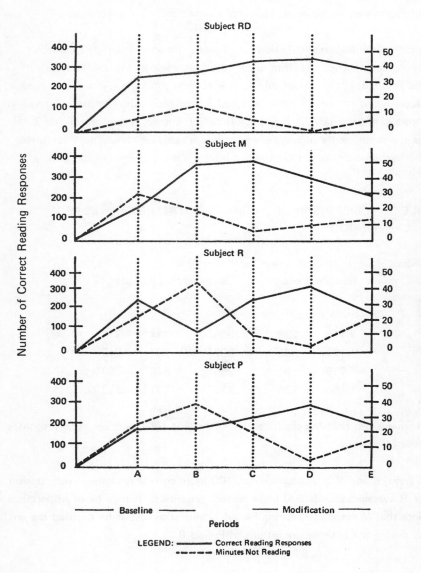

FIGURE 2. AVERAGE NUMBER OF CORRECT RESPONSES AND AVERAGE NUMBER OF MINUTES SPENT NOT READING PER PERIOD

Subject RD

Subject M

Subject R

Subject P

Number of Correct Reading Responses

Number of 5 Minute Periods Spent Not Reading

Baseline ——— Modification ———

Periods

LEGEND: ——— Correct Reading Responses
‑‑‑‑‑ Minutes Not Reading

Expensive reinforcers introduced the second week, requiring long term saving, were not effective in maintaining high response rates. Rates either rapidly decelerated or stabilized at a lower rate until the middle of the third week of Period D when three of the four students, short of the points necessary for very expensive items for which they had been saving, spent all points they had. At that time, responding again accelerated to near the high level observed the first weeks of Period D. A reinforcer too far removed from the response—too far in time from the final reinforcer—does not maintain the desired response (Kelleher & Gollub, 1962).

Maintenance reinforcement (Period E). As the number of reinforcements decreased gradually from one on the average of every 2 correct responses to one on the average of every 25 responses, without instruction to the student over 47 days, the significant difference between baseline response rates and changes in response rates during Period D modification procedures was maintained. A chi square test revealed that total responses under variable ratio schedules were significantly higher (.001 level) than baseline rate for three of the four boys, although significantly lower than rate under continuous reinforcement for two of the four boys.

Although research has demonstrated that response rates are characteristically higher under intermittent reinforcement than under continuous reinforcement (Ferster & Skinner, 1957; Kelleher & Gollub, 1962; Staats, Finley, Minke, & Wolf, 1964), there are several reasons why this failed to occur in the present study. During continuous reinforcement, the student probably responded near his physiological limit as he moved through the chain of requirements for writing, correcting, and recording the answer. Secondly, response requirements had become more complex, requiring much more silent reading per written response. RD and M, for whom response requirements changed greatly during Period C but not during Periods D and E, exhibited average daily responses not significantly different between these two periods. R and P, for whom response requirements changed greatly, exhibited significantly lower rates in Period E.

Observation of the number of minutes spent reading when learning conditions were motivating reveals a marked decrease in the number of intervals spent avoiding reading. When reading was reinforcing, the reading performance of the four students exhibited both higher rates and more intervals of reading during each session. The increase in minutes spent not reading during Period E for R and P is evidence of weakening reinforcers. Certainly for R the data exhibit the effect of a visit by his mother 2 weeks before the end of the period; she told him he must not buy any more candy or other edibles. For R, edibles had been the strongest reinforcers; consequently, his rate rapidly decelerated, but all points he did earn were spent on candy.

Maintenance reinforcement during transition (Period F). The chain of three silent and oral reading components, through which the child had to respond each session, using reading materials typical of the classroom, proved very effective in maintaining stable rates during the final 19 days in the experimental setting and the final 3 weeks of responding in the regular classroom. Only once out of the 19 days of the period did each boy fail to silently prepare his reading lesson carefully before having the opportunity to read orally for points. A lesson poorly prepared silently meant few points earned during oral reading.

This same three component chained assignment was used during the final 3 weeks of school within the regular classroom with equal effectiveness. At the time the students returned to the classroom, R moved out of the state. A followup letter from his mother stated he was reading above grade level in his classroom, and at home was reading "everything he could get his hands on." Reading performance back in the regular classroom actually occurred at a higher average rate than observed during the last week in the experimental setting. In the classroom, a student helper or the classroom teacher listened to the oral reading, tallied the number of words read correctly, and recorded the information in a common bankbook. The total number of correct responses was converted into "points to spend," using the same intermittant schedules from the experimental procedures. Twice a week each student was brought a supply of store items from which to make purchases. Plans for the final phase of the project require maintenance of these efficient, accurate reading performances, using systematic programing of learning conditions natural to the classroom.

Reading Progress

Change in reading performance was not only remarkable because of the amount of change in rate of making correct responses every day and the number of 5 minute intervals spent reading, but also because of the amount of measurable skill development. Overall changes in the instructional reading levels of the four boys ranged from one and one-half years to 4 years, following 5 months of instruction (Table 1). Comparison of pre- and postmeasures of instructional basal reading levels indicated: a) RD progressed from primer to book 4-1; b) M progressed from primer to book 3-1; c) R progressed from book 3-1 to 4-2; and d) P progressed from primer to book 2-2 by the time the transition period began. Each student read his final programed book with less than 5 percent error rate during both oral and silent reading.

Reinforcer preference. Of the three types of reinforcers available for purchase, the preferred reinforcers were generally edibles and expensive items, although individual preference patterns differed. The typical daily pattern for point spending included purchase of 50 to 200 points worth of edibles and saving of the remainder toward purchase of an expensive item valued between 500 and 1,500 points.

Summary and Conclusion

Learning conditions were individually programed in a group setting to provide sequential arrangement of reading material and systematic presentation of reinforcing events to optimize each child's performance. Arrangements of reinforcing events were designed first to accelerate performance rate, then to maintain the high rate. Learning conditions were considered optimal when the child's performance rate accelerated and stabilized at a higher rate and/or when the number of minutes spent avoiding reading greatly decreased.

When learning conditions were individually appropriate, each child averaged between 100 and 200 more correct responses every day and spent very few minutes avoiding reading. The students not only made more correct responses daily and worked longer, but also progressed in instructional reading levels from one and one-half to 4 years over 5 months of instruction. Behavior and performance in other academic areas within the regular classroom also improved markedly, according to *unsolicited* comments from the classroom teachers.

Conditions for learning were evaluated, through direct and continuous measurement of the student's performance under specified conditions, a) in terms of effectiveness of the conditions for reading, and b) for functional, ongoing decisions about future arrangements of these conditions.

The steps in modifying a behavior are components of a process of refining the independent variables of performance, i.e., refining reading materials for sequential skill development and refining motivational variables within the classroom for efficient performance. Both are critical to performance, as experimental results of this and other research well demonstrate. Response data from each boy indicated that attention to sequencing instructional materials without appropriate programing of motivational variables proved ineffective for establishing efficient performance.

When performance data from the child do not meet preset criteria, then learning conditions are not effective and must be changed. If the learning environment is programed appropriately, there is a high probability that the child will make more reading responses and at an accelerated rate because he is rapidly acquiring a history of reinforcement which motivates him to read. Positive reinforcement not only accelerates responding but also has the additional effect of establishing stimuli, present during reinforcement, as conditioned reinforcers, which come to maintain responding (Ferster, 1961). Specifically, the more initial pairings of the reading stimuli with events which are reinforcing to the individual child, the more motivating the reading stimuli themselves become (Staats et al., 1964; Goldiamond & Dyrud, 1966). Concomitantly, as the high rate of responding to successively more difficult material actualizes the establishment of a large repertoire of skills, "being correct" comes to gain strength as a reinforcer (Ferster, 1961).

When children encounter severe reading disabilities the teacher frequently looks to the cause of the problem as being biological or constitutional. The present investigation, however, demonstrates that rather than look to the etiology of the problem look to the systematic refinements in procedures of instruction that improve instructional conditions to the point where children who have severe reading disabilities can come to read normally in a rather short period of time. Whether or not we, as educators, recognize and systematically investigate the effects of classroom variables on performance, these variables are functionally influencing performance.

References

Bijou, S. W. Operant extinction after fixed-interval schedules with young children. JOURNAL OF EXPERIMENTAL ANALYSIS OF BEHAVIOR, 1958, 1, 25-29.

Bijou, S. W., & Baer, D. M. Operant methods in child behavior development. In W. Honig (Ed.), OPERANT BEHAVIOR: AREAS OF RESEARCH AND APPLICATION. New York: Appleton-Century-Crofts, 1966.

Bijou, S. W. & Sturges, P. T. Positive reinforcers for experimental studies with children—consumables and manipulables. CHILD DEVELOPMENT, 1959, 3, 151-170.

Birnbrauer, J. S., Wolf, M. M., Kidder, J. D., & Tague, Cecilia. Classroom behavior of retarded pupils with token reinforcement. JOURNAL OF EXPERIMENTAL CHILD PSYCHOLOGY, 1965, 2, 219-235.

Critchley, M. DEVELOPMENTAL DYSLEXIA. London, England: Whitefriars Press, 1966.

Ferster, C. B. Positive reinforcement and behavioral deficits of autistic children. CHILD DEVELOPMENT, 1961, 32, 437-456.

Ferster, C. B., & Skinner, B. F. SCHEDULES OF REINFORCEMENT. New York Appleton-Century-Crofts, 1957.

Ferster, C. B., & DeMyer, M. K. The development of performance in autistic children in an automatically controlled environment. JOURNAL OF CHRONIC DISORDERS, 1961, 13, 312-345.

Goldiamond, I., & Dyrud, J. E. Reading as operant behavior. In J. Money (Ed.), THE DISABLED READER. Baltimore: Johns Hopkins Press, 1966.

Haring, N. G., & Kunzelmann, H. P. The finer focus of therapeutic behavioral management. In J. Hellmuth (Ed.), EDUCATIONAL THERAPY. VOL 1. Seattle Special Child Publications, 1966.

Hermann, Knud. READING DISABILITY: A MEDICAL STUDY OF WORD-BLINDNESS AND RELATED HANDICAPS. Springfield, Illinois: Charles C Thomas, 1959.

Hewett, F. Teaching reading to an autistic boy through operant conditioning. READING TEACHER, 1964, 17, 613-618.

Homme, L. E., deBaca, P., Devine, J. V., Steinhorst, R., & Rickert, E. J. Use of the Premack principle in controlling the behavior of nursery school children. JOURNAL OF EXPERIMENTAL ANALYSIS OF BEHAVIOR, 1963, 6, 544.

Kelleher, R. T., & Gollub, L. R. A review of positive conditioned reinforcement. JOURNAL OF EXPERIMENTAL ANALYSIS OF BEHAVIOR, 1962, 5, 543-597.

Money, J. (Ed.) READING DISABILITY. PROGRESS AND RESEARCH NEEDS IN DYSLEXIA. Baltimore: Johns Hopkins Press, 1962.

aats, A. W., & Butterfield, W. A.   Treatment of nonreading in a culturally
prived juvenile delinquent: an application of reinforcement principles.
ILD DEVELOPMENT, 1965, 36, 925-942.

aats, A. W., Finley, J. R., Minke, K. A., & Wolf, M. M.   Reinforcement
riables in the control of unit reading responses.   JOURNAL OF EXPERI-
NTAL ANALYSIS OF BEHAVIOR, 1964, 7, 139-149.

aats, A. W., Staats, C. K., Schutz, R. E., & Wolf, M.   The conditioning of
tual responses using "extrinsic reinforcers."   JOURNAL OF EXPERIMENTAL
ALYSIS OF BEHAVIOR, 1962, 5, 33-40.

mmerman, E. H., & Zimmerman, J.   The alternation of behavior in a special
ssroom situation.   JOURNAL OF EXPERIMENTAL ANALYSIS OF BEHAVIOR,
62, 5, 59-60.

STUDY QUESTIONS

1. Give an everyday example of the fundamental principle that a response immediately followed by a reinforcing event has a high probability of being repeated.

2. What do Haring and Hauck include in an individual behavior analysis? Why do they *not* feel it is necessary to administer Binet, Bender, ITPA, WISC, and other kinds of tests? Why are they not concerned with the issues of multisensory or intact-modality learning?

3. Describe in layman's terms: the subjects, the procedure, and the results of this experiment.

4. Suppose a debate were to be held with Gibson, Haring and Hauck, and Engelmann on one team and de Hirsch, Frostig, and Silver and Hagin on the other. Name two major issues that would arise, and summarize each team's position.

18: A COMPARISON OF TEN DIFFERENT BEGINNING READING PROGRAMS IN FIRST GRADE

Emery P. Bliesmer
Betty H. Yarborough

Bliesmer and Yarborough compare the effectiveness of ten beginning first-grade reading programs. The results suggest that not only are there differences among methods, but that these differences follow a pattern which appears predictable on the basis of the fundamental nature of the reading process. The kinds of theoretical analyses of reading presented in earlier selections are seen to have implications in the classroom world of commercial reading programs.

 B. D. B

Reprinted with permission of the authors and publisher from PHI DELTA KAPPAN, June, 1965, 500-504. Copyright © 1965 by Phi Delta Kappa, Inc.

The current reemphasis on the study of initial or beginning reading instruction, the recent revision of several established basal reading series, and the simultaneous publication of several new commercially prepared reading programs prompted the public schools of one Virginia school division to investigate, during the 1963-64 school session, the relative effectiveness of ten approaches to teaching reading in the first grade.

The ten approaches studied differed in numerous ways, such as in suggested teaching materials, instructional techniques, order in which types of word or sound elements were introduced, and administrative procedures (e.g., grouping practices). Nevertheless, analysis of the approaches revealed two basic underlying psychological-pedagogical theories represented among them: 1) Five programs were based upon the belief that the child should be taught whole words and then, through various analytic techniques, recognition of letters and the sounds they represent (hereafter referred to as the *analytic* method); 2) Five approaches were based upon the belief that the child should be taught certain letter-sound relationships or word elements before beginning to read and then be taught to *synthesize* word elements learned into whole words (hereafter referred to as the *synthetic* method).

Analyses of the data resulting from this study indicate that the programs of initial reading instruction based upon one of the methods were more effective in grade one than were those based upon the other.

The major purpose of this investigation was to study and to determine the relative effectiveness of each of ten different approaches or programs for the teaching of beginning reading. The null hypothesis tested was that, other variables being relatively controlled, there would be no differences in mean reading achievement scores of ten groups of first-grade children when each group had been introduced to reading instruction by a different approach.

The pupils involved in this study were from twenty classrooms in four of the twenty elementary schools in the public schools of a suburban Virginia city. A total of 22,227 students were enrolled in the elementary and the high schools of this system at the beginning of the 1963-64 school year. The first-grade enrollment was 2,415 pupils.

he four schools involved were selected from two adjacent boroughs of the
ty. The two schools in each borough represented what supervisory, research,
nd administrative personnel of the school division considered to be relatively
omparable socioeconomic environments. Since the socioeconomic level in
ne borough was what might be considered somewhat typical middle class
nd the other tended toward a lower level, efforts were made to use each of
ne ten programs in one classroom in each of the two boroughs. These efforts
rere successful for nine of the ten programs. Both classes involved in a tenth
rogram, however, were from the lower socioeconomic area.

ll of the 596 pupils in twenty of the twenty-one first-grade classes in the
our participating schools were initially included in the study. The pupils in
ach of the four schools were assigned randomly to classes, or teachers, accord-
g to the usual practice in those schools. Complete data were obtained for
nirty-eight to fifty-four pupils in each program group, or for a total of 484
upils (248 for the analytic programs, 236 for the synthetic programs). Be-
ause the population in the school area is relatively mobile, 112 pupils were
st from the study.

he mean chronological age of the experimental subjects was 79.4 months,
rith a range by classes of 76.4 to 84.7 months. The mean Language IQ
ALIFORNIA TEST OF MENTAL MATURITY) was 95.2, with a range by classes
f 82.8 to 107.0. The mean Non-Language IQ was 98.9, with a range by
lasses of 92.3 to 107.4. The mean METROPOLITAN READINESS TESTS score
ras 57.5, with a range by classes of 37.2 to 72.0.

lo special selection or school placement of teachers was arranged for the
tudy other than that efforts were made to have experimental group teachers
rho had received ratings of at least "average" from supervisory staff members
ne previous year and to have no beginning teachers. Because of circumstances
eyond the control of school officials, one beginning teacher was included.
his teacher, however, was fully qualified in regard to certification and recom-
nendations (and received an "above average" rating from supervisory staff
nembers during the year of the study). The years of teaching experience of
ne other nineteen teachers ranged from one and one-half to forty-three. All
f the teachers were women.

One teacher left the system at the end of March, six weeks before the conclusion of the study. This teacher, however, continued to work in the classroom with her replacement until satisfactory orientation of the new teacher to the reading program in progress was effected.

Eight of the programs studied were the latest (new or revised) programs of various publishers, as follows:

1. (AM)[1]: ABC BETTS BASIC READERS (1963), American Book Company.
2. (EC): PHONETIC KEYS TO READING (1933), Economy Company.
3. (GI): GINN BASIC READERS, Revised (1959), Ginn.
4. (HO): READING FOR MEANING SERIES, Third Edition (1963), Houghton Mifflin.
5. (LI): BASIC READING (1963), J. B. Lippincott.
6. (MC): PROGRAMMED READING (1963). Webster Division, McGraw-Hill.
7. (SC): THE NEW BASIC READERS: SIXTIES EDITION (1962), Scott, Foresman.
8. (SI): STRUCTURAL READING SERIES (1963), L. W. Singer.

In addition to these eight programs, all of which involve commercially prepared materials, the following two programs or approaches were used:

9. (IN): A completely individualized or personalized approach in which many different books were used but no specific set of commercially prepared books or materials was followed.
10. (IS): An individualized approach supplemented with READING LABORATORY Ia and READING LABORATORY I: WORD GAMES, published by Science Research Associates.

The complete programs of the first eight approaches were used, including *all* accompanying and supplementary materials such as readiness books, workbook flash cards, recordings, filmstrips, and the like. One program, SC, also include use of the publisher's entire language arts program for grade one.

---

[1]These code designations for specific programs will be used in the remainder of this paper and in Table 1.

Of the five programs representing the analytic method, three are widely used basal reader programs (AM, GI, and SC). Each of these programs helps the pupil develop a small sight vocabulary before individual letters or sounds in words are pointed out. The other two were individualized reading (Nos. 9 and 10 above). It should be pointed out again that the latter two approaches did not employ the use of commercially structured procedures. From the readiness period until the conclusion of the experiment, pupils were provided reading instruction based upon teacher-recognized individual needs. The transfer from the readiness period into formal reading was developed in most cases through each pupil dictating "stories" which were recorded by the teacher and then read by the pupil.

Among the five programs based upon the synthetic method was one widely used basal reader program (HO). One new basal reader program (LI) was also included. The remaining three (EC, MC, and SI) have not been generally regarded as basal reader programs because the materials involved are used primarily in a consumable way. The synthetic programs studied differ markedly as to the order in which the letter-sound relationships are introduced, and all but one of the programs (SI) provides for the teaching of a few sight words; but each program promotes independence in reading by having pupils attack most new words at each stage of development through the synthesizing of word elements previously taught.

The ten approaches differed in the administrative implementation suggested by their authors. Three of the conventional basal programs (AM, GI, and SC) recommend small-group instruction. Two of the analytic programs (IN and IS) and one of the synthetic programs (MC) were based essentially upon individualized procedures that allow each pupil to progress at his own rate. Some small-group instruction for specific purposes was necessary, however. Four of the five synthetic programs (EC, HO, LI, and SI) encourage the use of whole-class instruction to the extent possible, especially in the pre-reading period during which letter-sound elements are taught. Each of these programs provides ultimately for small-group instruction, however, as the range of pupil achievement widens.

At the beginning of the 1964-65 school year, the principals of the four participating schools "drew" for the reading programs to be used in their respective
schools. The teachers in each school were then randomly assigned one of the
methods their principal had drawn.

The pupils in this study did not begin working with any of the actual programs
until approximately October 1 of the school year. Although the first month of
school was spent in developing the pupils' general readiness skills, no specific
publisher's reading readiness program was carried out until the experimental
programs were begun.

Two general in-service meetings were held in September to acquaint the twenty
teachers with the purpose and structure of the study and to establish certain
working principles. In addition, the two teachers for each program (except IN
and IS) had special extended training or assistance by a consultant from the
publisher of their materials. The four teachers using the IN and the IS approaches were assisted by one of the school division's supervisors. In addition,
the two teachers using the IS program also met with a representative of Science
Research Associates.

Each of the publishers from whom materials for the experiment were secured
was invited to maintain consultant services during the course of the experiment.
All publishers responded by sending consultants two or three times during the
year.

Four elementary supervisors in the school system, the director of reading, and
the director of research supervised instruction in the classrooms in which the
study was in progress. Teachers were told that no child was to receive more
than forty-five minutes of formal reading instruction per day. As far as supervisory personnel could determine, these instructions were followed.

The METROPOLITAN READINESS TESTS, Form S, were administered to all experimental subjects in September; the CALIFORNIA SHORT-FORM TEST OF

MENTAL MATURITY (1957 Edition), Primary, in October; and the STANFORD ACHIEVEMENT TEST, Primary I, Form W, at the end of May.[2]

The criterion measures used to test the null hypothesis were the STANFORD ACHIEVEMENT TEST scores (grade equivalents) obtained for the pupils in May. Scores for the following five subtests were used: Word Reading, Paragraph Meaning, Vocabulary, Spelling, and Word Study Skills.

Analyses of variance revealed significant differences in the control variables of chronological age, language IQ, non-language IQ, and total readiness score. Analysis of covariance procedures were then applied to adjust mean criterion scores. Analysis of variance procedures subsequently applied to adjusted criterion scores revealed significant F-ratios for each of the five criterion measures. Further tests of significance were then applied to determine which of possible pairs of treatments had yielded significantly different scores or results.[3]

This study was subject to many of the characteristic limitations of methods studies. The usual cautions with regard to interpreting results and to generalizing should be made. Desirably, this study would have been carried on through grade two and even grade three; but this was not possible for budgetary and administrative reasons which were known before the investigation began. While it is quite possible that differences found among groups at the end of grade one might no longer be found to obtain at the end of grade two or three, this does not invalidate the present results or findings, because it is also quite possible, of course, that differences at the end of grade one might continue to be found at the end of grades two and three.

---

[2]William Koontz, director of research, Chesapeake Public Schools, assumed major responsibility for the planning of the testing program and the compiling and initial programing of data. Milton Jacobson, Division of Educational Research, University of Virginia, assisted with later analyses and further programing plans.

[3]See E. F. Lindquist, DESIGN AND ANALYSIS OF EXPERIMENTS IN PSYCHOLOGY AND EDUCATION. Boston: Houghton Mifflin Co., 1953, pp. 90-96.

The adjusted mean criterion scores of each program or treatment group and the differences between adjusted mean criterion scores of various pairs of program groups have been presented in Table 1. The various reading programs are designated along the top and at the left side of the table, with the code designations which were presented in a previous section. The order of listing of programs, which is the same as that used in initial studies of the data before statistical analyses were performed, happens to be such that the five synthetic program groups are listed first and the five analytic program groups are listed last. Inspection of data presented in Table 1 will suggest various comparisons and groupings of treatment groups and will reveal some fairly definite patterns or trends.

When the means of the synthetic program groups (HO, LI, SI, EC, MC) are compared with those of the analytic program groups (IN, IS, GI, AM, SC), a great preponderance of differences among means (ninety-two out of 125, or 74 per cent) is found to be significantly in favor of the synthetic group. In only three instances are the obtained differences in favor of the analytic group, and none of these differences is significant at the .01 level. Further study of Table 1 reveals no instances in which the obtained differences with respect to scores on Word Meaning (WM), Word Study Skills (WS), or Spelling (SP) favor the analytic group.

A criticism frequently made of synthetic programs is that the rather close attention given to word elements may lead to inadequate development of comprehension skills. In the present study, however, there was only one instance (out of twenty-five) in which mean Paragraph Reading (PR) scores favored an analytic program; and this difference was not significant. Conversely, twenty comparisons reveal all significant differences in favor of synthetic programs. It would appear, therefore, that beginning reading programs which give attention to sound-symbol relationships prior to teaching of words, or which involve a synthetic approach initially (pupils actually building words from sounds), tend to be significantly more productive in terms of specific reading achievement in grade one (as measured by the criterion test) than do analytic reading programs which involve the more conventional approach of going directly from readiness procedures (using pictures) to the reading of whole words before either letter names or the sounds the letters represent are taught.

It is of further interest to note that among corresponding means of the first three synthetic programs (HO, LI, and SI) only one of the fifteen differences is significant, although one program begins with intensive instruction in consonant letter-sound relationships, one with short vowels being taught, and one with consonants and short vowel sounds being taught individually. This suggests that the order of introduction of letter sound elements and/or relationships may not be as important in the success of synthetic programs as that the number of letter-sound relationships taught be sufficient to equip pupils with means for independent decoding of words.

It may also be noted, from further study of Table 1, that the differences among the criterion measures of the five analytic approaches were significant in only six instances (out of fifty possibilities). These six significant differences all favored the IN approach, which appears to be more effective than each of the other analytic approaches in developing comprehension skills measured by the Paragraph Reading subtest. There were no significant differences among the other analytic approaches. It would seem, therefore, that methodology, rather than specific programs or materials used, is the more decisive factor in the overall effectiveness of reading instruction in grade one.

The use of data presented in Table 1 affords many other possible comparisons, and a number of additional inferences may perhaps be made. The study here reported has offered a unique opportunity to compare and analyze "methods" rather than merely or only specific publishers' materials. While a study longer in range and scope would have been desirable, it should be kept in mind that the first grade year is still a really crucial one in the development of foundations for good reading skill and is regarded by many authorities as perhaps the most vital aspect of the entire reading program. Although programs for further analyses are being planned, the preliminary analyses done thus far have been relatively extensive. It is believed that the results obtained in this study have definite pertinence and significance with respect to effectiveness of various approaches to initial reading instruction and validity of theories of methodology represented by these approaches.

TABLE 1. ADJUSTED MEAN CRITERION SCORES, AND DIFFERENCES AMONG MEANS, OF VARIOUS TREATMENT GROUPS

Program Groups[**]		Adjusted Mean Scores[***]	Differences Among Program Group Means								
			LI	SI	EC	MC	IN	IS	GI	AM	SC
(HO)	WR	1.89	−0.21	−0.07	0.19	0.08	0.22*	0.27*	0.43*	0.33*	0.44*
	PM	1.81	−0.17	−0.12	−0.11	−0.06	−0.03	0.21	0.19	0.39*	0.28*
	VO	2.47	0.30	0.54*	−0.10	0.54*	0.58*	0.67*	0.51*	0.72*	0.67*
	SP	2.48	0.17	0.23	0.35*	0.64*	0.74*	0.82*	1.10*	1.01*	0.87*
	WS	2.58	−0.06	−0.09	0.43	0.56*	0.72*	0.71*	0.95*	0.83*	1.11*
(LI)	WR	2.10		0.14	0.40*	0.29*	0.43*	0.48*	0.64*	0.54*	0.65*
	PM	1.98		0.05	0.06	0.11	0.31*	0.38*	0.56*	0.56*	0.45*
	VO	2.17		0.24	−0.40*	0.24	0.28	0.37*	0.21	0.42*	0.37*
	SP	2.31		0.06	0.18	0.47*	0.57*	0.65*	0.93*	0.84*	0.70*
	WS	2.64		−0.03	0.49*	0.62*	0.78*	0.77*	1.01*	0.89*	1.17*
(SI)	WR	1.96			0.26*	0.15	0.29*	0.34*	0.50*	0.40*	0.51*
	PM	1.93			0.01	0.06	0.26*	0.33*	0.31*	0.51*	0.40*
	VO	1.93			−0.64*	0.00	0.04	0.13	−0.03	0.18	0.13
	SP	2.25			0.12	0.41*	0.51*	0.59*	0.87*	0.78*	0.64*
	WS	2.67			0.52*	0.65*	0.81*	0.80*	1.04*	0.92*	1.20*
(EC)	WR	1.70				0.11	0.03	0.08	0.24*	0.14	0.25*
	PM	1.92				0.05	0.08	0.32*	0.30*	0.50*	0.39*
	VO	2.57				0.64*	0.68*	0.77*	0.61*	0.82*	0.77*
	SP	2.13				0.29	0.39*	0.47*	0.75*	0.66*	0.52*
	WS	2.15				0.13	0.29	0.28	0.52*	0.40	0.68*
(MC)	WR	1.81					0.14	0.19	0.35*	0.25*	0.36*
	PM	1.87					0.20	0.27*	0.25*	0.45*	0.34*
	VO	1.93					0.04	0.13	−0.03	0.18	0.13
	SP	1.84					0.10	0.18	0.46*	0.37*	0.23
	WS	2.02					0.16	0.15	0.39	0.27	0.55*
(IN)	WR	1.67						0.05	0.21	0.11	0.22*
	PM	1.84						0.24*	0.22*	0.42*	0.31*
	VO	1.89						0.09	−0.07	0.14	0.09
	SP	1.14						0.08	0.36*	0.27	0.13
	WS	1.86						−0.01	0.23	0.11	0.39
(IS)	WR	1.67							0.16	0.06	0.17
	PM	1.60							−0.02	0.18	0.07
	VO	1.80							−0.16	0.05	0.00
	SP	1.66							0.28	0.19	0.05
	WS	1.87							0.24	0.12	0.40
(GI)	WR	1.46								−0.10	0.01
	PM	1.62								0.20	0.09
	VO	1.96								0.21	0.16
	SP	1.38								−0.09	−0.23
	WS	1.63								−0.12	0.16
(AM)	WR	1.56									0.11
	PM	1.42									−0.11
	VO	1.75									−0.05
	SP	1.47									−0.14
	WS	1.75									0.28
(SC)	WR	1.45									
	PM	1.53									
	VO	1.80									
	SP	1.61									
	WS	1.47									

[**]HO: Houghton Mifflin
LI: Lippincott
SI: Singer
EC: Economy
MC: McGraw-Hill
IN: Individualized Completely
IS: Individualized Supplemented
GI: Ginn
AM: American
SC: Scott, Foresman

[*]Significant at .01 level. Positive differences favor program at left.

[***]Stanford Achievement Test Scores (Grade Equiv.)
WR: Word Reading
PM: Paragraph Meaning
VO: Vocabulary
SP: Spelling
WS: Word Study Skills

STUDY QUESTIONS

1. What do Bliesmer and Yarborough mean by "analytic" and "synthetic" methodologies? Give an example of each.

2. Which methodology was superior on word reading? on (Comprehension) paragraph meaning? on Vocabulary? on Spelling? on Word Skills?

3. Can you think of a reasonable explanation for the results of this study other than the superiority of one methodology over the other?

4. How would Bliesmer and Yarborough respond to the suggestion that it is better to teach whole words first, then introduce phonics? How would Engelmann react to that proposal?

19: INTENSIVE PHONICS VS. GRADUAL PHONICS IN BEGINNING READING: A REVIEW

Louise Gurren
Ann Hughes

Gurren and Hughes have undertaken an extensive analysis of available research on the teaching of reading. Their conclusions are consistent with the findings of Bliesmer and Yarborough in the previous chapter and with the nature of reading as depicted in this section. Teachers will be especially interested in the conclusions regarding the effect of intensive, early phonics training on comprehension, vocabulary, and spelling. The recommendations made by the authors, on the basis of controlled research, are of vital concern to all educators.

B. D. B.

Reprinted with permission of the authors and publisher from THE JOURNAL OF EDUCATIONAL RESEARCH, 1965, 58, 339-346

Large numbers of American schools have recently altered their reading programs by adding intensive phonetic training from the start of the program. At the same time, a number of scholars have carried out carefully controlled research to determine the practical value of such an addition. There seems great need that the results of such research should now be comprehensively reviewed so that they may serve as a guide to educators concerned with teaching reading as effectively as possible.

The present review is both selective and comprehensive. It is selective in that it excludes opinion surveys, word-count studies, purely theoretical discussions, correlational studies, and loosely controlled experiments. It is comprehensive in that it includes all the rigorous evaluations the authors could locate which compare actual performance of a group which has had intensive phonics from the start with that of a group which has not.

The Question

The rigorous comparisons in this review furnish direct evidence on the following question:

> Does the intensive teaching of all the main sound-symbol relationships, both vowel and consonant, from the start of formal reading instruction have a beneficial effect on reading comprehension, vocabulary and spelling?

For convenience, such intensive teaching will be referred to in this review as a "phonetic" approach. It forms one element of many very different reading programs without being the only element of any of them. For instance, it is basic to programs involving such materials as the following: the Economy Company basic reading series, the various linguistic materials in the Bloomfield tradition, the Hay-Wingo materials, various Boston University auditory discrimination and homophone materials, and others.[1]

[1] Four of the most recently published reading series also include, among other elements, an intensive "phonetic" approach: the new Lippincott series (1963), the Mazurkiewicz-Tanyzer i/t/a series (1963), the Open Court series (1963) and the Reardon-Baer parochial series (1960).

On the other hand, an intensive "phonetic" approach is definitely *not* an element of traditional basal programs such as the American Book Company program, the Ginn program, the Row Peterson program or the Scott, Foresman program. Such programs are often referred to as involving an eclectic or combination method, but it should be noted that the phonics in such combinations consists of gradual phonics rather than intensive phonics.

Thus a clear contrast exists between reading programs which do include an intensive "phonetic" approach and ones which do not. Rigorous comparisons of results from such contrasting programs should furnish a basis for deciding the relative value of the two approaches.

The Main Differences

Most "conventional" methods do include training in phonics, and some are even referred to as being very strong in phonics, but they still differ from "phonetic" methods in three ways:

> **Timing.** The "phonetic" methods teach all the main vowel and consonant sounds from the start of reading instruction in first grade, while the "conventional" methods delay the teaching of most vowel sounds and some consonant sounds until second grade.
>
> **Emphasis.** The "phonetic" methods involve constant phonetic review, while "conventional" methods involve much less.
>
> **Method of Attacking an Unfamiliar Word.** "Phonetic" methods train the beginning reader to pronounce all the sounds of an unfamiliar word in the normal order and to use context for confirming the result, while "conventional" methods train him to analyze the sounds of parts of the word (usually the first and last consonants) and then guess the rest from context.

Some "phonetic" methods provide specific training in blending sounds into whole words, e.g., the Economy method and the Hay-Wingo method, while others leave this to the ingenuity of the individual child or teacher.

354

ıe first step in preparing this review was to examine all the studies on phonics ıich could be located and to list all those which compared an intensive "pho- tic" instructional group with a conventional-method instructional group. A ɔup was considered "phonetic" if it received intensive teaching of all the ain sound-symbol relationships, both vowel and consonant, from the start of rmal reading instruction; it was considered "conventional" if it did not. The rious "phonetic" methods identified all include such intensive teaching, but ɘ not implied to be alike in other respects. The various "conventional" ɘthods all fail to include it, but are also not implied to be alike in other re- ɘcts.

ıe second step was to examine the research design of these studies and to ex- ıde from the tabulation all which were not rigorous in their design. In this ⱴiew, a comparison is considered rigorous only if it has the four following aracteristics:

1. *Appropriate Type of Comparison.* Compares the actual performance of a "conventional" group with that of a "phonetic" group of comparable IQ, a group which has had intensive sound-symbol teaching from the start of first grade.
2. *Proper Sample.* Uses whole groups with equivalent IQ, or uses random selection resulting in equivalent IQ, or matches as many pairs as possible by IQ.
3. *Adequate Testing.* Uses tests of appropriate difficulty, administers the same tests to both groups at the same stage, and gives reading scores and IQ's of both groups.
4. *Standard Tests of Statistical Significance.* Evaluates the differences be- tween the means in terms of t-values or F-values.

ınly 18 of the investigations contained comparisons which could qualify as rig- ʳous by this definition.[2] There were, however, 22 rigorous comparisons in the ℨ investigations, since two compared more than one pair of groups. One inves- ɟator compared the same pair of groups at two different grade levels. The ıdies were published in several articles in educational journals, two reports to

ᴧ full bibliography of the non-rigorous studies which were excluded from this review may obtained from the junior author, Ann Hughes, Director of Statistical Research, Reading ɘform Foundation, 36 West 44th St., New York 36, N. Y.

school boards, and ten doctoral dissertations, five of which received little or no attention from earlier reviewers.

The third step was to tabulate the statistically significant differences in reading comprehension, vocabulary and spelling for each of the 22 rigorous comparisons. This step was accomplished by examining the tables in each study and was therefore completely objective, having no dependence on the opinion or conclusions of the various investigators. The word *significant* is used throughout this review in its technical sense, to indicate statistical significance at or beyond the 5 per cent level. Subtests showing differences which were significant at or beyond the 1 per cent level were also noted.

The fourth step was to classify each rigorous comparison as a whole as favorable to intensive phonics or not. A comparison was considered favorable to a certain group if that group was *significantly* superior in at least half the subtests of comprehension, vocabulary and spelling given. This classification was therefore also completely objective, having no dependence on the opinion or conclusions of the various investigator or on the opinions of the present reviewers.

Findings

An analysis of the 22 rigorous comparisons is shown in Table 1. Each comparison in Table 1 represents a different sample, except for Bear's '64 follow up study, and each has been listed beneath the group it favors.

It should be noted that the authors of this review were unable to find *any* rigorous comparisons which favored a "conventional" group. In other words, there were no rigorous comparisons in which a "conventional" group was significantly superior in half the subtests of comprehension, vocabulary and spelling.

In evaluating results from achievement tests such as those used in the studies cited in Tables 1 and 2, it is necessary to remember the human variables. Even the most foolproof system can occasionally be poorly installed.

RESULTS OF 22 RIGOROUS COMPARISONS IN 18 STUDIES COMPARING "CONVENTIONAL" AND "PHONETIC" READING PROGRAMS

Favorable to Neither Group[a]	Favorable to the "Conventional" Group[a]	Favorable to the "Phonetic" Group[a]
3[b] Morgan & Light '63	None	E-1 Sparks '56
4 Sparks '56		E-2 Sparks '56
4 McDowell '53		E-2 Kelly '58
		E-3 Henderson '55
		E-3 Duncan '64
		E-4 Wollam '61
		L-1 Wohleber '53
		L-2 Wohleber '53
		L-3 Wohleber '53
		L-4 Dolan '63
		H-1 Bear '59
		H-6 Bear '64
		Q-2 Wood '55
		O-1 Russell '43
		O-1 Murphy '43
		O-1 Crossley '48
		O-1 Durrell et al '58
		O-1 Santeusanio '62
		O-3 Agnew '39
Total: 3	0	19

or basis of classifications, see section on procedure and Table 2. See
nnotated bibliography for special details.
Key to symbols:
   E, L, H, Q, O = Materials used by "phonetic" group, as follows:
   E = Economy Company's Phonetic Keys to Reading
   L = Linguistic, various modifications of Bloomfield's plan
   H = Hay J. and Wingo, C., READING WITH PHONICS, Lippincott, Co.
   Q = Queensland Readers, Australia
   O = Other "phonetic" materials
   1, 2, 3, 4, 6 = Grade level at which tested

Conversely, poor materials can occasionally be surprisingly effective in the hands of an inspired teacher. One cannot expect a superior method to produce superior results under any and all conditions. However, one *can* expect it to produce superior results most of the time.

Thus, if the "conventional" method were actually superior, most of the rigorous comparisons could be expected to fall in the "conventional" column, with a few in the other columns. If both methods were equally good, most of the comparisons could be expected to fall in the "neither" column, with a few in the others.

What actually happens, is that most of the comparisons in Table 1, 19 out of 22, fall in the "phonetic" column, while three fall in the "neither" column and not one falls in the "conventional" column. This distribution of results strongly indicates an actual superiority of the "phonetic" approach over the "conventional" approach. The three comparisons in the "neither" column cannot legitimately be considered to negate the 19 in the "phonetic" column since a certain amount of spill must be expected in any situation where there are human variables.

Table 2, which demonstrates why each of the 22 comparisons was so classified in Table 1, also provides material for evaluating the widespread belief that a "phonetic" approach aids in word attack but damages comprehension.

If it were true that a "phonetic" approach damaged comprehension, most of the comprehension subtests would be expected to appear in the "conventional" column in Table 2, with a few in the others. If neither approach actually tended to produce superior comprehension, most should appear under "no-significant-difference," with a few in the other columns.

Actually, more than half the c symbols fall in the "phonetic" column. Sixteen comparisons favor the "phonetic" group as to comprehension, while not one favors the "conventional" group.

TABLE 2. ANALYSIS OF SUBTESTS IN 22 RIGOROUS COMPARISONS IN 18 STUDIES COMPARING "CONVENTIONAL" AND "PHONETIC" READING PROGRAMS[a]

Method	Comparison	Subtests Showing No Signif. Difference	Subtests Showing Sig. Diffs. Favoring "Conventional" Group	"Phonetic" Group	Total Subtests Given[a]
Economy:	E-1[b] Sparks '56			c, v[c]	2
	E-2 Sparks '56	v		c	2
	E-2 Kelly '58			c	1
	E-3 Henderson '55			ccc, vvv, s	7
	E-3 Morgan & Light '63	ccc	c, v		5
	E-3 Duncan '64			c	1
	E-4 Sparks '56	c, v, s			3
	E-4 Wollam '61	c, v		v, s	4
Linguistic:	L-1 Wohleber '53	c		c, v	3
	L-2 Wohleber '53			c, v	2
	L-3 Wohleber '53			c, v	2
	L-4 McDowell '53	cccc, v	c, v	s	8
	L-4 Dolan '63	cc, v		cc, vvvvv	10
Hay-Wingo:	H-1 Bear '59	vv		cc, vvv	7
	H-6 Bear '64	c		v, ss	4
Queensland:	Q-2 Wood '55	c		c	2
Other:	O-1 Russell '43			c, vvvv, ss	7
	O-1 Murphy '43			v	1
	O-1 Crossley '48	v		cc, v	4
	O-1 Durrell et al. '58	c, v		c, v	4
	O-1 Santeusanio '62			c, vvv	4
	O-3 Agnew '39	cc		cc, v	5
Total no. subtests:		27	4	57	88

[a]Including subtests of comprehension, vocabulary and spelling, but not other tests such as phonics, letter names, work-study skills, speed, accuracy, oral reading, and word pronunciation. Word discrimination and visual discrimination subtests have been counted as vocabulary. Subtests showing differences significant at the .01 level are italicized.

[b]For key to symbols E-1, L-4, etc., see key to Table 1.

[c]c = comprehension subtest; v = vocabulary subtest; s = spelling subtest.

Discussion

The belief that early emphasis upon phonics may damage growth in comprehension is only one of a number of frequently voiced criticisms of "phonetic" methods. Further analysis of other information in the rigorous studies supplies an objective basis for evaluating several other criticisms.

1. Does the "phonetic" method slow down fast-learners? The criticism that a "phonetic" approach slows down fast-learners is not supported by the data. Of the six comparisons in Table 1 in which mean IQ's were above 110 (see annotated bibliography for IQ's), five favored the "phonetic" group, while one favored neither.

In addition, five investigators, Dolan, Wollam, Bear, Sparks and Duncan,[3] took the further step of stratifying their groups by IQ. In these subgroup comparisons in which the fast-learners in the "phonetic" groups were compared with the fast-learners in the "conventional" groups, all the significant differences in comprehension, vocabulary and spelling favored the "phonetic" approach. Four of the five investigators found such differences in comprehension, and three found them in vocabulary.

2. Is a "phonetic" approach too hard for slow-learners? In every instance where the slow-learners in the "phonetic" groups were compared with the slow-learners in the "conventional" groups, all the significant differences again favored the "phonetic" approach. Four of the five investigators found such differences in comprehension, and three found them in vocabulary.

---

[3]Bear divided his fast-learners into two levels. His moderately-fast level (IQ 101 to 120) showed significant differences on every subtest, both in first grade and in sixth, all favoring the "phonetic" children; his top level (above IQ 120) showed none. Sparks included both these ranges in a single category and found the same number and kind of significant differences as he had found in his total groups.

3. **Do "phonetic" groups read more slowly?** While speed is not included in our basic question, it deserves mention because it is a key goal of the "conventional" method. It is true that the "conventional" method tends to develop facile reading in pre-primers, but experimental evidence suggests that such early speed in easy materials may have little relationship to eventual speed. Seven of the rigorous comparisons in Table 1 included measures of speed. In two, the "conventional" group read significantly faster, Agnew '39 and McDowell '53; in two, the "phonetic" group read significantly faster, Wollman '61 and Dolan '63; in the other three, there was no significant difference in speed: Wood '55, E-4 Sparks '56 and Bear '64.

4. **Can the success of the "phonetic" groups be explained by the Hawthorne effect?** Much has been said about the factor of teacher enthusiasm for a new method, the so-called Hawthorne or honeymoon effect, which is said to help any experimental group. Little has been said about two compensating factors: first, possible teacher distaste for change and extra work, and second, the initial awkwardness of teachers using an unfamiliar method.

If the Hawthorne effect were actually dominant, then teachers who were new to the "phonetic" method could be expected to get better results than teachers using it for the second or third time (or habitually); i.e., we would expect "phonetic" pilot groups to be superior almost every time, while we would expect "phonetic" non-pilot groups to achieve superiority much less often.

This was not the case. Of the 13 "phonetic" groups in Table 1 which were pilot groups, ten were superior.[4] Of the eight "phonetic" groups which were *not* pilot groups, *all* were superior.[5] It seems logical to conclude that the "phonetic" method does not owe its success to novelty.

[4]Bear's pilot group was superior in two comparisons in Table 1, but counts as only one group.

[5]The eight comparisons in Table 1 in which the "phonetic" group was not a pilot group are the following: E-1 Sparks '56, E-2 Sparks '56, L-1 Wohleber '53, L-2 Wohleber '53, L-4 Dolan '63, Q-2 Wood '55, O-1 Russell '43, and O-3 Agnew '39. In each of these cases, the "phonetic" group had teachers with at least one year's previous experience with the "phonetic" approach.

5. Does the early advantage disappear later? The best evidence on whether an early advantage from a "phonetic" start evens out later would come from longitudinal (or follow-up) studies. Only two investigators from Table 1 measured the same groups of children both early and late and published both first-grade and sixth-grade scores: Bear and Henderson.[6] In both cases, the "phonetic" group had an early advantage and maintained it.

The widespread belief that an early advantage dissipates rests largely on the Sparks '56 study, summarized by Sparks and Fay in 1957, which has been widely misunderstood. The comparisons in Sparks '56 were not longitudinal, but multilevel, all four grades being tested the same year. (See Table 1) The only longitudinal study of any of these children was done by Fay, who followed the pilot group's progress in fifth and sixth grade, but did not follow the younger, more successful non-pilot groups.[7] It should be noted that the total longitudinal span here was fourth grade through sixth, not first through sixth. We know only that this particular pilot group showed no significant difference from its control group in either fourth, fifth or sixth grades. It would be unsound to assume that a significant difference had existed in first grade and had dissipated.

The authors of this review know of no instance where an early "phonetic" advantage (rigorously measured) has later disappeared.

[6]Margaret Henderson Greenman's "phonetic" pilot group was superior in each grade from first through sixth, though only the third-grade comparison included tests of significance. Her follow-up is described in her February, 1959, report to the American Educational Research Association Conference (obtainable from School District No. 4, Champaign, Illinois) and in an article by Theodore L. Harris in the September, 1962, JOURNAL OF EDUCATIONAL RESEARCH.

[7]Leo Fay's fifth- and sixth-grade follow-up of Sparks' pilot group was reported in the 1961 INTERNATIONAL READING ASSOCIATION CONFERENCE PROCEEDINGS, without scores or critical ratios.

6. Are "phonetic" groups usually superior in grade 3 and above? Although only Bear and Henderson made wide-span longitudinal studies, several others chose to make single comparisons at the third-grade level or higher. Altogether, there are ten rigorous upper-grade comparisons in Table 1: seven favor the "phonetic" group, and three favor neither. Not one favors the "conventional" group.

Thus the rigorous comparisons indicate that "phonetic" groups tend to be superior in later grades as well as in first and second grade.

Some Non-Rigorous Studies

Previous reviews on phonics have concentrated largely on a group of studies from the 1920's and 1930's which have been cited as supporting the "conventional" method. Several of these as well as some of their modern successors are irrelevant in that they did not actually compare a "phonetic" group with a "conventional" group, but made some other type of comparison and then hypothesized freely. Others used highly selected samples or failed to give IQ's. Fourteen such studies will be mentioned below, simply to point out why they cannot be considered rigorous as previously defined.

A. The studies listed below were omitted from Tables 1 and 2 because they did not employ appropriate types of comparison. The first four, for instance, failed to include any group which had been intensively "phonetic" from the start.

1. *Dolch and Bloomster,* 1937, ESJ.[8] All the children had gradual phonics. The only actual comparison was between bright children and dull children.

2. *Tate,* June, 1937, ESJ. All the children had gradual phonics except during the eight-week experiment in the spring.

[8]The dates listed are dates of publication. The initials NM refer to Gates' book, NEW METHODS IN PRIMARY READING. The other initials refer to the following periodicals: ESJ—ELEMENTARY SCHOOL JOURNAL, RT—READING TEACHER, JEP—JOURNAL OF EDUCATIONAL PSYCHOLOGY, PJE—PEABODY JOURNAL OF EDUCATION.

3. *Tate, Herbert and Zeman,* March, 1940, ESJ. The study compared gradual phonics with no phonics.

4. *Mills,* January, 1956, ESJ. Various children were given a single lesson in phonics by the experimenter. No attention was paid to methods used by regular teachers.

5. *Gates'* Carden study, March, 1961, RT. The study failed to include a "conventional" group for comparison.

6. *Tensuan and Davis,* October, 1964, RT. The study did not deal with English-speaking children.

B. The next three were omitted because they discarded most of one group or the other (or both) while matching. This procedure can result in a final sample which is not representative because it is loaded with over-achievers or under-achievers.

1. *Gates'* study of 25 matched pairs, 1928, NM. The comparison was not based on a proper sample, because the experimenter used only a selected fourth of his 111 "conventional" children.

2. *Gates and Russell,* October, 1938, ESJ. The comparison was not based on a proper sample because the experimenters used only a selected third of their "phonetic" group. They compared 146 children from four "conventional" classes with 51 children selected from four "phonetic" classes.

3. *McCollum's* report to the Berkeley School Board on 20 matched pairs, June, 1962. The comparison was not based on a proper sample, because the experimenter used only a selected third of each group.

C. The four studies below were omitted because they failed either to administer IQ tests or to report IQ's. This failure is a serious one, since IQ differences have been shown to produce differences in reading ability which have no connection with method.

1. *Sexton and Herron's* Newark study, May, 1928, ESJ.

2. *Gates'* split-class experiment, 1928, NM.

3. *Mosher and Newhall,* October, 1930, JEP.

4. *Garrison and Heard,* July, 1931, PJE.

D. The study below was omitted because inappropriate statistical techniques were used.

1. *Cleland and Miller,* February, 1965, ESJ. The test which was treated as a pretest was given during the second half of February, five months after the experiment had begun. The present reviewers applied ordinary t-tests to the raw data given in the original study (Harry B. Miller's doctor's dissertation, University of Pittsburgh, 1962), and discovered that the "phonetic" group was actually significantly superior to the "conventional" group both in February and in May.

In addition, six of the studies already listed failed to include tests of significance: Dolch and Bloomster; Tate; Tate, Herbert and Zeman; Gates '61; Sexton and Herron; and Gates and Russell. In another of these studies, Garrison and Heard, the tests of significance were improperly applied to scores from tests that were so easy that both groups averaged almost perfect scores. This was true of 11 of the 20 tests of comprehension, vocabulary and spelling.

Many of the non-rigorous studies just listed have other major faults, both of design and of interpretation, too numerous to explore in this review. Their irrelevance or statistical inadequacy has received little attention from advocates of the "conventional" method. No attempt has been made in this review to take into account the many non-rigorous studies which are frankly favorable to the "phonetic" approach.

Conclusions

1. It can be seen from Table 1 that rigorous controlled research clearly favors intensive teaching of all the main sound-symbol relationships, both vowel and consonant, from the start of formal reading instruction.

2. It can be seen from Table 2 that such teaching benefits comprehension as well as vocabulary and spelling.

3. It can be seen from the ten upper-grade comparisons in Table 1 that "phonetic" groups are usually superior in grades 3 and above.

Recommendations

Since the results of this comprehensive and objective review of rigorously controlled research indicate that a gradual phonics approach is significantly less effective than an intensive phonics approach in beginning reading instruction, the authors recommend that an intensive "phonetic" approach be generally accepted as one of the most essential components of a good reading program. It is specifically suggested:

1) that all the main sound-symbol relationships, both vowel and consonant, be taught intensively from the start of reading instruction.

2) that schools provide their teachers with suitable materials and in-service training for using an intensive phonetic approach, and

3) that colleges and universities offer training in the necessary techniques, both in summer workshops and in regular courses.

Annotated Bibliography

(The note after each reference gives group sizes, IQ levels, and the proportion and direction of significant differences on the subtests relevant to comprehension, vocabulary and spelling. Symbols are explained in the key to Table 1.)

1. Agnew, Donald C. THE EFFECT OF VARIED AMOUNTS OF PHONETIC TRAINING IN PRIMARY READING, Duke University Research Studies in Education No. 5. Durham, N. C.: Duke University Press, 1939. (Also condensed in Hunnicutt, C. W. and Iverson, W. J., RESEARCH IN THE THREE R'S. New York: Harper, 1958.)
(O-3) The majority of the relevant subtests, three out of five, showed significant differences favoring the 89 third-graders from Durham, where phonics was emphasized. There were no such significant differences favoring the 89 "conventional" third-graders from Raleigh. Mean IQ's were 111 and 112, respectively. Tests used: Gates Basic Silent Reading, Pressey Vocabulary, Otis IQ.

2. Bear, David E. "Phonics for First Grade: A Comparison of Two Methods," ELEMENTARY SCHOOL JOURNAL LIX (April 1959), pp. 394-402. (Summary of the author's "A Comparison of a Synthetic with an Analytic Method of Teaching Phonics in First Grade." Unpublished doctor's dissertation, Washington University, St. Louis, 1958.)
(H-1) The majority of the relevant subtests, five out of seven, showed significant differences favoring the 136 first-graders who had used Hay-Wingo materials. There were no significant differences favoring the 139 "conventional" first-graders. Mean IQ's were 112 and 113, respectively. Tests used: Gates Primary; Metropolitan Achievement Primary I; Durrell Visual Discrimination; California Test of Mental Maturity, Primary.

3. Bear, David E. "Two Methods of Teaching Phonics: A Longitudinal Study," ELEMENTARY SCHOOL JOURNAL LXIV (February 1964), pp. 273-279.
(H-6) In this follow-up of Bear's '59 study, the majority of the relevant subtests, three out of four, showed significant differences favoring the 96 sixth-

graders who had used Hay-Wingo in first grade. There were no significant differences favoring the 90 "conventional" sixth-graders. No significant difference was found between the mean IQ's of these diminished groups. Tests used: Gates Reading Survey, local spelling tests.

4. Crossley, Beatrice A. "An Evaluation of the Effect of Lantern Slides on Auditory and Visual Discrimination of Word Elements." Unpublished doctor's dissertation, Boston University, 1948.
(O-1) The majority of the relevant subtests, three out of four, showed significant differences favoring the 204 first-graders who had systematic auditory training. There were no significant differences favoring the 212 "conventional" first-graders. Mean IQ's were 106 and 105, respectively. Tests used: Gates Primary, Boston University test of visual discrimination, Kuhlmann-Anderson IQ for Grade One.

5. Dolan, Sister Mary Edward. "A Modified Linguistic Versus a Composite Basal Reading Program," READING TEACHER XVII (April 1964), pp. 511-515. (Summary of the author's "A Comparative Study of Reading Achievement at the Fourth Grade Level under Two Methods of Instruction: Modified Linguistic and Traditional Basal." Unpublished doctor's dissertation, University of Minnesota, 1963.)
(L-4) The majority of the relevant subtests, seven out of ten, showed significant differences favoring the 403 Detroit fourth-graders who had followed a modification of Bloomfield's plan. There were no significant differences favoring the 407 Dubuque "conventional" fourth-graders. Mean IQ's for the boys were 104 and 106 respectively. Mean IQ's for the girls were 111 for both groups. Tests used: Gates Reading Survey; Bond, Clymer, Hoyt Diagnostic Test Bond, Clymer, Hoyt Developmental Tests; Lorge-Thorndike Non-Verbal IQ.

6. Duncan, Roger L. "A Comparative Study: Two Methods of Teaching Reading," TULSA SCHOOL REVIEW XXI (September 1964), pp. 4-5. (Also condensed in SCHOOL MANAGEMENT VIII (December 1964), pp. 46-47.)
(E-3) Duncan applied the median test to second- and third-grade scores of the 882 children in the Phonetic Keys pilot group and the 878 "conventional" children. He found highly significant differences favoring the "phonetic"

oup on every subtest of comprehension, vocabulary, spelling and language at
ith levels. He applied t-tests only to third-grade comprehension and language
id found significant differences on both, again favoring the "phonetic" group.
ean IQ for both groups was 103. Tests used: Metropolitan Achievement
imary II, Metropolitan Achievement Elementary, Kuhlmann-Anderson Intel-
ience.

Durrell, Donald D. and others. "Success in First Grade Reading," JOUR-
AL OF EDUCATION CXL (February 1958), pp. 1-48. (Summary of doctor's
ssertations at Boston University by Alice Nicholson, Arthur V. Olson, Sylvia
. Gavel and Eleanor B. Linehan.)
)-1) Half the relevant subtests, two out of four, showed significant differences
voring the 314 first-graders who had systematic training in letter names and
ionics. There were no significant differences favoring the 300 "conventional"
·st-graders. Mean mental ages were 81 and 82 months, respectively. Tests
ied: Detroit Word Recognition, Boston University tests, Otis Alpha, Califor-
a Test of Mental Maturity.

Henderson, Margaret G. PROGRESS REPORT OF READING STUDY 1952-55.
iampaign, Illinois: Board of Education, 1955. (Also condensed in CHICAGO
:HOOLS JOURNAL, January-February 1956, pp. 141-147.)
:-3) All seven relevant subtests showed significant differences favoring the
7 third-graders who had used Phonetic Keys to Reading over the 195 "con-
·ntional" third-graders. Mean IQ's were 109 and 106, respectively. Tests
ied: Metropolitan Achievement Elementary, Stanford Elementary, Iowa
asic Skills, California Test of Mental Maturity.

Kelly, Barbara C. "The Economy Method Versus the Scott, Foresman
iethod in Teaching Second-Grade Reading in the Murphysboro Public Schools,"
)URNAL OF EDUCATIONAL RESEARCH LI (February 1958), pp. 465-468.
:-2) The one relevant test showed a significant difference favoring the 100
icond-graders who had used Phonetic Keys to Reading over the 100 "con-
·ntional" second-graders. The mean mental ages were 100 months and 101
onths, respectively. Tests used: California Achievement, California Test of
ental Maturity.

10. McDowell, Rev. John B. "A Report on the Phonetic Method of Teachir Children to Read," CATHOLIC EDUCATION REVIEW LI (October 1953), pp. 506-519.

(L-4) The majority of the relevant subtests, five out of eight, showed no significant difference between the 142 fourth-graders who had used a modification of Bloomfield linguistics and the 142 "conventional" fourth-graders. (Of the other three relevant subtests, one showed a significant difference favoring the "phonetic" group, and two showed significant differences favorin the "conventional" group.) Mean IQ's were 116 and 115, respectively. Tests used: Iowa Silent Reading, Metropolitan Achievement, California Test of Mental Maturity.

11. Morgan, Elmer F. and Light, Morton. "A Statistical Evaluation of Two Programs of Reading Instruction," JOURNAL OF EDUCATIONAL RESEARCH LVII (October 1963), pp. 99-101.

(E-3) The majority of the relevant subtests, three out of five, showed no significant difference between the third-graders who had used Phonetic Keys to Reading and the "conventional" third-graders. (The other two subtests showed significant differences favoring the "conventional" group.) Group sizes were not given, but combined groups totaled about 150. Mean IQ of both groups was 102. Tests used: Gates Basic Reading, California S-Form IQ. The second and third comparisons in the study did not include IQ's and therefore do not qualify as rigorous.

12. Murphy, Helen A. "An Evaluation of the Effect of Specific Training in Auditory and Visual Discrimination on Beginning Reading." Unpublished doctor's dissertation, Boston University, 1943.

(O-1) The one relevant subtest showed a significant difference favoring the 144 first-graders who had systematic auditory training over the 73 "conventional" first-graders. Mean mental age was 71 months for both groups. Tests used: Detroit Word Recognition, Detroit First Grade IQ, Pintner-Cunninghan IQ.

13. Russell, David H. "A Diagnostic Study of Spelling Readiness," JOURNAL OF EDUCATIONAL RESEARCH XXXVII (December 1943), pp. 276-283.

(O-1) All seven relevant subtests showed significant differences favoring the 61 first-graders who had "much phonics" over the 55 "conventional" first-graders. Mean IQ's were 104 and 105, respectively. Tests used: Gates Primary, Gates Reading Diagnosis Tests, New Stanford Dictation Spelling, informal spelling test, Detroit First Grade IQ, Pintner-Cunningham IQ.

14. Santeusanio, Nancy C. "Evaluation of a Planned Program for Teaching Homophones in Beginning Reading." Unpublished doctor's dissertation, Boston University, 1962. (Summary in DISSERTATION ABSTRACTS XXIII (February 1963), pp. 2820-2821.)
(O-1) All four relevant subtests showed significant differences favoring the 202 first-graders who had training in homophones over the 202 "conventional" first-graders. Mean IQ for both groups was 106. Tests used: Metropolitan Achievement Primary I; Boston University Visual Discrimination Test; Lorge Thorndike IQ, Level 1.

15. Sparks, Paul E. "An Evaluation of Two Methods of Teaching Reading." Unpublished doctor's dissertation, Indiana University, August, 1956. (Summary in an article with the same title by Sparks, Paul E. and Fay, Leo C. in the ELEMENTARY SCHOOL JOURNAL LVII (April 1957), pp. 386-390.)
(E-1) Both the relevant subtests showed significant differences favoring the 124 first-graders who had Phonetic Keys to Reading over the 122 "conventional" first-graders. Mean IQ's were 110 and 105, respectively. Tests used: California Reading Test, Primary, Form CC; Otis Alpha IQ, Short Form.
(E-2) One of the two relevant subtests showed a significant difference favoring the 122 second-graders who had Phonetic Keys to Reading. There were no significant differences favoring the 104 "conventional" second-graders. Mean IQ's were 105 and 108, respectively. Tests used: California Reading Test, Primary, Form CC; Otis Alpha IQ, Short Form.
(E-4) None of the three relevant subtests showed a significant difference favoring either the 84 fourth-graders who had formed the Phonetic Keys pilot group or the 89 "conventional" fourth-graders. Mean IQ for both groups was 106. Tests used: Gates Reading Survey; Stanford Achievement Intermediate Spelling; Otis Alpha IQ, Short Form.

N.B. Sparks' third-grade comparison made use of tests that were too easy to measure the ability of the better half of either group: California Reading Test, Primary, Form CC. Therefore the third-grade comparison does not qualify as rigorous.

16. Wohleber, Sister Mary Louis, R.S.M. "A Study of the Effects of a Systematic Program of Phonetic Training on Primary Reading." Unpublished doctor's dissertation, University of Pittsburgh, 1953.

(L-1) The majority of the relevant subtests, two out of three, showed significant differences favoring the 65 first-graders who had used a modified linguistic program. There were no significant differences favoring the 65 "conventional" first-graders. Mean IQ's were 114 and 115, respectively. Tests used: Gates Primary, Detroit Advanced First Grade IQ.

(L-2) Both the relevant subtests showed significant differences favoring the 80 second-graders who had used a modified linguistic program over the 80 "conventional" second-graders. Mean IQ's were 105 and 106, respectively. Tests used: Gates Advanced Primary, Otis Alpha IQ.

(L-3) Both the relevant subtests showed significant differences favoring the 79 third-graders who had formed the linguistic pilot group over the 79 "conventional" third-graders. Mean IQ's were 105 and 106, respectively. Tests used: Gates Advanced Primary, Otis Alpha IQ.

17. Wollam, Walter A. "A Comparison of Two Methods of Teaching Reading." Unpublished doctor's dissertation, Western Reserve University, 1961. Abstract available from author: Superintendent of Schools, Alliance, Ohio.

(E-4) Half the relevant subtests, two out of four, showed significant differences favoring the 301 fourth-graders who had used Phonetic Keys to Reading in grades one through three. There were no significant differences favoring the 306 "conventional" fourth-graders. Mean IQ's were 107 and 109, respectively. Tests used: Diagnostic Reading Tests, Survey Section, Lower Level; sixty-word sample from spelling manual; California Test of Mental Maturity.

18. Wood, W. AN INVESTIGATION OF METHODS OF TEACHING READING IN INFANTS' SCHOOLS, Bulletin No. 9. Brisbane, Australia: Research and

Guidance Branch of the Queensland Department of Public Instruction, March, 1955.

(Q-2) One of the two relevant subtests showed a significant difference favoring the 168 second-graders who had used the usual Queensland Readers, a program which included an intensive "phonetic" approach. There were no significant differences favoring the 193 second-graders whose teachers were experimenting with gradual phonics. Mean IQ's were 110 and 107, respectively. Tests used: A.C.E.R. Reading Comprehension; Ohio Department of Public Instruction Reading for Meaning Test; Terman-Merrill Binet IQ, Form L; Melbourne General Ability Test.

N.B. A later Queensland study, in 1958, did not include IQ's and therefore does not qualify as rigorous.

STUDY QUESTIONS

1. Compare Gurren and Hughes' use of the terms "intensive phonics" and "gradual phonics" with Bliesmer and Yarborough's "synthetic" and "analytic" and with Bateman's "auditory" and "visual."

2. What do Gurren and Hughes mean by "rigorous comparisons?"

3. Cite the three major conclusions reached by the authors. Give an example of the evidence that supports each conclusion.

4. Their recommendations have not yet been widely implemented, although there is a detectable movement in that direction. What factors impede immediate and total implementation?

20: READING—A NON-MEANINGFUL PROCESS

Barbara D. Bateman

Bateman suggests that reading is not the visual, meaningful process it has been said to be, but that it is a rote, non-meaningful, auditory process. Reading disability is viewed, by implication, as the result of inappropriate programs for teaching reading, derived from a faulty analysis of the task of reading.

B. D. B.

Reprinted with permission from COLLEGE OF EDUCATION CURRICULUM BULLETIN, 1967, 23:278, Eugene, Oregon: University of Oregon, pp. 1-5.

The concept that the activity popularly and commonly known as reading can and should be viewed as a non-meaningful process is by no means a new one, nor is it one that should be considered grossly heretical. In the teacher's manual accompanying Lippincott's BASIC READING series (McCracken & Walcutt, 1963) this position is clearly and forcefully stated:

> *The written words are in fact artificial symbols of the spoken words, which are sounds. So reading must be the process of turning these printed symbols into sounds. The moment we say this, however, someone is sure to ask (and probably in a tone of the greatest anxiety), "But what about meaning? Do you propose to define reading as mere word-calling, without regard for meaning?" Yes, we do.* (p. iv)

Jastak (1946) and Bloomfield and Barnhart (1961) have also clearly and emphatically pointed to the distinction between a) reading as a process of converting letters to sounds and b) the ultimate goal of this process, which is to obtain meaning from the resultant sounds. Teachers sometimes refer to these as "word calling" and "comprehending." It appears unfortunate that the former, which is herein called reading, is sometimes viewed as a "necessary evil." In our eagerness to help children reach the eventual goal of obtaining meaning or comprehending what they have read, we perhaps have sometimes neglected the all-important prior stage of mastering the mechanical, rote process of letter-to-sound conversion. One might well ask why another statement of this position is necessary when it has been stated earlier and so well by others. It has been observed that many, if not most, elementary teachers and reading specialists are reluctant to consider seriously the possibility that initial reading instruction could or should neglect to emphasize meaning. Cases have been encountered where teachers who are using materials such as the Lippincott series, espousing this point of view, have denied ever hearing of such a position!

Others assert, after an initial presentation of the concept of reading as a non-meaningful process, that all it means is that word recognition is also important but they prefer to define reading as more inclusive. While it would be easy to pretend the issue vanishes by being labelled a matter of "semantics," the fact is that how one views the basic nature of the reading process should have a determining role in how reading is taught. It is because of these important implications for reading instruction that it seemed time to look once again at the differences between the process of reading and the purpose of reading.

Two lines of evidence—clinical and research—will be advanced in support of the position that reading should be viewed as a rote, automatic, conditioned non-meaningful process which precedes (and thus is separable from) comprehension.

Logical and Clinical Approach

Clinical work with children who have difficulty in reading leads to the observation that very, very few of them have difficulty in comprehending symbols such as the spoken word "dog." But they almost all share a pronounced difficulty in converting the letters d-o-g into the spoken sounds "dog." One way to view this distinction would be to think in terms of two stages as shown below:

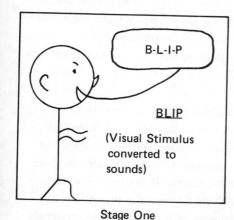

Stage One

Reading or Converting symbols to sounds.

Stage Two

Comprehension or attaching meaning to the sounds produced in Stage One.

Stage One is the *process* of reading. It differs only in quantity, not quality, from what the rat does when he learns to jump to the circle but not to the triangle (differential responses to visual stimuli). Stage Two is that of comprehending or attaching meaning to the symbols which have been identified in the previous step. This second stage should indeed be taught to children and taught very directly and explicitly, but it is the contention of this paper that in the early stages of so-called reading instruction, the child has quite enough to do in Stage One and his task ought not be unduly complicated by simultaneously requiring Stage Two. The process of learning to drive a car (this same illustration was used by McCracken & Walcutt, 1963) is perhaps analogous. It is certainly true that we learn to read for the eventual purpose of obtaining meaning. But, we would consider it somewhat ill-advised to combine teaching a novice to drive with a meaningful task such as driving a dignitary to the airport during rush-hour traffic when the time schedule is tight. We recognize that the mechanics of driving must be practiced *without* the pressure of any immediate purpose beyond mastering the mechanics. It is also true in both driving and reading that after the mechanical (Stage One) part has been mastered it seems to disappear. As adults we are seldom aware of the actual process of converting printed symbols to sound equivalents as we read, just as we frequently shift gears, brake, and accelerate without consciously attending to those behaviors. This is one of many instances in which introspective knowledge of how we as normal adults perform a given task does not necessarily provide helpful guides in teaching that task to young children who have not yet become proficient in it.

In order to check the accuracy of the contention that children who have trouble in reading are in need of instruction in Stage One, not Stage Two, it would be very simple for classroom teachers to administer two forms of a test like the Gates Reading Tests (e.g., Advanced Primary Paragraph Reading) in two different ways and compare the scores. If the teacher were to read the paragraphs aloud to the class ("Draw a line under the little cat.") and have them do the required comprehension of the spoken word (symbol) and make the appropriate marks on the test, Stage Two would be measured.

If a comparable form of the test were then administered in routine fashion, the child would be required to perform both Stages One and Two. The difference between the two scores would thus constitute a measure of the need for instruction in Stage One.

Earlier it was indicated that Stage Two, attaching meaning to symbols, should be taught directly. However, obtaining meaning from printed letters is only *one* kind of comprehension and we are advocating that it not be taught until after the child is comfortable with the process of converting printed letters to sounds. However, the world is full of many symbols and signals which children need to learn to comprehend. We would suggest that teaching the meanings of facial expressions, moss on a tree, traffic flow, etc. (e.g., in terms of what it means or tells us about the time of day, the direction of the downtown area, the socio-economic class of the area, etc.), are all legitimate educational pursuits and that they do not differ from the teaching of the meanings of words which have been previously *read*. In short, we are urging that reading be taught as a rote, conditioned, mechanical process of converting letters to sounds and that the comprehension of *many* symbols (including sounds combined into words) be taught as a separate process. It is a highly significant, but widely overlooked fact that reading disability is usually defined as a discrepancy between proficiencies in comprehending symbols (mental age, loosely translated) and in converting visual symbols to sounds and then obtaining meaning from them (reading as traditionally measured, including both Stages One and Two). Thus, by *definition,* reading disabilities occur in Stage One! If a child is strong in Stage One (word-calling) but poor in Stage Two (comprehension), as does occasionally happen, we say he has a problem in "comprehending what he reads," acknowledging in spite of ourselves that we really do equate word-calling with reading, as well we should.

An important qualification to this discussion is that a very substantial percentage of children, perhaps 3/4 of them, seem to acquire the skills of reading and comprehending almost by "osmosis." The method of instruction seems to matter very little compared to the fact of exposure. While in theory we would argue that reading should be taught to *all* children as the non-meaningful process it really is, in practice it would probably matter only to those few children who actually need systematic reading instruction because they do not learn by "osmosis."

Research Approach

The distinction we have made between Stage One and Stage Two as symbol conversion or identification versus symbol recognition or comprehension, appears to parallel that made in the psycholinguistic model of Illinois Test of Psycholinguistic Abilities (ITPA). In the test, two levels of language are assessed—the representational or meaningful and the automatic-sequential or rote, non-meaningful. The ITPA has generated recent research which is quite relevant to the concept of reading as a non-meaningful process. Two of the earliest studies utilizing the ITPA (Kass, 1962; Bateman, 1963) found that reading achievement correlated positively with the non-meaningful language subtests, and not with the meaningful ones. In fact, Kass found a negative relationship between reading achievement and the ability to comprehend *meaningful* visual stimuli. Ragland (1964) also reported that retarded readers performed better than non-retarded readers on the comprehension of meaningful visual stimuli. Additional data (see Part II of this bulletin) also indicate that good readers and poor readers are differentiated psycholinguistically by their performances in the use of language at a non-meaningful level. These four studies just mentioned included mentally retarded, partially seeing, dyslexic, and normal subjects.

Evidence which bears on the validity of the assertion that reading can and should be taught as a symbol-sound conversion process can also be adduced from new research on methodology in reading instruction. But it is first necessary to point out that "Stage One instruction," in our terminology, is most closely approximated in today's practice by intensive phonics programs in which the *initial* instructional emphasis is on symbol-sound conversion with comparatively little attention to meaning per se. These systems have been described as synthetic—"in which the child is taught certain letter-sound relationships or word elements (Stage One) before beginning to read (Stage One plus Stage Two)." (Bliesmer and Yarborough, 1965, p. 500)

The other widely used approach embodies an initial emphasis on meaning and learning whole words prior to the introduction of specific letter-sound relationships. It is often called the analytic approach or the look-say method. In our terminology, it requires the child to perform Stage Two first and then later introduces him to Stage One.

Bliesmer and Yarborough (1965) compared ten different beginning reading programs in first grade—five of these were synthetic (phonics) and five were analytic (whole word and meaning). Reading achievement was measured by five subtests of the Stanford Achievement Test: Word Reading, Paragraph Meaning, Vocabulary, Spelling, and Word Study Skills. When the means of the two programs were compared on these five measures, 92 differences were significantly in favor of the phonics programs and none significantly favored the analytic programs (125 total comparisons). With specific regard to comprehension skills, 20 of 25 comparisons significantly favored the phonics program and none significantly favored the analytic programs. This study was well controlled (e.g., programs were randomly assigned to teachers, in-service training was provided by consultants from the program publishers, covariance procedures were applied to adjust mean criterion scores, etc.) and the authors' conclusion that ". . . reading programs which give attention to sound-symbol relationships prior to teaching of words . . . tend to be significantly more productive . . . than do analytic reading programs which involve the more conventional approach of going directly from readiness procedures to the reading of whole words" is well founded.

In an excellent review of all available rigorous (carefully defined by the authors) comparisons of reading achievement of groups which had early intensive phonics with groups that had not, Gurren and Hughes (1965) found that the evidence "clearly favors intensive teaching of all the main sound-symbol relationships from the start of formal reading instruction" and that "such teaching benefits comprehension as well as vocabulary and spelling." Of the 22 rigorous comparisons of "conventional" and "phonetic" reading programs, 19 were favorable to "phonetics," 3 to neither group, and one to "conventional." Sub-analyses revealed that 16 comparisons favored the "phonetics" in specific regard to comprehension, while none favored the "conventional."

In summary, it is this observer's opinion that logical analyses of the reading process, clinical experience, and research data all point unmistakably toward the currently unpopular notion that reading can and should be taught as the formation of a series of rote, non-meaningful, conditioned bonds between visual stimuli (letters) and vocal responses (sounds). This non-meaningful *process* is, of course, carried on for the eventual *purpose* of obtaining meaning from the symbols, but this fact ought not remain an obstacle to teaching the process of reading.

If one were to test the merit of this position (and one certain merit, however small, is that it *is* testable) he would perhaps carry the position to its extreme and employ a program in which a) the symbol-sound relationship were always constant, e.g., i/t/a, and b) *all* "meaningful words" were excluded until after the child had thoroughly mastered the conditioned associations using only in- dividual sounds and nonsense combinations. Teachers often ask how long it would take for the child to master the 44 sound-symbol bonds in i/t/a, espe- cially if all meaningful words were excluded. Research would of course be required to answer this with certainty, but if the best application of known principles of learning were systematically employed, a couple of months would appear to be a reasonable guess.

Another objection frequently raised to this type of proposal is that the children might not be "motivated" to learn 44 rote associations. This, too, would have to be tested, but it would seem that careful application of reward and precise structuring to insure task success could eliminate such anticipated difficulties.

The nature of the process of learning the 44 sound-symbol associations advo- cated here should be no different from that of learning 44 children's names, or 44 baseball players' batting averages, or 44 models of automobiles. In all cases an arbitrary label is assigned and if one forgets that label, there is no way to meaningfully deduce it. It is in just this sense we urge that the pro- cess of converting letters to sounds, which we have called reading, should be viewed as a rote, non-meaningful process.

References

Bateman, Barbara D. Reading and psycholinguistic processes of partially seeing children, CEC Research Monog., Series A, No. 5, 1963.

Bliesmer, Emery P. and Yarborough, Betty H. A comparison of ten different beginning reading programs in first grade. PHI DELTA KAPPAN, June, 1965, 500-504.

Bloomfield, L. and Barnhart, C. L. LET'S READ: A LINGUISTIC APPROACH. Detroit: Wayne State University Press, 1961.

Gurren, Louise and Hughes, Ann. Intensive phonics vs. gradual phonics in beginning reading: a review. JOURNAL OF EDUCATIONAL RESEARCH, 58:8, April 1965, 339-346.

Jastak, Joseph. WIDE RANGE ACHIEVEMENT TEST and MANUAL, 1946. (Available from Psychological Corporation, 552 Fifth Ave., N.Y., N.Y.)

Kass, Corrine E. Some psychological correlates of severe reading disability. Unpublished doctoral dissertation. University of Illinois, 1962.

McCracken, Glenn and Walcutt, Charles C. BASIC READING: TEACHER'S EDITION. Philadelphia: J. B. Lippincott Co., 1963.

Ragland, G. G. The performance of educable mentally handicapped students of differing reading ability on the ITPA. Unpublished doctoral dissertation. University of Virginia, 1964.

STUDY QUESTIONS

1. Is it true that how one views the essential nature of the reading process influences how one teaches reading? Do all teachers of reading have a position on the nature of reading?

2. What is meant by the assertion that reading disabilities, by definition, occur in Stage One (word recognition or decoding)?

3. Give one example of each type of evidence used by Bateman to support her view of the nature of reading.

4. Distinguish between the process of reading and the purpose of reading.

9398   49

109